THE
OMNISCIENT
BUYER

WINNING CUSTOMERS IN A WORLD OF INFINITE BUYER INTELLIGENCE

ANDY HALKO

For permission requests, contact: andy@andyhalko.com

First Edition: 2025

ISBN: 979-8-9989728-2-9

Printed in the United States of America.

This book is a work of nonfiction. While every effort has been made to ensure the accuracy and completeness of the information contained herein, the author and publisher assume no responsibility for errors, inaccuracies, or omissions.

Buyer-Centric™ and BuyerTwin™ are trademarks of Andy Halko and/or affiliated entities. All other product names and brands are the property of their respective owners.

For more insights and resources, visit:

www.andyhalko.com

For Aurora Rose & Sonoma Lily.

My future. My world. No matter what they do,

I hope they continue to carry my entrepreneurial heart.

TABLE OF CONTENTS

Getting the Most from Omniscient Buyers

Your buyers now know more than you think.

And they're faster than you expect. Armed with AI that sees through your polished pitch decks and sugarcoated promises.

This isn't business as usual.

It's a new era of audiences with access to more information delivered in the most consumable form in human history. Before you go any further, know this:

If you're not ready to rethink everything, put this book down.

But if you are—if you're willing to challenge every assumption you've held about influence, trust, and control...

Keep reading.

Why Am I Writing This?

Because AI is the great equalizer that just leveled us all. Your buyers aren't guessing anymore.

They're not waiting for your sales deck to fill in the blanks.

They're armed to the teeth with AI-powered insights you can't outrun or outspin.

They've analyzed your company and summarized it into a neat table.

They have a full list of your competitors with side-by-side comparisons.

Alternatives and their benefits? Right there.

Every online comment or review is summarized and quantified.

Even if your pricing isn't "public", it's been found or predicted.

They know which of your promises hold up—and which ones crumble under scrutiny. And all of this happens in the blink of an eye.

I'm writing this book because pretending you still have the upper hand is a delusion you can't afford.

The old playbook in marketing and sales of controlling the narrative, obscuring details, drip-feeding information—has collapsed.

Why? Because every tactic built on you as the gatekeeper or guide is gone.

Artificial intelligence didn't just tip the balance. It obliterated it.

You can't out-bluff an algorithm. You can't overwhelm a buyer who can verify everything you say before you even finish your sentence. You no longer win by being the proprietor of information anymore.

But you *can* win on clarity. On credibility. On adapting as the ground shifts under all our feet.

This book is your wake-up call—and your blueprint. Read it if you're ready to compete in a world where your buyers see everything.

About The Author

I've spent over two decades building businesses, advising founders, and studying what makes people say yes.

What started as a messy, underfunded agency became a lab for growth strategy. I've been in the room when the big deals closed—and when they fell apart. I've led teams through pivots, layoffs, breakthroughs, and burnouts. I've lived the chaos that strategy books sanitize.

Over the years, a pattern emerged. The difference between companies that win and those that stall?

It's how deeply they understand their buyer.

That obsession became my compass. It led to hundreds of interviews, thousands of strategic sessions, and eventually, a system. That system is now embedded inside BuyerTwin, the platform I built to turn static personas into living, evolving buyer intelligence.

Today, AI has changed the game. Your buyers aren't wandering the funnel—they're storming in with answers. The power dynamic has shifted.

This book is my response to that shift.

It's not theory. It's the blueprint I use with teams navigating the new rules—where AI is the front door, and your narrative better be strong enough to make it through.

I wrote this because marketing and sales have been forever changed.

Not because of automation, efficiency, personalization, or any change in how we reach or influence buyers.

But because our buyers are now fundamentally different from who they used to be. What worked before will never work again in this world.

Who This Book Is For

Not everyone is ready to face the impact that AI has had on buyers and customers.

This book is for you if:

- You lead a business and feel the ground shifting under your feet.

- You sense your customers know more than your team—and you're not sure how to catch up.

- You're tired of tactics that used to work but now fall flat.

- You want to trade spin for substance and rebuild real trust.

- You believe transparency isn't optional but the only strategy left.

- You're willing to rethink how you sell, market, and communicate in a world where your buyers are omniscient.

This isn't for you if you're looking for comfortable reassurance.

If you want to keep pretending AI is just another passing trend, put this book back on the shelf.

But if you're ready to confront reality—and use it as fuel— **You're in the right place.**

The Assumptions We're Starting With

Let's begin on common ground. Not theory—just facts you already see unfolding in your own business.

These assumptions are baked into every chapter ahead:

1. **AI isn't a novelty anymore.** It's a standard tool your buyers use daily, whether you've embraced it or not.

2. **The pace of change is unrelenting.** You can't wait to see how the dust settles. Advancments are happening each day and the only option is to evolvo.

3. **AI does not leave anyone untouched.** No matter your industry or role, AI is impacting you and your buyers.

4. **You are here because you're open to change.** You wouldn't be reading this if you were satisfied with business as usual.

If any of this sounds unreasonable to you, you'll struggle with what comes next. But if you recognize them as reality, you're already ahead of most.

How to Read This Book

This book is structured as a progression—each part builds upon the foundation laid by the previous one. Think of it as a map through the upheaval AI has created and a guide to rebuilding your advantage.

Here's how the journey unfolds:

Part I: The Great Disruption
You'll start by seeing the forces that ended the information asymmetry you once relied on. You will see how AI empowered buyers, eroded trust, and made old tactics obsolete.

Part II: A Buyer Transformed
Next, you'll step into the mind of today's omniscient buyer. You'll learn how instant expertise, real-time fact-checking, and the hunger for transparent value shape every decision they make.

Part III: The Mindset Shift
Then we'll dismantle the outdated playbook and replace it with a mindset built for this new era. Radical honesty, collaborative discovery, and empathy will become your tools for earning trust and standing out.

Part IV: Marketing In An AI-First World
Here we'll focus on visibility, communication and engagement for buyers who are leading their own process guided by AI.

Part V: Sales In An AI-First World
Following that, we'll dive into how sales teams need to adapt to these buyers that have every piece of info or analysis at their disposal.

Part VI: The AI Buyer R.A.D.A.R Framework

This part offers you practical strategies to redesign your experiences, retrain your teams, and future-proof your business for whatever comes next.

Read these sections in order—each chapter is a stepping stone. By the end, you won't only have a new perspective but also a plan you can act on.

This isn't passive reading. It's an invitation to rethink, rebuild, and lead.

The Promise (And the Warning)

I won't pretend this will be comfortable. It probably won't be.

AI is already scary. Looking at how it changes the people you want to engage and influence—rather than just treating it— as a tool can be unsettling.

You'll see things you wish weren't true—about your messaging, your processes, your blind spots. You'll realize how much your success once relied on your buyers *not* knowing everything. And yes, you might feel a flicker of panic when you see how far ahead some of them already are.

That's normal.

But here's the promise:

If you stay with it—if you confront the discomfort instead of retreating— you'll come out stronger on the other side. You'll earn trust the old playbook could never buy.

You'll build resilience no algorithm can erode.

And you'll rediscover the most powerful advantage left: a company willing to tell the truth in a world drowning in noise.

If you're ready, let's begin.

Part I

The Great Disruption

Your monopoly on truth is over.

There was a time when buyers came to you empty-handed, hungry and dependent on you for insight.

You could ration information.
You could shape perceptions.
You could control the narrative.

That time is gone.

AI has flooded the market.

Knowledge now flows—instant, infinite, precise.

The Buyer Who Knows Everything

They research while you sleep.
They compare in seconds before your pitch begins.
They enter your funnel armed with conclusions already drawn.

You can't bluff.
You can't distract.

The Omniscient Buyer is here.

Still believe you steer the narrative?

You don't.

At best, you're a participant in a conversation you no longer dictate.

And whatever you say is compared with what their AI told them.

Your credentials? Skepticism.
Your promises? Scrutiny.
Your intentions? Doubt.
Your ideas? Double-checked.

This is not evolution.

This is the *Great Disruption*.

Adapt.

Or get left behind.

Chapter 1

The New Reality

Most companies are racing to integrate AI into their organization for scale, speed and survival.

Automate processes.
Boost productivity.
Cut costs.

But while you're busy retooling the inside, you've likely missed the real revolution that AI has completely disrupted the people coming to you.

The proliferation of AI has given you're buyers and customers infinite intelligence and transformed them into something you've never seen before.

You Used To Hold All The Cards

For most of business history, you owned the facts. You controlled the narrative. Buyers came to you with curiosity and left with whatever version of the truth you decided to share with them.

Picture the 1950s:

Ad Men in smoke-filled boardrooms, crafting slogans to bend perception.

A family huddled around the television, absorbing every polished claim as gospel.

A salesperson knocking on the door with a suitcase of samples—and no challenger to their pitch.

Information flowed one way: from the seller to the buyer.

Your brochures, your pitches, your glossy presentations—these were the gatekeepers. You decide what buyers knew. And when they knew it.

Even as dial-up internet sputtered into the 80s and 90s, the dynamic didn't change much. Information online was scattered, slow, and unreliable. Online opinions lacked trust. Most buyers still depended on brochures, catalogs, and commissioned experts to tell them what mattered.

This information control laid the foundation for the traditional sales playbook.

- Highlight strengths.
- Gloss over weaknesses.
- Answer questions selectively.
- Keep the buyer dependent.

Entire industries were built on this imbalance. Car dealerships thrived on hidden markups. Healthcare systems buried pricing in complexity. Enterprise software companies obscured implementation costs behind layers of jargon and "customization."

It wasn't always malicious. Sometimes, it was simply tradition. A belief that too much transparency would confuse customers or erode margins.

But whether intentional or not, the dynamic was clear: You held the knowledge. They held the uncertainty.

And for decades, that uncertainty was your leverage.

Early Stages Of Information Balance

As internet access became mainstream and every company had a website, information control shifted. Suddenly, information wasn't locked behind a salesperson's desk. Specs, reviews, and competitor comparisons trickled online—piecemeal but revolutionary.

In the early 2000s, search engines made it easier to hunt for answers. Buyers began arriving to sales conversations more prepared. Less willing to accept your single narrative alone.

Companies responded by flooding the web with polished content, hoping to maintain their grip on the story.

Then came social media.

Review sites multiplied.

Forums and comment sections empowered ordinary people to share unfiltered experiences. One negative post could spread faster than your best marketing campaign.

Trust migrated from brands to peers. From official brochures to user-generated content. From corporate declarations to third-party validation.

By the 2010s, buyers were no longer passive recipients of information.

They were researchers. Investigators. Comparative analysts.

Studies at the time revealed that B2B buyers completed as much as 60 to 70 percent of their research before ever reaching out to a salesperson.

Buyer started showing up much more prepared and capable. However, even as their access to information increased, friction persisted.

It took effort to sift through conflicting claims. It required hours to assemble a clear picture. The information further shifted into buyers hands —but it didn't come easily.

Nonetheless, the seeds were planted. Buyers were learning they didn't have to take your word for anything.

All they needed was a way to gather and process the truth faster.

AI would soon give them exactly that.

The Moment the Dam Broke

AI didn't continue the evolution.
It collapsed the timeline to zero.

It was the moment the dam burst—and knowledge flooded every corner of the buying process.

Overnight, the barriers that had slowed buyers disappeared.

All the friction—hours spent browsing pages, combing through reviews, deciphering jargon, comparing specs—collapsed into a single prompt.

What used to take days now took seconds.

A buyer can now prompt AI to:

- Summarize every review of your services from the last five years.

- Benchmark your features and pricing against ten competitors—instantly.

- Uncover every known drawback your sales team prefers not to discuss.

- Generate a list of probing questions to test your credibility on a call.

For early AI adopters, this is how they currently make purchases. They no longer rely on your website or your sales collateral. They have an impartial advisor that is faster, more thorough, and immune to persuasion.

But this shift isn't confined to a few outliers. It's spreading—fueled by tools that grow more powerful and more accessible every month. What feels like an emerging trend today will soon become the baseline expectation.

If your buyers aren't doing this yet, they will. And when they do, they won't go back.

That's what makes this moment different from every disruption that came before.

You are not preparing for some distant future.
You are living inside the early stages of it right now.

Where you once decided what buyers knew, buyers are beginning to decide what you are worth before the first meeting, before the first email reply, before you even know they're looking.

This isn't an incremental change. It's the start of an irreversible transformation. One that will accelerate whether you're ready or not.

The Universal Impact

No industry is exempt.
No sector is safe.

AI-enabled transparency is not selective.
It touches everything.

In **B2B software**, enterprise buyers are already running AI-powered comparisons before your first discovery call.

In **healthcare**, patients use AI to translate medical jargon into plain language—and to uncover the real costs hidden behind codes and disclaimers.

In **retail**, shoppers are prompting AI to surface alternative suppliers, validate reviews, and reveal the true origins of your "exclusive" products.

In **consulting**, buyers are building RFPs and sample implementation plans in mere seconds and bringing them to you to buy into.

Small purchases. Big investments. It doesn't matter. The tools are available to anyone with an internet connection and a question.

And complexity is no longer a shield. In the past, companies relied on the idea that certain decisions were too complicated for buyers to fully untangle.

Enterprise contracts.

Engineered solutions.

Compliance requirements.

SaaS implementations.

The more complex or opaque, the more the buyer needed you.

That protection is dissolving. AI doesn't get overwhelmed by dense documentation or convoluted pricing models. It thrives on them—digesting thousands of pages, surfacing patterns, and highlighting inconsistencies in moments.

This is why the impact is universal. If you sell anything—software, services, products, ideas—your audience is evolving faster than your playbook.

The transformation doesn't wait for your permission. It doesn't care about your industry's conventions or your comfort with the status quo.

It simply moves forward. And it takes your buyers with it.

The New Reality

Your buyers have it all.

Information. Analysis. Ideation. Everything.

Not in theory. Not in some speculative future.

In practice, today.

Your new reality is to assume they know almost everything: your strengths, your weaknesses, your prices, even your track record.

Everything.

The old tactics—control, obscure, deflect—don't just fail. They backfire.

When buyers can see the entire landscape, any attempt to correct, hide or spin becomes a signal of distrust. In a world of infinite knowledge, credibility is your only leverage.

What do you need to adapt to?

- Every interaction that happens requires radical transparency.

- Claims will be tested in seconds.

- Advantages must withstand instant scrutiny.

- Expectations will fully replace questions.

Most companies haven't even considered this new reality or are pretending this won't change anything. They imagine there's time to adapt slowly. They believe the old ways will hold a little longer.

They won't.

If your full focus is on internal AI adoption, you will be left behind. While you optimize internally, your buyers are evolving without you.

Learning faster.

Trusting less.

Expecting more.

This isn't an incremental shift you can ignore. It's the foundation that every other change in this book will build upon.

Welcome to the age of the omniscient buyer.

Chapter 2

Now Buyers Know More Than You Do

You used to be the authority. The expert. The gatekeeper.

You had the expertise, the experience, the relationships and everything else that made you the source they needed.

Buyers came to you for answers because they had no other choice.

But not anymore.

While your marketing team is still grabbing coffee—and your sales team is syncing calendars, the buyer has already asked an AI to:

- Compare your offering to everyone else in the market.

- Summarize a thousand reviews.

- Expose your weaknesses.

- Predict your pricing over the next 5 years.

- Draft the right questions to challenge your claims.

They walk into the first conversation knowing more than most of your team. They don't have to trust your narrative.

They can verify it—or dismantle it—on demand.

This is the omniscient buyer. They aren't theoretical. They aren't niche.

They are multiplying every day. And if you're still selling as if they don't exist, you've already lost ground.

In this chapter, we'll explore how this new buyer thinks, what they can do, and why their expectations will redefine your entire approach to persuasion.

People Have Always Wanted Transparency & Control

Long before AI, buyers were learning to question, compare, and verify.

Search engines trained them to find answers themselves. Review sites taught them that real experiences were more reliable than polished claims. Social media showed them that one bad customer story mattered way more than a stream of marketing messages from you.

For a long time now, every buyer has been trying to get as far as they can in making a decision before reaching out.

Your buyer is already conditioned to do their homework.

But there were limits.

- **Information was fragmented** - review sites, competitor sites, online documents, industry information, all separated.

- **Research was time-consuming** - all these pages first needed to be found and then synthesized

- **Expertise still mattered** - you didn't understand all the jargon or intricacies.

AI removed those limits in one move.

With a single prompt, a novice can operate like an expert. They can compress days of research into a few seconds. They can see patterns that used to be hidden behind complexity and noise.

This is how the omniscient buyer was born—not from sudden technological shock, but from a steady march toward self-sufficiency that finally found its perfect catalyst.

They are not a different kind of customer. They are simply the inevitable next version. And they will never go back to depending on you as their primary source of information.

The Capabilities Your Buyer Now Has

For years, you could count on one simple fact: even the most motivated buyer still had limits.

Limits on time.
Limits on expertise.
Limits on patience.

Sure, they could research. They could ask colleagues. They could skim reviews and study white papers.

But it was messy, incomplete, and often overwhelming. In other words, your advantage was safe.

Now AI has taken over.

It didn't just give buyers more information.

It gave them the power to process, organize, and weaponize that information faster than any human team could hope to match.

Consider just a few of the ways buyers now use AI:

- **Instant Side-by-Side Comparisons**
  A prospect asks an AI to create a table of your product's features versus every major competitor, with strengths, weaknesses, and user ratings highlighted in color-coded columns. They spot gaps you hoped no one would notice.

- **Sentiment Summaries**
  Before the first meeting, they prompt AI to distill thousands of reviews into three bullet points: what people love, what they tolerate, and what they hate.

- **Pricing Transparency**
  Even if you bury your fees in complicated tiers, AI can decode them, benchmark them against the market, and highlight where you overcharge.

- **Preemptive Objections**
  They prompt AI to draft the ten most challenging questions to pose to your sales team—questions designed to test honesty and expertise.

- **Risk Profiling**
  AI surfaces legal disputes, data breaches, or regulatory issues associated with your company that you thought were buried deep in the web.

- **Implementation Realities**
  Buyers prompt AI to uncover stories about your onboarding process—how long it *really* takes, how often it fails, and what hidden costs arise later.

- **Unbiased, Unemotional Evaluations**
  A procurement team can feed your entire RFP response into an AI model that scores your fit against their internal criteria—before you ever get to defend yourself.

- **Voice of the Customer Analysis**
  AI scours social media for unfiltered opinions, then clusters sentiment trends you'll never see in your NPS surveys.

- **Dynamic Monitoring**
  After shortlisting you, buyers set an AI to track news, pricing updates, and customer feedback in real time. One negative headline triggers a reconsideration.

- **Active Listening & Verification**
  An AI is listening to calls and in real-time summarizing and surfacing information related to what you say.

This is already happening. Not a prediction. A reality.

Enterprise buyers have entire workflows built around these capabilities. Individual consumers have AI copilots embedded in their browsers. Even small businesses can access this power through free or low-cost tools.

And here's the part you–trying to sell to them–struggle to accept:

Once a buyer experiences this level of clarity and speed, they never want to buy any other way again.

Infinite Knowledge Brings Confidence

For all its power to expose half-truths, AI also introduces a more subtle danger:

It makes people feel so confident in the answers that they stop questioning the source altogether.

Because AI is fast, thorough and feels neutral.

When buyers prompt an AI, they aren't sifting through dozens of conflicting reviews or scrolling past banner ads. They get a clean, authoritative answer—delivered in the calm, confident tone of an all-knowing guide.

Think of a product on an ecommerce site with 5,000 reviews. Before a buyer might look at the one star reviews, some of the five star and read nuances that signaled what felt true or not. Now ecommerce sites automatically condense all those reviews into three sentences that sound definitive, not nuanced.

They see clear positive affirmations, citations and bullet points in summaries. But here's the truth nobody wants to admit:

Most buyers don't verify what the AI tells them.

They don't trace every link. They don't cross-reference every claim.

They accept the output as fact because it feels easier, faster, and smarter to do so.

And AI tools are designed to encourage that trust.

- They are engineered to sound objective and definitive—even when they're making probability-driven guesses.

- They promote that they have been trained on millions of documents and data points.

- The easily let you follow up with more questions that continue to deliver more definitive answers.

I've never seen an AI say "I don't know."

In other words, AI doesn't just inform buyers. It *guides* them and sometimes subtly nudges them toward conclusions they wouldn't have drawn on their own.

This is the paradox: AI has created a generation of buyers who feel omniscient but often accept first answers uncritically.

And that makes their trust more brittle than ever. Because when you attempt to give them a reality that diverges from their AI's assurances, they question your motives first.

You're not just competing with other sellers anymore.
You're competing with the illusion of perfect answers.

And when your story conflicts with the buyer's AI, it is the one seeing as all knowing and unbiased. Not you.

AI Confidence Becomes Unadulterated Ego

Knowledge doesn't just change what people know. It changes how they feel about what they know.

Before AI, even well-researched buyers arrived with some humility. They might have had questions. They might have admitted uncertainty and left room for your expertise.

Now, that humility is gone.

AI has birthed a new buyer mindset—one defined by unshakable confidence. They don't just think they understand your industry or product. They believe they understand it as well—*or better*—than you do.

When every question has an instant, polished answer, why would they defer to your expertise? When the most complex topic can be explained in terms that are best for their understanding. When every claim can be checked in seconds, why would they tolerate ambiguity?

They don't believe you're the authority anymore.

At best, you are a secondary source—someone expected to validate what the buyer already believes.

They don't arrive with curiosity. They arrive with conclusions.

And if you challenge those conclusions without evidence, you don't look wise. You look defensive. It may feel like you have ulterior motives.

This is why sales teams are starting to walk out of meetings feeling blindsided. The buyer wasn't looking for education or persuasion. They were looking for confirmation.

I call this phenomenon: The AI Ego.

The AI Ego is a psychological manifestation where instant access to algorithmic knowledge inflates a buyer's sense of expertise far beyond their actual experience.

It's *synthetic* confidence, manufactured in milliseconds. It feels earned, but it's simply the byproduct of frictionless information.

When the AI Ego takes hold:

- Buyers feel in the lead, not you.

- They stop asking open-ended questions.

- They expect you to agree with their conclusions.

- Any contradiction sounds like evasion.

The omniscient buyer doesn't wait for you to prove your knowledge.

They expect you to prove you're worthy of theirs.

The Experience of Buying Now

If you haven't been on the other side of the table lately, it's hard to appreciate just how transformed the buying experience feels.

It's not just that information is easier to find. It's that every step—research, comparison, validation—has collapsed into a seamless, almost effortless flow.

A buyer doesn't start by clicking through twenty websites anymore. They start by prompting their AI.

One query can do what used to take days:

- List every viable vendor.

- Summarize key differentiators.

- Surface common complaints.

- Generate questions to separate hype from substance.

- Tell me what's best for my unique situation.

From that moment, their expectations are set. The AI has already created a frame of reference you may never see—and you may never get to challenge.

When they do land on your site, they're scanning, not exploring. They're looking for confirmation, not discovery.

If they schedule a call, it's not to learn. It's to see if you match the picture their AI has painted.

This is what buying feels like now: Faster. Simpler. More decisive.

It feels empowering. It feels efficient. It feels objective—even if it isn't.

And because it feels that way, buyers trust it more than any salesperson, any piece of collateral, any polished pitch.

This is why so many marketers and sales people are caught off guard: While you're trying to build rapport and lay groundwork, your buyer is already halfway to a verdict.

They don't feel like they're discovering or deciding. They feel like they're verifying a conclusion that was delivered to them without friction.

That's the experience of buying now—a streamlined process that leaves little space for persuasion and no patience for uncertainty.

The Myths Marketing & Sales Still Cling To

Even as AI reshapes the buying landscape, most revenue focused teams continue to comfort themselves with the same tired assumptions.

They tell themselves their prospects still want to engage with their brand. That customers don't have time to do this level of research. They insist their product is too complex to be compared so easily. They believe their relationships or brand reputation will insulate them from disruption.

These are comforting stories. But they're myths—and dangerous ones at that.

Myth #1: "Our buyers are too busy to research this deeply."
That used to be true.
Time was the great limiting factor.But AI obliterated that.

What used to take days now takes minutes—or less. Your buyer can get an executive summary of your entire market in the time it takes to drink a coffee.

They're not too busy. They're too efficient to wait on you.

Myth #2: "We're too complex for AI to simplify."
No, you're not.

Complexity doesn't protect you anymore. It makes you easier to decode.

AI thrives on dense information. The more data you feed it—pricing tables, feature lists, legal fine print—the clearer it can make the picture for your buyer.

What once made your solution seem unapproachable now becomes elegantly digestible in a single command: "Explain it to me like I'm 5."

And it will.

Myth #3: "Our brand trust will carry us."
It won't.

Trust used to come from repetition, visibility, and name recognition.

Now, it comes from something much harder to fake: **verifiability**.Your buyer doesn't have to take your word for anything. If your claims don't align with what their AI uncovers, they won't hesitate to walk away.

Myth #4: "They'll still rely on us to guide their thinking."
Not anymore.

Today's buyer doesn't show up looking for guidance. They expect you to validate what they already believe. If you don't—or can't—they'll find someone who will.

These myths are comforting because they let you believe you still have time. That you still have the advantage. That you can wait a little longer to adapt.

But you don't.

The omniscient buyer isn't a theoretical threat. They're already here—and they're reshaping your market whether you're ready or not.

What Happens Next

If you think this is the peak, you're mistaken. We're not at the end of the transformation. We're at the very start.

- Every month, AI tools get faster, more accurate, and more accessible. What was once the domain of early adopters is quickly becoming standard practice.

- Browser extensions and chatbots are integrating AI research into the buying process by default.

- Procurement teams are embedding AI into their RFP workflows.

- Consumers are using AI assistants to scan product reviews and auto-generate comparison charts without even realizing it.

This isn't just a technological shift. It's a cultural one.

In the next few years, two things will become true:

1. Every buyer will have access to instant answers.

2. Buyers will trust those answers more than they trust you.

And that means the old playbooks—persuade first, educate slowly, reveal selectively—won't just be outdated. They'll be liabilities.

You're not preparing for a future that might arrive someday. You're adapting to a present that's already here—and accelerating.

The omniscient buyer is the new default. They will define how you sell, how you build trust, and how you survive in the years ahead.

The question isn't whether you'll change. It's whether you'll change in time.

Chapter 3

Your Illusion of Control

For decades, you were taught to control the narrative and the outcome. And you did.

You crafted the narrative. You decided when to reveal the details. You sequenced your message to lead buyers step by step toward a sale.

It worked—because buyers needed you to make sense of what they couldn't see.

I've made it clear by now, *hopefully*, that that advantage is gone.

Buyers don't wait for your story to unfold. They don't need your carefully curated journey. They leap straight to verdicts, armed with more context than you could ever provide.

It may be hard to accept, but any perception of control is just that—a perception.

AI has quietly removed your grip on how buyers learn, how they compare, and what they believe. Every claim you make is instantly weighed against an ocean of evidence. Every asset you produce—your webinars, your white papers, your landing pages—feels biased and time-consuming to buyers who can get instant, seemingly objective answers elsewhere.

You're not the guide anymore. At best, you're a participant in a story that's already half-written by the time they reach out.

In this chapter, you'll see why your old playbook—control the narrative, own the funnel, shape perception—doesn't just fail in this environment.

It backfires.

And you'll learn what it means to engage buyers who are no longer looking for a story. They're looking for confirmation that their conclusions are right and that you're worth listening to at all.

When Marketing & Sales Were In Control

If you look closely you will see that nearly every modern sales and marketing discipline was designed to guide—and sometimes manipulate—buyers who didn't know enough to challenge the story.

Think about how many of the tactics you were taught only worked in a world where your audience lacked context:

The Marketing Plays

- **Gated content:** Because prospects couldn't get credible information elsewhere, they were willing to trade their contact details just to learn.

- **Nurture campaigns:** You drip-fed knowledge in a sequence you controlled, believing you were moving buyers from "unaware" to "ready."

- **Case studies:** You decided which success stories to highlight—and which failures to bury.

- **Comparison guides:** You framed your competitors on your terms, knowing buyers rarely validated the claims.

The Sales Frameworks

- **Sandler Selling:** You controlled the "up-front contract," setting the terms of what the buyer would see and when. You decided when and how information was disclosed.

- **SPIN Selling:** You asked leading questions to steer buyers toward problems you could solve—problems they often hadn't researched yet.

- **Challenger Sales:** You taught prospects something new to create "commercial insight"—which only worked if they hadn't already read everything you were about to share.

The Timing Advantage

- You scheduled demos when you thought buyers were ready to be persuaded.

- You controlled the pace of the conversation—fast to outflank competitors, slow to build desire.

- You engineered urgency by rationing information.

All of these techniques relied on a simple, unspoken assumption:

You knew more than they did.

You were the keeper of the map. The interpreter of complexity. The filter through which truth passed.

And because buyers didn't have the tools to cross-check every word, they accepted your word as truth.

That was the foundation of your playbook. Not just what you said—but when you said it, how you packaged it, and what you deliberately left out.

It worked—until the moment buyers could know everything before you ever opened your mouth.

Buyers Show Up Absolutely Convinced of Their Right

Give people a little information, and they act like experts. Give them an AI that sounds authoritative, and they'll believe it's the gospel.

We've spent years training ourselves to be overconfident consumers.

Social media taught us that every opinion deserves an audience—and that the loudest voice wins. Algorithms feed us content that agrees with what we already believe, so we think we're right more than we are.

Now, when buyers prompt an AI to get fast, polished answers, they don't see it as a starting point. They see it as confirmation.

It feels objective.

It feels complete.

It feels indisputable.

And that feeling is addictive.

When you can compress a week of research into thirty seconds, why would you ever question whether you missed something? When you can get a verdict in a tidy bullet-point summary, why would you not feel like you have it all under control?

Humility is gone. AI makes us all powerful.

In many cultures across the world right now admitting you don't know something is seen as weakness. Hesitation looks like incompetence. Asking for help looks like surrender.

AI has become the perfect tool for this illusion—always ready with an answer, never hesitating, never revealing how little it really understands.

So buyers leap straight to conclusions. They arrive convinced. Not curious. Not open. **Convinced.**

And in their minds, marketing won't tell them anything new nor will sales be a helpful guide. Instead those are barriers—obstacles between them and what they've already decided is true.

Because why waste time listening to a pitch when your AI already told you what to think? Why tolerate persuasion when you can declare certainty before the conversation even starts?

This is what you're up against: A buyer who has been conditioned to see questioning as unnecessary and self-doubt as a flaw.

They don't think they need you. They think they already know.

And the scariest part? Most of the time, they'd rather be confident and wrong than uncertain and right.

Your Metrics Are Now Useless

Look at your dashboards and you'll see all the familiar metrics:

Downloads. Webinar signups. Email opens. Demo requests.

It's now just B.S. Smoke and mirrors.

Those metrics might feel like proof that your story is working. Evidence that your influence is intact.

But their actions are just a formality—another box buyers tick.

- They aren't attending your webinar because they need your insight. They're recording it because their boos forwarded it to them.

- They aren't downloading your white paper to learn. They're getting it to upload into AI and summarize.

- They didn't open and read your email–your message became a bullet point in a daily summary AI provided them.

- They didn't read your page, they clicked a reference link in an AI summary just to see if the source still exists.

This is called **Synthetic Engagement.**

Interactions with your brand that harvest artifacts to feed into the machine, where no human ever evaluates the information directly or sees the story in totality.

Every metric you celebrate may be nothing more than Synthetic Engagement—phantom key performance indicators.

- That page view? It might be a screenshot being fed into an AI model to pull out pricing, compare features, and highlight inconsistencies—while you think the buyer is reading every word.

- That case study download? It's getting dropped into an AI prompt, analyzed alongside five competitors' cases, and reduced to a single bullet point of relevance.

- That form completion? An automated AI agent did it because it was instructed to get 10 quotes.

We've built a whole discipline around the illusion that attention equals trust. That participation means agreement. That interest means openness.

It doesn't.

Buyers today are going through the motions while outsourcing the effort to their AI. You see these motions as engagement but everything really serves their AI.

So, you think you're shaping perception because the buyer is visible in your metrics, still clicking, still replying. But in reality, they're just waiting for you to stop talking so they can move on with their verdict.

What looks like interest is often just inertia. What feels like momentum is often just politeness.

In a world of Synthetic Engagement, what you measure isn't what matters. What you think is influencing isn't even being consumed.

When Your Story Doesn't Match The One They Have

Imagine walking into a courtroom where the jury has already reached a verdict—and you're the last to know.

That's what it feels like to sell today.

By the time you open your mouth, your buyer has a story they trust.

Their story feels objective. Their knowledge feels comprehensive.

It all feels like the truth, even if it's just an algorithm's best guess.

And any word you say that doesn't fit is treated with skepticism.

They *don't* wonder whether their version might be incomplete. They *don't* ask if their AI missed something important.

"Maybe *you* aren't an expert," they start thinking. Or they assume you've got a motive to answer differently. You're the biased narrator. You're the one trying to salvage a position they've already decided is weaker.

Because often the first story a buyer believes is the one they defend.

It doesn't matter how credible your facts are—what matters is that you arrived second. You aren't a logic-driven machine.

Now there is a collision.

Your narrative meets theirs. Those claims clash with what they've researched and concluded. In that moment, it's your word versus their AI.

It will happen in every industry:

- A software vendor corrects a competitor comparison the AI provided, and the buyer assumes spin and desperation.

- A consultant challenges an AI-generated budget benchmark, and the buyer assumes they are just over priced.

- A sales rep explains why the service list is outdated, and the buyer assumes evasion.

Because when stories collide, it isn't about who's right. It's about who the buyer decides to trust. And once that trust tilts away from you, no amount of persuasion will bring it back.

Everything Is Happening Without You Now

I already stated that trends showed buyers were doing more and more leg work before reaching out.

Now that line has moved even farther. You don't see them on your site or get them on a call until they've done the lionshare of their discovery and decision making.

Those buying activities—option research, short list building, comparison, validation, timeline estimates—all done before they even hit your site let alone your funnel.

It's invisible. It's without your knowledge or consent.

You're not in the room when the first impression locks into place. You're not there when your story gets stripped of nuance, condensed into bullet points, and compared to a competitor's.

You're not consulted nor notified. **You're simply judged.**

And when you finally are brought into the conversation, you assume you're starting from neutral ground. You're not.

You're trying to overwrite a perception that feels complete, objective, and final—even if it's none of those things.

This is the new reality:

Perception is formed way before they read the narrative you crafted or you're invited in for a conversation. And by the time you do arrive, it's often already too late.

The Path Forward

You can't out-sequence AI, neither can you out-script a buyer who arrives already convinced nor reclaim control over pre-formed perceptions.

The old playbook—craft the narrative, dictate the journey, ration the information—isn't just obsolete. It's toxic.

And yet, most teams haven't realized the change or won't admit it.

Marketing wants to still imagine they are persuading and informing. Sales will bulk at the idea that buyer knows more than they do. Executives will tell themselves their brand reputation is immune.

They'll call it best practice.
They'll call it discipline.
They'll call it consistency.

But it's really just fear of change. Fear of irrelevance.

Because letting go of the illusion of control feels like admitting you're powerless. Potentially not needed. And no one wants to admit that.

But ignorance isn't neutral. Denial won't slow down a change that's already happened. It's a choice to stand still while your buyers move past you at lightspeed.

The instinct to over-explain, to reassert authority, to correct and contradict—these reactions don't rebuild credibility. They erode it.

The only path forward is to accept that control is gone and replace it with something buyers actually value:

Transparency.
Responsiveness.
Humility.

In this environment, the fastest way to stand out isn't by building a taller wall around your narrative. It's by inviting buyers to test your claims openly—and proving you have nothing to fear from their scrutiny.

This won't feel comfortable. It may feel like surrender. But it isn't. It's the only strategy left when perception no longer belongs to you.

If you can let go of the illusion of control, you'll find something more durable in its place:

The ability to meet buyers where they already are—and earn the trust they no longer give freely.

And in a world where every fact can be checked, every claim can be challenged, and every story can be replaced in seconds, trust isn't just important.

It's everything.

That's where we go next.

Chapter 4

When All Trust Is Gone

Trust is not only paramount to business, it's oxygen. Marketing and sales can't survive without it. They can't even begin without the ability to build (or at least project) it.

As we clarify the evolution of what buyers have become and plan out a new strategy for marketing and sales in the coming chapters, much of the underlying concepts revolve around trust.

This chapter exists for the core purpose to establish some baselines for the importance and shifting landscape of trust.

So, if AI is the new gatekeeper... If buyers aren't reaching out till the end of their process... If they test all our claims in their AI engine... Or if they eventually outsource significant parts of the buying process to AI entirely...

Then ask yourself who is building trust with them?

Is it us or is it AI?

And if AI has become the new arbiter of trust, can we influence AI in a way to transfer that trust to us?

I believe trust is the foundation of marketing and sales outcomes, so let's really explore it.

Trust is the Catalyst of Action

Every decision to buy begins as a vacuum of trust. When a buyer first sees your name—in an ad, a search result, a social post...

They feel nothing. No loyalty. No belief. No conviction. *Not yet.*

Compare that to a referral or influencer mention. In those cases, their journey starts with some foundation of trust.

But when they start with none, every interaction does exactly one thing:

It either builds trust or dilutes it.

Everything becomes a test. Do they look credible? Is what they say consistent in different places? Does it feel like they have earned trust with others before?

I've always believed conversion is threshold of trust. Visitors move through every interaction gaining or depleting trust until there is enough built to drive action.

A closed sale is a threshold of trust too—proof, validation, risk reduction and manifesting confidence in value until they feel safe enough to say yes.

When you looked credible, people believed you. If you sounded authoritative, they deferred. When you claimed expertise, they gave you the benefit of the doubt.

In marketing and sales, trust doesn't accumulate evenly. It accelerates.

Small moments—an honest answer, a clear price, a transparent admission of limitations—create a foundation. When that foundation is strong enough, action becomes inevitable.

Trust is the catalyst that turns intention into commitment.

But when trust is weak, buyers stall. They don't convert. They delay decisions. They look for alternatives. Or they do nothing—because doing nothing feels safer than risking regret.

This has always been true. It's more true than ever now. Because in a world where AI can validate or contradict every word you say, buyers need *more* proof, *more* reassurance, *more* signals of credibility to reach the threshold where action feels safe.

Trust Was Already Hard To Gain

Long before AI entered the conversation, trust was eroding everywhere you looked.

We stopped believing in our institutions. The media fractured into partisan echo chambers. Corporate scandals made us question every promise. Scams and spam have become the norm.

Every breach, every manipulated headline, every phishing attempt chipped away at the assumption that anyone could be taken at face value.

When social media arrived, it accelerated the decline.

We watched curated feeds shape reality, watched misinformation spread faster than any correction could catch up. We saw how easy it was to manufacture credibility with a polished profile and the right number of followers. Platforms even experimented on us to see if they could manipulate our emotions.

At the same time, technology made it easier to look credible while being untrustworthy.

- Brands began to buy fake reviews.

- Influencers started selling endorsements they didn't even believe in.

- Companies gamed algorithms to bury complaints and amplify praise.

And consumers learned a simple lesson:

If you don't question everything, you'll end up fooled.

We learned to be skeptical because skepticism felt safer than the risk of being manipulated. We taught ourselves to assume everyone has bias, question motives, and triple-check the facts. And eventually, that vigilance turned into a natural state of constant distrust.

This is important because as we explore your buyer's trust, we have to understand where it stands today.

Skepticism is already a cultural reflex.

AI Amplifies Your Buyer's Mistrust

AI is becoming your buyer's source of trust.

Your buyer doesn't have to wonder if your pricing is competitive. They can ask an AI to pull data from a dozen competitors and benchmark you in seconds.

They don't have to guess if your reviews are real. They can prompt an AI to find patterns that expose manipulation.

They don't have to take your word for anything—because their AI will check it while you're still talking.

Before AI, verification of any claim had friction. You had to research, cross-check, ask around, dig.

Now, every claim you make is now tested by a machine that presents as if it has infinite knowledge, *feels* impartial, and lightning-fast.

So, why not use it to verify every claim made?

This is why AI isn't just another tool. It's a verification accelerant.

It compressed the timeline between promise and proof. It removed the last excuses for taking you at your word. And it set a new buyer expectation, you can't walk back:

Every claim should be validated instantly, or it shouldn't be trusted at all.

AI Companies Will Fight For Credibility

We've clarified so far that trust is the buyer's doorway to action, they come to us naturally skeptical, and they can now easily attempt to verify evey claim we make with AI.

At the moment, most buyers will trust AI more than they trust you. More than they trust your competitors. More than they trust almost any human source.

While many take every AI response as gospel, that trust is actually fragile. Some people already do question its outputs.

There will be more moments where that credibility is tested for those that do have a high level of trust.

- A few more high-profile AI hallucinations.
- A wave of lawsuits over biased outputs.
- An exposé about hidden incentives in training data.

AI companies won't go down without a huge fight though. They understand exactly how valuable that trust is.

Their entire business depends on being perceived as objective. They know the machine's credibility is what keeps humans coming back. And they will spend billions of dollars to protect that perception.

They will develop sophisticated systems to detect hallucinations more quickly. They will invest in PR campaigns to reassure the public. They will release endless updates, promising more transparency, accuracy, and fairness.

Not because they care about your buyer's well-being. Because maintaining trust is their business model.

And that means the machine's authority isn't likely to collapse any time soon. If anything, it will become more entrenched. Because the companies behind AI have more incentive—and more resources—to preserve that trust than any brand you will ever compete with.

So while you're fighting to earn credibility one buyer at a time, the platforms shaping their perceptions will be waging an industrial-scale campaign to stay indispensable.

And they will excel at it.

When Only the Machine is Trusted

The platforms behind AI understand something most companies haven't yet grasped:

Trust is their most valuable asset—and they must do everything to protect it.

Because if buyers stop believing the machine, the entire model collapses. The recommendations, the comparisons, and the search answers all become noise.

That's why AI companies are investing billions to ensure their authority never gets questioned:

- They are building self-correcting systems that learn from every mistake faster than any human team could.

- They are training models to preempt objections before they arise.

- They are designing interfaces that deliver answers with the kind of clarity and confidence humans rarely muster.

- They are publishing research, transparency reports, and "trust layers" engineered to reassure the public that their conclusions are neutral.

- They are providing positive reinforcement with every answer to tear down your walls.

And it's working. We can see it.

Because, while every other source of credibility—news outlets, brands, institutions—has fractured under the weight of bias and scandal, AI appears frictionless and uninvolved. It feels like the only place left where truth isn't up for debate.

It's a campaign, not an accident.

The machine isn't passively trusted. It is actively working to remain the sole arbiter of what buyers should believe.

And that means you're now competing against an opponent with unlimited scale, endless reinforcement loops, and a vested interest in making sure no human claim ever feels more reliable.

If you think you can out-compete AI companies for trust and authority, you're not optimistic—you're delusional.

In this new environment, you don't get to decide whether the machine is trusted. You need to work to influence what the machine says and how well you handle situations where its story is different than yours.

AI is The Arbitor of Trust

It used to be obvious who controlled your reputation. You could see the outlets that shaped perception: journalists, analysts, review sites, and search engines.

You learned how to play their game. You even hired SEO consultants to reverse-engineer algorithms. You published case studies to influence analysts. You crafted web pages knowing exactly how they would appear in search results.

Even when you didn't like the rules, at least you understood them.

With AI, its not so straight-forward.

AI is an algorithm where every output for every question is different. Its always changing. The information that informs it is invisible.

When a buyer asks the machine about your company, you don't know which sources it pulls from. You don't know how it weighs credibility or prioritizes context. You don't know what version of your story it's assembling.

It feels impartial to your buyer. To you, it's a black box.

And unlike search, there are no guaranteed entry points. No blue links you can optimize. No page titles you can control.

Often the machine doesn't present a list of sources. It delivers a verdict. A confident, frictionless answer that feels definitive—no matter how incomplete or distorted it is. Even if sources are provided, they are minor footnotes.

This is the shift most brands are unprepared for:

Your credibility no longer lives on your website. It lives in a system that's difficult to audit, predict, or manipulate the way you once did.

AI is the gatekeeper. And if your story isn't discoverable, corroborated, and aligned with the machine's version of reality, your story doesn't matter.

Radical Transparency Wins

You don't have to like this new reality. You just have to decide whether you'll compete in it.

Because when AI becomes the first place buyers look for answers, your only sustainable strategy is to make the answers about you impossible to dispute.

Radical transparency isn't a marketing slogan. It's the baseline expectation in a world where every claim can—and will—be verified in seconds.

This is not about gaming the algorithm. You won't be able to.

It's about removing every excuse buyers have to doubt you:

- Publish evidence in formats AI can ingest and cross-reference.

- Share your pricing, your process, and your performance data without spin.

- Proactively answer the questions and objections you know the machine will surface.

- Keep your story so consistent across every channel that the algorithm has no gaps to exploit.

- Release your secrets so that they are revealed in AI outputs.

Most companies will resist this. They'll cling to creative messaging, secrecy, half-truths, and carefully packaged narratives. They'll tell themselves transparency is a liability.

And that's why they'll lose.

Because in this environment, the brands that win won't be the ones with the most polished story. They'll be the ones with nothing to hide—and the receipts to prove it.

Radical transparency isn't just how you survive the trust recession. It's how you turn credibility into your most unassailable advantage.

Don't worry, later in this book we'll talk about how to achieve it.

A Final Warning On Trust & AI

It's tempting to think this is just another phase. A trend you can wait out. A wave of hype that will settle back into something more familiar.

It isn't.

This is a permanent shift in who buyers trust, how they learn, and what they expect.

AI won't lose relevance. It won't grow less sophisticated. It won't stop rewriting the rules of credibility.

And the longer you pretend you can operate by yesterday's standards—guarding information, rationing access, relying on polish over proof—the faster your relevance will evaporate.

Trust has always been the catalyst of action. Now it's the only thing standing between your brand and irrelevance.

The companies that adapt will be the ones buyers believe. The ones that don't will spend the next decade wondering why no one listens to them anymore.

A Buyer Transformed

An AI-Influenced Buyer is different from anything you have ever seen before. They've evolved.

Buyers don't reach out to you because they're curious—they're often already convinced. They don't ask you to teach—they just want you to confirm. Their confidence feels unshakable even when it's shallow.

You're not facing a better-informed version of the old buyer. You're facing a new species entirely. One shaped by an environment where knowledge is infinite, verification is effortless, and the machine feeds them just what they need.

This transformation is bigger than data or technology. It's psychological, emotional, cultural, worldwide.

It's the reason every sales conversation feels different now. It's why your marketing doesn't land the way it used to.

And it's why, if you keep treating these buyers like their predecessors, you'll spend the next decade watching your relevance decay.

Part II isn't a eulogy for the old buyer. It's an unflinching look at who these new buyers are—and the hidden tensions that will shape every decision they make.

Because if you don't understand the psychology of the omniscient buyer, no strategy, no pitch, no technology will save you.

This is the blueprint for decoding the minds you're about to face.

Chapter 5

Instant Expertise & Overconfidence

They don't come to you empty-handed anymore.

They show up certain.

Certain they've already figured you out. Certain, they know exactly how your product stacks up, why your pricing is inflated, and which of your promises will fall apart under scrutiny.

Because in five minutes, an AI has filled their heads with curated summaries and confident verdicts.

They think that's expertise.

But here's the truth: instant knowledge isn't wisdom. It's a veneer—thin enough to crack under the slightest pressure.

And if you're not ready to expose the gap between what they think they know and what actually matters, you'll lose to their illusion.

This is the age of synthetic expertise. We need to adapt to this new reality or get outpaced by false certainty wrapped in bullet points.

The Rise of Synthetic Expertise

It used to take months—sometimes years—for a buyer to feel like they understood your business. They'd read white papers, talk to peers, collect brochures, sit through demos, and slowly build a sense of competence.

Or often they just plain trusted your expertise, knowing that they didn't have the time to gain it themselves.

That timeline and ability to *gain* expertise—or at least prompt and get answers—has collapsed to a few minutes.

It's all just a few prompts away from being explained in the simplest terms that the buyer can understand.

- *Explain it to me like I'm 5.*
- *Tell me the steps to get this completed.*
- *How does this work in my [industry]?*
- *Who are the top players and what do they each do different?*
- *What might fail or be a challenge?*

The illusion of mastery is instant—and it's addictive.

Because buyers no longer have to wrestle with ambiguity. They don't have to sift through conflicting sources or wonder if they've missed something important.

The machine makes it feel complete, objective, authoritative.

And that feeling is powerful.

It feels earned—even when it isn't.

Because when an AI serves you a clean, bullet-pointed verdict, it does more than compress information. It manufactures a sense of competence. It gives you the same psychological reward as real expertise: the relief of certainty, the confidence of having the answers, the quiet thrill of feeling like the smartest person in the room.

In the past, buying something complex used to feel humbling.

You had to admit what you didn't know. You had to ask questions. You had to sit with uncertainty. You had to accept you wouldn't understand it all.

No more. AI knows your personality and learning style. It presents a wealth of information in a format that you'll understand best.

Think about the cultural and psychological shift this triggers.

For most of human history, not knowing was an uncomfortable but essential state. We were wired to stay cautious, to keep questioning, to keep gathering evidence. Uncertainty made us alert. It kept us humble.

But instant knowledge hijacks that wiring. It gives our brains the dopamine hit of certainty without the hard work of understanding. It rewards speed over depth, conviction over curiosity.

And the more people experience this on-demand confidence, the less tolerance they have for ambiguity **or for any seller who challenges their conclusions.**

Buyers walk in believing they're fully prepared, because the machine made them feel that way.

That's why you'll hear them speak with an unshakable confidence that sounds like experience but is really just the byproduct of a fast, curated download.

Some buyers will be transparent about it. They'll tell you outright that they've run your entire offering through an AI and come prepared with questions.

Others will pretend the insights are their own.

For any subject matter expert, hearing someone with Synthetic Expertise won't be that hard to see.

Their line of questioning will expose the truth. The same patterns always surface—confidence without context, granular details they shouldn't know yet, and conclusions delivered like foregone facts.

Shallow confidence that erodes upon any depth.

For sales, delivery and service teams that often stand in for a subject matter expert, they will be experiencing a new environment of buyer and customer confidence that may take them off guard.

Confidence manufactured by speed, but hollow at the core.

It's the reason so many sales conversations will feel combative from the first minute. And customers on service calls will be attack with summarized lists of highly technical points they don't actually understand.

When that happens, you're not just dealing with a skeptical buyer. You're facing a silent verdict you may never get the chance to contest.

But the even scarier scenario?

They never bother to ask at all. Synthetic expertise convinces buyers they don't need clarification. They don't need your perspective. They don't need to hear your story. They go through their process convinced that the answer they got was the truth—complete, final, beyond dispute.

You're not educating anymore.
You're defending.

You're not guiding discovery.
You're reacting to conclusions drawn in seconds.

This is the new baseline. Every buyer thinks they've already solved the puzzle. Your job now isn't to supply more data. It's to reveal what their AI briefing left out—and why it matters.

The Invisible Gaps in Synthetic Expertise

AI loves to project an air of completeness.

It scrapes every article, every review, every public document it can reach—and distills them into a clean, authoritative summary.

Your buyer walked in with confidence.

They'd spent hours with an AI, prompting it like a trusted advisor. They'd seen the bullet points that sounded spot on. They'd asked the machine to simplify the complex—and it delivered.

Now, they're walking into your conversation with the quiet confidence of someone who believes they already know how this goes.

But what they've built isn't real expertise. It's a projection.
A convincing, articulate, polished illusion that omits the hardest parts.

Because no matter how advanced the language model, it will always lack what matters most: the context only earned through lived experience.

So, if we want to start managing overconfident buyers, we need to see exactly what AI leaves out.

1. Reality vs. Theory

AI knows what should happen. Not what does.

It pulls timelines from case studies. Steps from documentation. Confidence from public consensus.

But it's never seen a client stall because procurement forgot to file paperwork.

It's never watched a kick-off derailed by an unexpected re-org. It's never had to say, "This was supposed to take 30 days… but now it's 90."

When your buyer asks AI, "How long does onboarding take?" they're given an answer that feels safe: "Typically 30–45 days depending on complexity."

But complexity isn't just a configuration variable.
It's a team member going on leave.

It's legacy systems throwing silent errors.
It's a champion losing influence mid-rollout.

AI doesn't experience delays. It doesn't hit walls.
So it doesn't know how to account for them.

This isn't just a knowledge gap.
It's a friction gap.
And AI doesn't feel friction.

2. Emotional Intelligence

AI can read the logistics of the room. But it can't feel the tension inside it. It can parse tone. It can flag sentiment. It can surface complaints from online reviews.

But it doesn't know what a buyer looks like when they're under pressure. It doesn't know how a hesitant "maybe" can mean "absolutely not" if you're listening closely enough.

It doesn't see how internal politics shape every conversation, even when no one names them.

A buyer might say, "I've reviewed a lot of feedback about your customer support." What they mean is: "My team's worried they'll be left hanging when things go wrong."

That fear never made it into the data. But you've heard it before. You've addressed it before. You've earned trust in high-stakes moments—and you know exactly how to surface the concern, address it with empathy, and turn it into confidence.

AI can simulate tone. You can sense what's unsaid.
And that difference defines the whole relationship.

3. Tacit Knowledge

AI knows the steps. You know where people get stuck.

It can explain how to build a strategy. You've built strategies that collapsed. Then rebuilt them smarter.

It can list common risks. You've seen rare ones explode because someone forgot the edge cases.

Tacit knowledge is hard to describe because it was never written down. It's the pattern you start to recognize after the tenth failed implementation. It's the shortcut you take because the official route is riddled with delays. It's the part where someone says, "Follow the instructions," and you quietly think, "No one who's actually done this would follow those instructions."

AI never lived that. So it doesn't know what to skip, what to question, or where to dig deeper.

It delivers the illusion of mastery.
But it has no scar tissue.
And scar tissue is where real expertise lives.

4. Unwritten Signals

AI answers what it's asked. It doesn't know what's worth asking.

It doesn't know how a change in executive tone mid-call should alter your sales motion.

It doesn't catch when a buyer mentions a previous vendor's failure—and downplays it too quickly.

It doesn't notice that the third stakeholder hasn't spoken in 20 minutes but suddenly objects at the close.

Buyers prompt AI for checklists.
"What should I ask this vendor?"

They get smart questions. Thoughtful ones, even.

But not the one that breaks the case open. Not the one that reveals the real risk. Not the one that disarms the performative confidence and exposes what's actually keeping the buyer up at night.

AI can't ask that question. Because it doesn't know how to notice the tension behind the words.

These aren't gaps in information.
They're gaps in intuition.
The buyer doesn't know what they missed.
And the AI never told them to look.

5. Strategic Rationale

AI can describe what you built. But not why you built it that way.

It lists your features. It compares your pricing. It notes that your platform doesn't serve small businesses or that you left out a buzzy integration. Then it draws a conclusion: something must be missing.

What it can't see is what you learned when you did serve that segment—and why you walked away.

It can't know that you killed off three features to double down on the one that actually solved the problem better.

It can't explain why you raised prices and lost some deals—only to provide a higher level of service that customers really need.

AI sees what is.
Only you can explain why.
And in complex buying decisions, the why is often the deciding factor.

Your buyer isn't trying to be arrogant.
They just think they've done their homework.

But they've only read the syllabus. They haven't done the lab work.
They haven't seen how it breaks. They haven't stood where you've
stood—at the edge of a failed rollout, a dropped handoff, a misaligned
team—and learned what makes the difference between success and
damage control.

AI gave them structure.
You give them truth.

Your job isn't to out-fact the machine.
It's to expose what the machine can't see.
To bring context to the surface.
To reveal the real cost of conclusions drawn too fast.

Because the buyer doesn't just need more answers.
They need perspective.
And that only comes from you.

This is why synthetic expertise is so dangerous. It doesn't just leave out
context—it actively convinces buyers that no context is missing.

The brain loves a clean story. When the machine provides a confident
narrative, buyers don't feel the need to question it. They assume the
unknowns don't matter—or don't exist at all.

Avoid Playing Offense Against Their AI

We know their information isn't perfect or its so perfect it isn't realistic.

But if you begin to slam their efforts and play offense, some buyers
won't smile and thank you for your corrections.

They'll silently think you are trying to manipulate them. Or that you are unhappy they know more. Even that you don't know what you're talking about.

They gained power through the AI's manufactured expertise and have a sense of ownership over it.

We'll talk about how to handle this overconfidence in future chapters, but for now, understand that buyers often will no longer feel like they are novices looking for your guidance like they once did.

Chapter 6

Every Vendor, Every Option, Instantly

Once, it was enough to be the most visible.

If you ranked first, you won. If you bought the right placement, you looked credible. If you showed up everywhere, you stayed top of mind.

Prominence was your advantage, and most of your competitors stayed hidden in the margins.

Not anymore.

A single prompt can expose every option in your category. Every alternative. Every upstart competitor you hoped no one would notice.

AI doesn't care how long you've been at the top. It doesn't care how much you paid to stay there. It just levels the field.

And when every choice is presented side by side in an instant, prominence won't be the only winning strategy.

Friction Kept Buyers From Digging Too Deep

For decades, your position mattered more than almost anything else.

If you were the first search result, you won the click. If you were the featured vendor in a paid directory, you got the call. If you were the brand everyone had heard of, you got the shortlist by default.

Visibility was a moat.

If a better solution was buried five pages deep in Google search results. If some new innovative competitor was posting on social with 10 followers. If there was an alternative approach no one was talking about.

Few people ever dug that deep. Call it lazy. Call it busy.

Just know that those competitor's lack of prominence was your protection. Even if you weren't the best, you were often the easiest to find.

And when time was limited, convenience won. Buyers had to put in the work to uncover their options. They had to search, filter, cross-reference, and ask around. That effort alone protected incumbents and established brands.

This is why so many companies built empires on prominence. Not because they were the only option—but because they were the most frictionless option.

AI reads all 50 pages of a search results when your buyer wouldn't go past the 6th result on page 1.

AI is the Ultimate Discovery Engine

AI didn't just compress research. It obliterated the walls around it. The machine gobbles vast amounts of information and delivers them in an instant.

A 100 pages of search results. Easy.
Every directory of solution providers. Instant.
20 videos of how to do it yourself. Transcribed.

Those alternatives your buyer was too busy to find before just got delivered to them with barely any effort at all.

Type one prompt—"Show me every vendor who solves this specific problem"—'and the algorithm doesn't just return a multi-page list.

It delivers what it thinks answers the question best no matter how deeply it was buried in the internet.

AI presents a detailed table of options including that competitor that used to be on the third page, the new startup with no marketing budget, and the niche specialist you've never considered. All presented next to your brand like an equal.

And at the end of the table, their engine asks if they want a detailed plan to do it themselves instead of hiring.

When a buyer prompts their copilot, it doesn't care about location, ad spend, rank, alphabetical order or anything else. It cares about fit.

"Which vendor offers the best combination of pricing, features, and customer success for my [specialty industry]?"

It doesn't care if you have thousands of inbound links from decades of being in business. It doesn't care that you paid a premium for special placement in an industry directory.

This can be a win for some how used to be buried. For those who have dominated on visibility, it flattens the market into a single playing field where the moat of prominence disappears.

You relied on the friction that came with deep research.

When that friction goes away, so does your insulation.

The buyer sitting across from you isn't comparing you to the same three companies you've always pitched against.

They're comparing you to everyone. All at once. And they're doing it before you even know they're looking.

The Psychological Impact Of AI Infinite Discovery

When buyers first experience infinite discovery, it can feel exhilarating.

What once was a ton of effort is so fast, simple and thorough.

"Provide me a list of 20 companies that solve my specific problem and create a table that compares years in business, team size, price, industry experience, etc."

And it's delivered.

To look through 40 plus sites and multiple comparison charts to gather all that information was days of effort before.

It's the famous 'Easy Button'.

This will bring people back over and over again at the start of any task they have. It's not only just plain efficient, it's addicting.

Those perfectly curated tables also create the illusion of objectivity, a feeling that the right choice is obvious because it's all laid out in a grid.

Why do your own research or fact checking when the AI just provided detailed pros and cons that look more thorough that anything you could produce manually.

Familiarity & Brand Loyalty At Risk

When it is easier and faster to discover alternatives, the downside of looking at your options is eliminated.

Often buyers would go to the company they knew or had heard of because the effort to research and vet felt daunting.

Instead of thinking: *"We already know them—let's start there,"* buyers think: *"Let's see who stacks up best." Because its easy to do.*

Before, familiarity helped overcome the friction of research and evaluation. Now that research and evaluation are infinite and easy, familiarity isn't as important.

Answers Become Conversations

Most AI interfaces are chats. This is a big paradigm shift from pages of results.

Sure, in search engines, you could run another search or click on suggested searches it provided, but this just added to your effort. Maybe your first search was too broad and the 20 minutes you spent figuring that out by click on results was just how it worked.

AI responses are not just fast but also connected.

"Provide me a list of 20 companies that solve my specific problem and create a table that compares years in business, team size, price, industry experience, etc."

Is now followed by:

"Narrow that down to ones that specifically work with my tech stack."

"Show me some more options that have over 50 employees."

"Can you remove any that have worked with my competitors"

All of which happens in a fraction of what previously was multiple searches and browsing through results.

That ease of expanding and narrowing the AI answers encourages buyers to dig for more options than they every would have before.

Controling Your Visibility Just Got Harder

Google dominated search for decades. Billions of searches were the pathway for millions of buyers to find what they needed.

First page rank equaled customers.

That's why Search Engine Optimization was a massive industry of tactics and techniques to attempt to manipulate rankings. But when being honest, the best SEO experts would admit that Google kept its ranking algorithm close to the vest. We all had a good idea what influenced rank, but no one ever got to see the exact formula.

So, with enough ongoing effort you could reach the first page. Or us paid search to buy top visibility instantly.

Now, AI prompting is overtaking search. It's just easier and better. Even search engines are delivering AI overviews as much as ranked pages for you to explore.

The issue is that AI doesn't work like search.

AI by its very nature is more random—the same prompt in the same AI engine produces a new response every time. You can't audit or reverse-engineer this algorithm the same way.

In addition, there is yet to be a dominate AI engine. Google had 80% market share of search, so it made sense to focus efforts there. We don't know if there will be a dominate AI player and if there is, who it will be.

Right now, this is great for buyers. Instant, objective answers. But for anyone looking for visibility to those buyers, it feels like a black box.

An industry is about to explode around optimizing for visibility in AI engines. I have no doubt some dominant AI engines will emerge and experts will find some patterns.

But, we do need to understand that the way AI works is very different and we are still in the infancy stages of its evolution.

What This Means For You

You can't rely on prominence or name recognition anymore. Your search rank, directory placement and reputation will be replaced by an AI response.

Even the process of achieving visibility will be more difficult.

And buyers are going to see a much broader view of your competitive landscape. Their going to view their options in new ways that just were too time consuming before.

Now that your buyer has an infinite vantage point, there is only one option.

Make your value so clear, so verifiable, and so differentiated that no algorithm can bury it—and no buyer can ignore it.

Chapter 7

Outsourcing The Entire Buying Journey To AI

The buying process has always been a series of steps. Whether you are purchasing a small consumer item or a complex B2B solution.

Buyers aren't just handling discovery in their AI engines, They are handing them the keys to the entire process.

From drafting requirements to shortlisting vendors to negotiating final terms, the machine doesn't just inform decisions—it makes them.

And by the time you're invited in, most of the real choices have already been made.

The Delegation Of Everything

By now, we've established that using AI to buy is easy, fast, thorough and psychologically satisfying.

Deciding is hard work. Especially for any purchase of significance.

People are researching, reading, compiling, comparing, conversing, verifying, collaborating, approving, contracting.

If you're paying any attention to changing buyer habits with AI, you are probably focused on the discovery part of their journey.

But, it's not just discovery.

Comparison.
Education.
Evaluation.
Verification.
Negotiation.

AI does it. Every step in the process has the potential to be delegated.

A single prompt replaces weeks of effort:

- *"Create a shortlist of the best vendors."*

- *"Draft an RFP for this solution."*

- *"Benchmark pricing across the market."*

- *"Summarize common implementation risks."*

- *"Evaluate if this recommended solution will work."*

- *"Review this contract and redline unfavorable terms."*

That work your buyer used to do, AI obliges instantly. Buyers don't think of this as delegation. They think of it as efficiency.

This delegation is happening across the entire journey you either tried to influence or collaborate with buyers on.

Buyers even use AI to inform and work with other decision makers. *"Write a summary of my findings to send to finance."* Replaces a meeting or phone call to review all the options.

Leading AI adopters are already outsourcing as much as they can.

But the laggards are not far behind.

AI Creates the Requirements

In the old model, defining what mattered was a collaborative effort.

You'd run discovery calls, uncover hidden priorities, and educate buyers on trade-offs they hadn't considered.

That was your chance to shape the problem before you sold the solution. To influence what the solution might need or look like.

With AI, that opportunity often disappears before you even know a buyer exists. Because now, why get requirements from a biased vendor?

Buyers outsource it to AI:

- *"Generate an RFP for enterprise data platforms."*

- *"List must-have features for a cloud-based security solution."*

- *"Summarize key selection criteria for pricing consultants."*

- *"Build an ROI questionnaire for our current vendors."*

And the AI responds with thorough, bullet-point certainty.

All packaged as if they were facts rather than guesses stitched together from scraped content.

This is how you end up with buyers who walk in convinced:

- That the plan they created includes everything.

- That your solution is missing critical capabilities.

- That your pricing is too high before they understand your model.

- That your delivery timelines are unacceptable before you can explain why they matter.

Requirements used to be a conversation.

Now, they're a pre-written script you had no hand in drafting.

And if you don't learn to challenge without criticizing the buyer's work, you'll spend every deal defending yourself against an algorithm's half-informed checklist.

Algorithmic Shortlists

In the old buying process, getting on a shortlist took work.

You built relationships. You earned referrals. You invested in visibility so you'd be top of mind when the time came to decide.

That investment paid off because discovery was manual, and buyers leaned on familiar names to save time and reduce risk.

Today, shortlisting is a one-prompt operation:

- *"Show me the top ten vendors that meet these criteria."*

- *"Rank them by price, customer satisfaction, and feature completeness."*

- *"Highlight which ones are growing fastest."*

- *"Review these proposals and give me the top three."*

- *"Analyze these reports and tell me which vendors we should re-evaluate."*

AI doesn't care about your reputation in the market. It doesn't care how much you've invested in being seen.

It pulls data from a thousand sources, weighs them by algorithms you'll never see, and produces a ranked list that feels definitive.

What makes this shift so dangerous is that not only do you not know exactly why the AI didn't put you on the shortlist, but your buyer might actually not know either.

There's no fallback discovery process. No polite outreach from the buyer asking you to join the conversation. No second chance to be considered.

Once the AI generates the shortlist, the human brain does what it always does–it assumes the list is complete.

If you're not on it, you might as well not exist.

The Invisible Challenger

AI is now part of every conversation.

You made the shortlist. Now you jump on a call with the buyer to talk and they are ready with a list of questions generated by their AI to vet you like a leading expert.

The prospect prompted their AI *"What 10 questions should I ask to ensure vendors can accomplish my goals?"* and they don't get soft ball questions. The AI dug through it's vast resources to deliver penetrating, uncomfortable queries meant get to the root of the matter on the first call.

You novice buyer sounds like an expert investigator.

Not only are you presented with a new level of questioning, but AI is listening to confirm and validate your responses. Calls being recorded, transcribed, summarized, evaluated in an instant by AI.

Five minutes after the call, the AI delivers a document to the buyer that has condensed your answers, uncovered discrepancies, and suggests new questions to go even deeper.

AI Scored Proposals

Typically, submitting a proposal meant you could shape how it was read. You'd highlight strengths in person. You'd walk buyers through your logic. You'd present a narrative and contextualize pricing and timelines.

Evaluation was as much about dialogue as it was about documentation.

Now, your proposal isn't read first by a human.

It's uploaded, scored, compared, and summarized—**by an algorithm.**

They prompt the AI:

- *"Score each vendor against our requirements."*

- *"Flag any discrepancies or missing features."*

- *"Identify which proposal delivers the best value."*

- *"Research their recommendations and tell me which won't produce ROI this quarter."*

The machine spits out a ranking, complete with bullet-pointed rationales that feel authoritative.

But here's what the buyer often doesn't realize:

Those scores are only as reliable as the data they were derived from. If your proposal didn't use the exact keywords the AI was trained to look for, you get dinged. If you frame your differentiation in nuanced ways, the algorithm misses it. If your approach can't be easily summarized in a table, it gets ignored.

You walk into the conversation already labeled:

"Too expensive." … *"Incomplete."* … *"Less aligned."*

And you're forced to defend yourself against a verdict the buyer has accepted as objective truth.

In this environment, it's not enough to have the best proposal.

You have to make sure the machine understands it—because that's who evaluates you first.

Negotiation by Prompt

Even if you clear every hurdle. Even if you make the shortlist, prove your value and ace the proposal.

You still walk into a negotiation that's already been scripted. Because buyers aren't just using AI to discover options. They're using it to engineer their entire strategy to extract more from you.

It starts with a simple prompt:

- *"What concessions are typical in this industry?"*

- *"What hidden fees should I challenge?"*

- *"What tactics work best to negotiate lower pricing?"*

- *"Give me 5 talking points to negotiate costs 10% lower."*

The AI provides a list of discount thresholds, identifies common areas where vendors overcharge, and employs psychological levers to create urgency and secure better terms.

You're not sitting across from a buyer who's learning as they go. You're facing someone armed with a playbook designed to undermine your position before you even speak.

This is why so many negotiations will feel like the other side is reading from a script— because they are.

Even the intern sounds like a national debate team champion.

And once those tactics are in play, you're no longer negotiating with a human who feels uncertain. You're negotiating with an algorithm that convinces them they're right.

If you thought buyers were empowered before, you haven't seen anything yet.

The Illusion of Control

If you asked most buyers, they'd tell you this new process makes them more independent. More informed. More objective. More in control.

And on the surface, it feels true.

After all, they have every option, every benchmark, every negotiation tactic at their fingertips.

But look closer, and you'll see the irony that they've outsourced their judgment to a machine they don't understand.

When the AI drafts its requirements, that becomes the blueprint. It ranks their vendors, which becomes the shortlist. Now, when it scores proposals, that becomes the verdict. If AI suggests concessions, that becomes the deal breaker.

What feels like empowerment is often just submission. Submission to an algorithm trained on public data and old assumptions.

And because it all feels clean and rational, buyers rarely question it.

They don't wonder:

- *"What did the AI miss?"*

- *"What biases shaped this output?"*

- *"What nuance did it flatten?"*

The buyer believes they're fully in control... but are really just following instructions. Sounds a bit dystopian.

When you finally get your chance to speak, you're not up against a blank slate. You're up against a certainty manufactured by code.

And if you can't puncture that illusion, you'll never regain influence.

Your Role: The Late-Stage Validator

This is the new reality you have to accept:

By the time you're invited into the conversation, most of the evaluation has been done and very little uncertainty exists.

The AI has defined what good looks like. It has decided which options deserve consideration. It has created a rubric table for your offer. It drafted the negotiation plan.

You're not the guide anymore. **You're the validator.**

Your job isn't to help the buyer figure out what matters. It's to confirm that the machine's assumptions are correct—or to prove, carefully, that they aren't.

This requires a different skill set:

- The ability to reframe expectations without sounding defensive.

- The clarity to surface nuance in ways that don't feel like excuses.

- The courage to challenge the script buyers trust more than you.

Because when the entire buying journey has been outsourced, your only chance is to become the one variable AI can't replicate:

A human who can explain the gap between what sounds right and what is true.

In a world where algorithms do the thinking, your credibility depends on breaking through the illusion, delivering more than the AI has, or changing the paradigm.

Chapter 8

Real-Time Fact-Checking

There was a time when buyers needed hours—or days—to process what you said. They'd take notes, circle back with questions, and reflect before making a call.

That breathing room is gone. Every word you say is captured, summarized, and fact-checked before you finish your sentence. The machine isn't just recording. It's judging.

And in this new reality, there's no space to think, no time to clarify, and no tolerance for anything that can't be verified instantly.

Live AI Note-Takers as Silent Witnesses

It used to be just you and the buyer in the conversation. You'd share your story, answer questions, and trust they'd remember the parts that mattered.

Now, there's always a third participant.

The AI note-taker is silently analyzing every word.

But it doesn't stop at transcription. People have been recording calls forever, but often the collected virtual dust because no one wanted to take the time to re-listen.

AI recordings and note takers remove the effort and deliver a lot more:

- They tag and summarize your statements in real time.

- They cross-check your claims against what you've said before.

- They surface inconsistencies as you speak.

For buyers, this changes everything. They no longer have to stay fully engaged. They don't need to capture nuance or think carefully about their answers in the moment. They can skim, half-listen, or move on, knowing the machine will package everything later.

And while you're still talking, the AI is already drafting:

- Follow-up questions to challenge your assumptions.

- A list of objections you haven't even heard yet.

- A timeline of everything you promised.

Before, buyers would pause, reflect, and process. Now they leave the meeting with a simplified version of what just happened, condensed into bullet points that feel objective.

And the most important shift?

It's not just a recounting. It's a silent referee.

It reassures buyers:

"I'll remember exactly what was said."

"I'll let you know if they leave anything out."

"I'll let you know what to ask them next."

"I'll keep them honest."

That's why, no matter how accurate or transparent you are, you're no longer the trusted narrator.

Every meeting is a deposition. And the machine is the judge who never forgets—and never stops listening.

No Buffer Between Your Claims and Their Reaction

In sales, time could be your ally. After a conversation, buyers needed space to process:

- They'd review their notes.

- They'd talk with their team.

- They'd reflect on what they heard before responding.

- They'd do some light research without going past the first page of Google results.

If something you said was unclear or inconsistent, you often had a chance to follow up— to clarify, to reframe, to prove your credibility.

Now, as soon as the meeting ends, buyers already have:

- A complete summary of your statements.

- A list of flagged discrepancies.

- Links to references you made on the call.

What used to take days now takes 2 minutes.

The moment you sign off, the machine re-packages everything you said and pushes it to their team. Five minutes after the end of the call, buyer follow-up questions come two dozen at a time because the AI handed it to them in seconds.

While you were preparing your typing up your thank you for their time, the buyer has already moved to evaluation.

There's no buffer or breathing room anymore. No pause to gather context. No time to inject nuance.

In this environment, your words don't just have to be accurate.

They have to be *instantly* defensible.

Endless Question Engines

When buyers relied on their own notes, your conversations kept their depth. They might not capture every detail, but they also didn't reduce everything to black-and-white conclusions.

Questions were genuine and often emotionally driven.

But what happens when a buyer has an expert ready to coach them through their evaluation of you?

- *"Create a list of questions I'm not thinking of."*

- *"Highlight any areas where the solution wouldn't work for me."*

- *"Tell me if the pricing they mentioned makes sense."*

And the machine delivers probing questions designed to expose gaps, structured objection frameworks to push for concessions, and follow-up emails that sound informed and authoritative.

This doesn't just change the tone of your next conversation. It creates an environment where every interaction feels like a cross-examination.

Instead of asking genuine questions to learn, buyers show up ready to confirm what their AI has flagged. Instead of curiosity, you get expert interrogation.

In some cases, you'll be lucky if the buyer reads the questions before forwarding them on.

Those questions were provided by the AI in the calm language of the machine and feel neutral, even when they're engineered to corner you.

This goes beyond pre-call and even live listening. AI email assistants will read your response and provide questions to follow up on. Did they read your email or was it easier to just click send on the generated response?

This is why follow-ups will feel different now.

You're not responding to human curiosity.
You're responding to a script designed to test you.

The Compression of Consensus

Internal alignment can take time. After a meeting, buyers often share notes with their teams, debate options, and gather feedback from stakeholders. It could take days or weeks for a consensus to form, and for decisions to move forward.

Now, that entire cycle can happen in hours with the AI assisting every single person joining the process.

It generates clean, shareable briefings that circulate instantly.

Your pitch is now a bullet-point record of your claims, a list of perceived strengths and weaknesses, and oversimplified summaries of your differentiators.

Within 30 minutes, stakeholders who never attended your meeting feel like they were there. They don't read your proposal themselves. They don't listen to your explanations. They just absorb the distilled verdict.

This compression has a hidden consequence. By the time you follow up, the consensus is already set.

- The buyer's team has agreed on what you did and didn't say.

- They've prioritized objections you haven't heard yet.

- They've decided where you fit in the pecking order.

- They've run multiple comparisons with other calls.

You once had time to shape perception, build trust, and respond to questions before they hardened into decisions.

Now, not only do you have zero control over how AI packages up all your documents and pitches, but even team members you've never met are using those summaries as prompts—to fact-check the diluted claims they've been handed.

Now, all of that happens—without you—in a single afternoon.

The Zero-Trust Environment

Every step of this process has the same effect: It erodes the benefit of the doubt.

When buyers have AI transcribing, summarizing, and cross-referencing everything you say, they aren't working to build trust with you. They will wait for the machine to tell them whether what you said can be trusted.

What used to be small inconsistencies:

A date you misspoke.
A metric you rounded.
A timeline you adjusted.

Now become evidence. Evidence that you're hiding something. Evidence that you're careless. Evidence that your story can't be trusted.

And because AI packages these flags in neutral, clinical language, it feels objective.

It may even consult outside sources to identify any inconsistencies it can, as that is what it was tasked to do. A block of text from three years ago buried on a page is used as a counterpoint to your words.

- *"Potential discrepancy identified between the demo and CIO's explanation regarding X feature."*

- *"Clarification recommended about their timelines as they don't match public reviews."*

- *"These three statements are inconsistent with the prior sales deck."*

- *"Their API documentation indicates the claim from your call isn't accurate."*

To the buyer, this isn't skepticism. It's diligence.

But to you, it's a zero-trust environment where every statement must be precise, verifiable, and consistent with everything you've ever said.

This is why selling feels harder, even when you're telling the truth.

You're not just competing with other vendors.

You're competing with infinite data at the speed of light. One off bullet point and their AI can make a cold hard evaluation you never see.

Your New Standard: Instant, Verifiable Clarity

In this new environment, credibility isn't something you build over time. It's something you prove, moment by moment.

You can't rely on a polished pitch to earn trust. You can't count on follow-ups to fix misunderstandings. You can't assume buyers will extend grace when you get a detail wrong.

Every claim must be defensible the second it leaves your mouth. Every data point must be backed by evidence you can produce on demand. Every promise must be consistent with the last hundred things you've said—because the machine will remember even if you don't.

This is your new baseline:

- No vague answers you'll clarify later.

- No loose language you hope will be forgiven.

- No stories that can't be verified.

- Ensuring public information, no matter how buried, is up-to-date and accurate.

Because in a world where AI fact-checks faster than you blink an eye, has access to every word in the world and processes information in seconds, **clarity isn't optional.**

It's the only thing that keeps you credible.

Chapter 9

Buyers Expect Everything Right Now

Time has always been an expected requirement of any process.

People new it might take a day to get something back and that was ok.

Not anymore.

AI has taught us that answers are instant. Comparisons happen in seconds. Certainty arrives with a single prompt. Complete clarification is provided in every answer.

Once buyers experience that kind of speed, their patience for anything slowly evaporates.

This isn't just about response times. Once a buyer has been conditioned by AI to expect instant progress at every step...

It becomes a psychological intolerance for any friction at all.

And if you think you can still buy yourself time—if you think a thoughtful delay will be forgiven—prepare to watch your credibility disintegrate.

The On-Demand Benchmark

Every buyer you meet is carrying a hidden expectation.

It's not enough to be responsive.

You have to be as fast and seamless as the AI that guided every step of their buying journey so far.

Think about the contrast. AI produces answers now—typing them out on the screen in a way that feels instantaneous.

AI shows people what frictionless feel like. Then they get to you...

The human variable.

The only part of the process that still takes hours, days, or weeks.

This is why what might still be considered normal:

- *"I'll check on that and follow up tomorrow."*

- *"Let me connect you to our team lead for that answer."*

- *"We'll send the proposal by the end of the week."*

These common expectations are going to start to feel intolerably slow.

Because in the buyer's mind, you're not just slower than you used to be. You're slower than everything they've experienced without you in the loop.

Human interactions feel like a bottleneck to progress.

And that contrast is what kills your momentum. The machine is setting the benchmark and you don't have the luxury of time for delay.

You have to be ready to match the pace or risk being left behind.

Slow Now Feels Suspect

Resonable response times and slight delays rarely raised red flags.

If you took a day to reply, they assumed you were being thorough. If you needed time to pull together details, it signaled care, not weakness.

Patience was built into the process.

But, we're all being conditioned by AI to expect instant clarity. To generate any answer, plan, counterpoint or solution in seconds.

When you're the only part of the process that takes time, your delay doesn't feel thoughtful.

It feels like you're scrambling behind the scenes. Like you don't know the answer. Like you're stalling to cover gaps you hope they won't notice.

This isn't rational. It's just psychology.

Speed is becoming a proxy for competence.

Buyers won't say it out loud. But here's the quiet narrative running in their heads:

> *"They haven't responded yet. What are they trying to figure out to answer me?"*

> *"If they're this slow now, how responsive will they be if we become a customer?"*

> *"They must not care enough."*

> *"I'll just ask my AI instead."*

The expectation isn't fair. It's just where we are headed. Playing catch-up with trust you haven't even realized you've lost.

If you need time, you must explain why that time serves the buyer, not you. Because with everything else delivered instantly, your speed puts you at risk of losing their confidence.

Lost Patience Is A Loss For Everyone

With a reasonably patient buyer, you had time to do things right.

Time to read between the lines of what a buyer said—and what they didn't. Time to research their industry, their challenges, and their ambitions. Time to get perspective from colleagues or past customers. Time to prepare a response that felt tailored, precise, and genuinely insightful.

That was the kind of thoughtfulness buyers valued. It was the signal that you were credible and committed.

But when patience collapses, thoughtfulness goes with it.

They expect your responses to be quick, even if that means you have no chance to do more than skim their needs and generate templated responses.

Ironically, the AI that gives them 20 follow up questions in an instant will be the same AI that provides you the answers to respond.

As the sales team trying to keep up, you skip over clarifying questions. Instead of thinking, you are generating responses for speed.

And when it becomes a volleyball game of instantly generated questions and answers? All thoughtfulness and thoroughness are gone.

You're matching their speed so they don't get impatient, but in the end, you lose the human element. Gut instinct. Contextual understanding. Empathy.

And when both sides settle for shallow, everyone ends up making decisions they'll regret.

AI Makes Fast the Default Setting

You don't get to choose whether speed matters.

It already does.

Your buyer has been conditioned to expect progress in seconds, not days. Their patience isn't coming back.

That doesn't mean you have to answer every question instantly, or rush to the shallowest possible response.

But it does mean you can't pretend you have time you don't. Speed is now the baseline—the cost of entry if you want to be taken seriously.

If you're slow, buyers assume you're unprepared. If you hesitate, they assume you're uncertain. If you delay, they assume you don't care enough to keep up.

You can fight that reality.
You can resent it.
You can wish it were different.

Or you can adapt.

In the next part of this book, you'll see exactly how to decide when to move fast, when to slow down, and how to build a process that delivers credibility at the buyer's pace—without compromising your standards.

Chapter 10

They Want To Do It For Themselves

For decades, sales have relied on one core assumption…If the purchase was big enough, complex enough, or important enough, buyers would always want help.

But AI is eating complex for breakfast.

It hasn't just made buyers *more* informed. It's made them more self-reliant—and more resistant to human involvement of any kind.

This is the same cultural drift that made phone calls feel intrusive, in-store shopping feel inefficient, and live support feel like a last resort.

But now, it's reaching even the most complex purchases. The idea that a buyer needs to be guided through the process is fading. Instead, they expect to self-educate, self-evaluate, and self-execute—without you in the room.

And if you try to insert yourself too soon, you won't be seen as helpful.

You're seen as *friction*.

The Self Service Cultural Shift Started Long Ago

For years, consumer habits were the canary in the coal mine.

People stopped calling customer service when they could chat asynchronously. They stopped walking into stores when delivery was a click away. They stopped asking salespeople for recommendations when they could search on their phone in store.

B2B was the last holdout. Complexity and risk were too high. The stakes were too big to trust a fully self-service process.

But AI is quietly closing that gap.

When a machine can compile the research, benchmark the pricing, draft the contracts, answer complex questions, and even prepare an onboarding plan, human involvement feels less essential, even in a million-dollar decision.

For a rising generation of buyers, human contact is avoided. They don't want to pick up a phone. They prefer the chatbot. They don't want to talk to sales, they want to just sign-up or buy.

They want everything on their own time and terms.

Complexity Is No Longer a Barrier

Solution or product complexity has protected sales teams from becoming self-service portals.

It was the reason they were indispensable.

After all, no machine could possibly handle the nuance of enterprise deals, the mess of integrations, or the politics of a custom contract—right?

Wrong. That world is vanishing—faster than most companies realize.

AI isn't just making buyers feel more capable. It's transforming once-daunting complexity into something that feels effortless.

Let's look at examples of how this is playing out right now...

Enterprise Software

It can take months scoping new software. Stakeholders sit through endless discovery calls mapping requirements no one fully understands.

Dozens of hours go into building configuration and integration checklists. Sellers deliver mountains of detail.

Now, an AI agent ingests process documentation, has access to corporate goals, can cross-reference it with current product capabilities, produce a draft implementation plan, and maybe even deliver sample code for customization.

All complete with timelines, dependencies, and risks outlined in less than a day. What once required a small army of consultants is now a conversational prompt.

Engineered Solutions

Sales engineers are often a key to complex purchase. In some industries strategy or design is required before the real solution is quoted.

While online configuration tools have allowed buyers do some self-service, it often hit a wall of complexity.

New AI configuration tools will let buyers configure even the most complex engineered solutions with ease. Need a new part for a product? An AI configurator produces mock-ups and specs, each accompanied by benchmarks and forecasts.

What once was an intellectual barrier is accessible online.

Heavily Regulated Environments

In industries like pharmaceuticals and defense, compliance used to be the ultimate reason for a high-touch, consultative approach.

Vendors justified months of meetings to align on regulatory requirements, document every decision, and prepare exhaustive audit trails.

Not now. AI can ingest entire policy frameworks, map them to your solution requirements, and produce fully documented compliance plans.

Instead of waiting for legal and regulatory teams to weigh in, buyers can get a first-pass validation and risk assessment in hours—without ever scheduling a call.

Negotiated Term Solutions

Enterprise contracts were notorious for requiring human finesse.

Payment schedules, volume discounts, performance guarantees—every element was a negotiation shaped by personal relationships and compromise.

Not a barrier now. AI-powered procurement platforms can generate baseline agreements, model pricing scenarios, and suggest the optimal terms for both parties.

What used to take a month of calls and draft exchanges happens in a single workflow, with the buyer only stepping in to approve the recommendation.

Large-Scale Capital Equipment

Buying multimillion-dollar machinery once demanded site visits, feasibility studies, and lengthy engineering assessments.

Buyers can feed operating requirements, capacity targets, and facility data into an AI configurator that models multiple scenarios, recommends equipment configurations, and estimates installation timelines.

Where expertise and physical presence were once the default, virtual tools now deliver 80% of the confidence without requiring an office presence.

Complexity was the last excuse for why buyers couldn't self-serve.

That excuse is quickly becoming obsolete thinking.

The solutions that once required your presence now require nothing more than an interface and an algorithm. And as these capabilities improve, the window for sellers to add irreplaceable value will keep getting smaller.

The question now isn't if your buyers will want to do it themselves.

It's how are you going to allow them to?

AI Makes Self-Service Feel Personal

A strong argument against self-service was that it felt generic or cold.

Buyers accepted automation for simple transactions, but in complex decisions, they wanted personalized experiences and warmth— someone who knew their history, understood their context, and made them feel like more than an account number.

AI is quietly erasing that trade-off too. Nothing has to be generic anymore. AI can make anything feel.

An AI assistant can remember every past interaction. It can surface relevant details—contract milestones, prior conversations, historical preferences—without making the buyer repeat themselves.

It can adapt its tone, mirror the buyer's language, and anticipate questions before they're asked.

It can cross-reference internal data with public information to produce recommendations that are so specific, they feel handcrafted, even if no one ever touched them.

For buyers, this creates an experience that feels responsive, intelligent, and quietly affirming. They don't feel like they're talking to a machine. They feel like they're talking to something built exclusively for them.

And when that happens, the assumption that self-service is impersonal loses all credibility.

If the choice is between a fast, always-on assistant that never forgets and a salesperson juggling a dozen other accounts, the machine might actually feels more attentive.

This is the reality most companies haven't internalized:

Buyers won't tolerate AI-driven self-service. They will prefer it—because it feels like the kind of personalization humans promise but rarely deliver.

Why Buyers Would Rather Not Talk to You

Most sales people believe human connection is what buyers crave. They're convinced a real conversation is the key to trust, understanding, and ultimately, a deal.

After all, they've built careers on relationships.

They're extroverts. Small talk is fun.
Conversation gives them energy.

They assume everyone else feels the same way. But that assumption is more about ego than reality. Because for many buyers, human interaction doesn't feel like a benefit.

It feels like a drain.

Being sold to isn't fun no matter how personable the sales person is.

Every meeting is another mental tab to keep open. Another hour stolen from work they already don't have time to finish. Another performance where they must appear informed and decisive, even when they aren't sure.

Buyers don't always articulate it, but this is the truth:

Your sales meeting costs them energy.

Fending off manipulation. Asking the right questions. Presenting some version of themselves they might not naturally be. Repeating answers they told five other sales teams.

This is why AI feels like such an upgrade.

Not because it's always better, but because it's easier—less intrusive.

With a machine, buyers never have to admit they don't know something. They never have to pretend to be comfortable. They never have to worry that showing uncertainty will be used against them later.

They can stay guarded.
They can stay efficient.
They can stay in control.

If you're in marketing or sales, this may feel uncomfortable. It challenges the story you tell yourself about your role.

That buyers want your expertise.
That your personality makes the process better.
That human connection is what elevates the experience.

Sometimes that's true. But more often, it's projection.

It's the assumption that because *you* enjoy interaction, the person on the other side must enjoy it too. And in an age when AI can deliver nearly everything without the social tax, that assumption is collapsing.

Buyers haven't just learned to tolerate self-service.

They've learned to prefer it—because it demands less of them, not more.

Chapter 11

The Machine Becomes the Only Buyer

AI is often something buyers prompt when they need help.

It's transactional: Ask a question. Get an answer. Move on.

But AI is quickly evolving into something more autonomous. More integrated. More invisible...

AI Agents.

Agents don't just react to prompts. They act on their own, monitor, anticipate, and respond autonomously. They detect when a contract is about to expire. They auto-generate RFPs, send them, collect responses, and rank proposals—without a human ever logging in.

The software buyers already use—procurement platforms, CRM systems, vendor portals—are all being rebuilt around this agentic model.

AI is no longer an enhancement to the buyer's process.
It's becoming the engine completing the entire process.

This is a shift most vendors are absolutely not prepared for yet.

You're not just working with a buyer assisted by AI. You're dealing with autonomous intelligence that can do most–if not all–of the process without a human in the loop.

When buyers disappear behind their AI, you don't just lose the relationship. You lose the chance to shape the decision at all.

The Shift from Assistive to Autonomous

AI has primarily entered the buying process as just an assistant. A tool buyers reached for when they need help summarizing reviews, drafting a comparison table, or checking pricing benchmarks.

They still make the calls. Decide when to engage. They're in control.

But assistive AI is only the beginning. Now, it's evolving into something more powerful—and less visible.

Autonomous AI doesn't wait for a prompt.

It observes, anticipates, and acts on its own.

Instead of a buyer needing to think, *"I should see who else is out there,"* their procurement agent is already scanning the market for alternatives.

Every day. Without a human.

Instead of someone remembering a renewal is due in six months, the system flags it, drafts a competitive RFP, and starts evaluating options.

Buying doesn't need to happen in discrete steps anymore.

AI Agents make it an always-on process:

- Monitoring contracts and vendor performance.

- Comparing new entrants.

- Re-ranking preferred partners.

- Preparing decisions before a human ever logs in.

- Contacting vendors, collecting inputs and evaluating them instantly.

We're not talking about AI assistance. This is about your buyer being completely replaced by AI for most of the process.

You're no longer competing for a person's attention.
You're competing for an algorithm's recommendation.

The Embedded AI Buying Agent

Most people think of AI as something separate—a browser tab or app you open when you need it. But that's changing fast.

AI is being integrated into the platforms buyers already use...

- AI integrated into email, calendars and documents.

- AI in procurement platforms.

- AI in project tools and vendor management systems.

- AI in contract and billing systems.

It's not an add-on anymore. It's everywhere. And it's always on.

When AI lives inside the systems buyers already trust, the process stops feeling like a decision at all. It becomes hidden and automatic.

Evaluation starts before you ever see a signal.

That procurement platform AI just flagged your company and you are compared, scored, or even dismissed without anyone clicking "begin."

Since these platforms are built for efficiency, the criteria and formulas are set by the company that made them.

- Predefined templates decide what a "good" vendor looks like.

- Benchmarks pulled from public data you never agreed to.

- Scoring rubrics you can't challenge or recontextualize.

And the most disorienting part?

Every tool becomes a gatekeeper—a rigid one. A human buyer might have bent a rule or overlooked a missing checkbox if the fit felt right.

The AI doesn't. It enforces the defaults, regardless of how shallow or arbitrary they may be.

When that happens, you're not just losing visibility. You're losing any chance to reshape how you're measured.

The Always-On Evaluation Cycle

In the past, buying was a project.

Someone decided it was time to look for options. A team assembled. Vendors were considered. And when the contract was signed, the process ended—at least for a while.

That cadence is changing.

When AI agents do the work, buying becomes a perpetual process rather than a discrete event. Evaluation doesn't pause because the contract is signed. It keeps running in the background, quietly ingesting signals you can't see.

Every time you submit a deliverable, a competitor publishes price changes, or the strategy for the business changes, it triggers an automatic AI agent to evaluate the right solution.

What used to trigger a formal, months-long buying cycle now initiates an automated re-evaluation without a human even in the loop.

And when AI is the one monitoring your relevance, loyalty and relationship aren't factored in.

Humans resisted switching because it felt risky and exhausting. Maybe relationships and familiarity bought you time and forgiveness.

But AI doesn't care about continuity. It doesn't feel loyalty or guilt or the need to justify decisions to colleagues. It simply re-scores the options and surfaces whatever looks better.

Even the organizational friction that once protected you is dissolving.

Where changing vendors meant navigating politics and retraining teams, agentic systems now make switching feel effortless. What used to take weeks of negotiation and planning happens automatically in a single workflow.

In this environment, you rarely get a signal that you're being reconsidered. You don't have a chance to intervene, to re-educate, or to remind the buyer why they chose you. You only find out after the system has already drafted a recommendation to move on.

This is what it means to sell in the always-on buying cycle.

Your relevance isn't something you establish once. It's something you have to re-earn in the background, again and again, whether you know it or not.

The Disappearance of Relationship Capital

For as long as there have been buyers, relationships have been your safety net. When performance dipped or a competitor undercut your pricing, familiarity kept you in the room.

Personal trust bought you time to respond, time to re-justify your value, time to protect the deal.

That buffer is disappearing.

When an AI agent is responsible for scoring options, it doesn't care how long you've been working together. It doesn't give weight to the history you've built or the goodwill you've earned.

It only knows the data.

If another vendor looks better in the spreadsheet, that's the recommendation it surfaces, without hesitation.

Even when a human buyer reviews the AI's output, your relationship carries less influence than you expect. Because when the algorithm presents a ranked list, rejecting it feels irrational.

It's easier to defer to the model. It feels safer to trust the numbers.

The result is subtle but profound: Your human connections matter less every day. Not because buyers don't like you, but because liking you feels subjective.

And in a world where AI does the measuring, anything subjective feels like a risk they don't want to defend.

When You're Just The Final Approval

With Agentic AI and multiple steps of the journey automated, you've lost the control and interactions that gave you some advantage before.

You helped define the problem.
You shaped the requirements.
You guided the buyer through the trade-offs.
You had a chance to make your case, refine it, and earn trust.

But when buyers become *just AI*, you don't get that.

The buying process begins with a deep research agent. It drafts a shortlist. It ranks the vendors. It flags preferred pricing and highlights every perceived weakness.

When a human buyer finally steps in, their role is little more than to review the recommendation and click "Approve."

You're not invited in to educate. You're not invited to differentiate. You're only there to confirm what the machine has already decided.

And if you're hoping that moment is an opportunity to reframe the conversation, you'll be disappointed.

Because the buyer isn't starting from zero. They're starting from a conclusion they trust more than your opinion.

In that environment, your influence is reduced to the margins. You're no longer a guide. You're a final box to be checked.

The New Playbook: Selling to Machines

If you're still building your strategy around the idea that AI isn't part of the buying process and even taking it over, you're already behind.

Eventually some buying will become just AI; you being scored by an algorithm you'll never meet.

That means your old advantages—rapport, charisma, relationship capital, entrenchment—matter less.

Clarity, consistency, and machine-readable proof matter more.

In this environment, discoverability isn't optional. Speed isn't optional. Structured evidence isn't optional.

And you don't get to wait until the buying process starts.

Because by the time you're invited in, the machine has already decided whether you're worth considering at all.

Part III
The Mindset Shift

We've just walked through the greatest shift in marketing and sales in centuries. Hopefully, I've painted a vivid picture of how AI is demolishing what marketing and sales used to be.

It's tempting to stall here. To continue diagnosing, lamenting, and dissecting what these new buyers look like and how your world has changed.

But if you stay in that posture—if you keep clinging to fear or nostalgia—you'll miss the only opportunity that still matters:

To become something buyers can't replace.

So, this is where the book shifts gears.

From here forward, we focus on what you can build next and adapt. This isn't a call to repackage the same behaviors in a shinier wrapper. It's a mandate to install a different operating system—one built for a world where:

- Every buyer shows up over-informed.

- Every claim will be tested before you finish speaking.

- Every narrative you craft is just one data point among thousands.

- Every advantage you once held can be benchmarked in seconds.

The old mindsets—control, opacity, deference—are liabilities now.

The only path forward is to adopt the mindsets that *thrive* when AI is infused into every buying decision:

- Consistency so relentless that AI delivers a clear narrative.

- Machine-readiness so thorough that algorithms can't misinterpret your value.

- Transparency so complete that AI has nothing left to expose.

- Curation so rigorous that your story becomes the default reference.

- Speed so reliable that buyers trust you to keep pace with their expectations.

- Collaboration so open that they see you as a partner, not a pitch.

- Empathy so grounded that no automation can replicate it.

These aren't tactics. They are operating principles.

Part III will show you how to adopt them—so you don't just survive the omniscient buyer, you become the company that that embraces the new reality.

Welcome to the rebuild.

Chapter 12

Auditing AI Before You Optimize For It

AI doesn't browse. It synthesizes.

Instead of scattered research, buyers get instant, confident conclusions—pulled from everything you've said, everything others have said about you, and everything you've tried to hide or outgrow.

It's not a series of messages, content, and media discovered one at a time to a buyer. It's an instant snapshot—conjured by an engine you don't control, in a conversation you don't see.

And in that instant summary, your preferred narrative is flattened, distorted, or simply erased.

All that work you have done to create assets that your buyers will read or engage with is dissected, cataloged and reassembled in real-time in an entirely new form.

This chapter is about learning how to audit that instant snapshot and uncover what buyers' AI tools are really saying about you. Where the gaps are. Where the hallucinations start. Where your competitor's words are louder than your own.

To begin to shape your AI story, you have to understand what it is now.

AI Is Telling A Story You Can't Predict

AI isn't providing sources. It works to deliver certainty.

When your buyer asks a question, AI doesn't reply with a trail of links. It replies with a confident, summarized opinion. It's not a reference. It's a conclusion.

That conclusion is built from hundreds of fragments:

Your website, your competitors' positioning pages, customer reviews, Reddit threads, PDFs from 2017, Glassdoor complaints, industry reports, and third-party roundups you've never even seen.

AI isn't curating. It's constructing.

It's blending all those signals into a single, clean output that sounds definitive. It compresses nuance. It resolves contradictions. It fills in gaps.

All the phrases you worked so hard to craft across a range of assets are extrapolated into individual words, sequenced, weighted and then poured into an ocean of other fragments.

Each prompt reconstructs these fragments differently every time.

This variability makes auditing a challenge. No spreadsheet can hold the variations that are produced. But that doesn't mean we shouldn't evaluate our presence in AI, it just means we have to adapt our instruments to its unpredictable nature.

Buyers Are Probably Prompting Differently Than You Expect

Before AI became mainstream, any research process was painstaking.

You put one thing into search and often had to dig through multiple pages to try to synthesize the information yourself. Possibly, a site had an answer to your specific question, but part of the process was determining the truth versus fiction.

A question in a search box has become replaced by a conversation.

Continued prompts to get deeper, clarify, understand, or see the information from different perspectives.

In just minutes, buyers are building detailed stories.

Here's a simplified example for context:

Buyer Prompt	*"I am a 20-person machine shop in Illinois, and I need a consultant who can help improve our floor efficiency to get more product out with the same machines.* *Who should I talk to?"*
	AI responds with a detailed list and comparison table of vendors that are hyper-specific to their scenario are provided by the AI
Buyer Prompt	*"Does [Company] have experience with [specific machines and software] producing [my part]?"*
	AI provides a declarative answer based on your website, PDFs you uploaded years ago, vendor mentions, and other relevant information.
Buyer Prompt	*"What is the average time to ROI for a company like mine using [Company's solution]?"*
	The AI doesn't know exactly, but it makes assumptions and a prediction based on thousands of references for hiring consultants in manufacturing.
Buyer Prompt	How much should I expect to spend and what is a timeline for a project like this?
	Once again, the AI doesn't hesitate and provides a declarative response pulling from competitors and Reddit threads.

You have to assume your buyers will ask specific, high-stakes questions and continue their narrative to build complete clarity.

It's not like search where people were restricted by having to browse the results and sites returned.

It's instant. It's effortless. It's deep.

As people continue to use AI, their prompts will get smarter and their conversations longer.

We're not evaluating a 1-100 rank based on a specific keyphrase, we're evaluating a narrative in a dynamic conversation.

AI Pulls From Places You Forgot or Never Controlled

As we get into evaluating our AI presence, it's important to clarify that responses are not direct translations of the story you have created for yourself.

That paragraph your buyer's assistant just generated about your implementation speed? It might've come from:

- A Reddit thread from a few years ago

- A G2 review you never responded to

- A long-forgotten webinar transcript

- A comparison page your competitor published

- A five-year-old case study that's no longer relevant

AI doesn't just pull from your primary pages.

It pulls from your ecosystem of dead pages, offhand comments, scraped PDFs, forum chatter, competitor comparison tables, and any voice that has a digital microphone.

And when there's nothing recent?
It guesses.

When your website is vague?
It substitutes context.

When you haven't said it clearly?
It borrows someone else's opinion.

If your competitor says you're expensive, that sticks.

If an old blog post says you serve a vertical you no longer touch, that lingers.

If a review says your UI is "dated," and you haven't published proof otherwise – well AI keeps repeating it anyways.

Silence is filled by a story you don't control. And the most dangerous part?

AI *doesn't tell your buyer where it found the answer.* It just says it confidently.

AI Surfaces Information You Have Been Trying To Hide

Marketing and sales have relied on controlling the flow of information. Maybe you didn't want pricing out there or you wanted to get a prospect on the phone before you shared your proprietary process.

But is delivering some answer no matter how much you have tried to hide or obscure. It's impossible to operate under the illusion that you get to reveal information on your terms.

> **A prompt for pricing even though you just have ranges on a third level page.** AI pulls benchmarks, review comments, and industry data to predict your price exactly anyway—and then provides a comparison to everyone else.

> **A prompt for what industries you've had the most success in, but you didn't want case studies out there.** AI still provides an answer, but instead of a story you craft, it creates one based on 20 different sources.

A prompt on whether you've had some issue that you hoped no one knew about. AI found the support forum, scraped the Reddit thread, read the 2-star review from two years ago, or even took it from an internal document someone uploaded.

You can try to hide. You can attempt to mitigate what employees upload. But the reality is the buyer will get an answer one way or another. It's just whether you influenced the answer or not.

Analyzing The Questions Buyers Are Asking

Few companies are even thinking about their buyers' AI prompts and the narratives they assemble. They never stop to consider that a single AI query can instantly surface every gap, contradiction, or outdated claim in their story.

Marketing & sales can't operate under these old assumptions.

When you understand the actual prompts buyers use, you gain three critical advantages:

1. You see your narrative the way buyers see it. Not as a linear story, but as a series of discrete questions that must all be answered consistently.

2. You prepare your team for the narrative. Marketing, sales, and customer service are ready for the types of statements from buyers that will need to be confirmed or denied.

3. You build a foundation for shaping the narrative. As we move further into the strategies to actually control your narrative in AI engines, these audits serve as the starting point.

Let's start by looking at the types of buyer prompts.

The 7 Categories of Buyer Prompts

Most of the questions your buyers ask will fall into predictable categories.

Prompt Category	Why Buyers Ask This
Discovery	They want to know who exists, fast. If you're not mentioned, you don't exist.
Credibility	Buyers seek proof from others before believing you. Social proof fuels AI summaries.
Fit and Use Cases	They want to know, "Are you for me?" AI fills in gaps when your positioning is vague.
Comparisons	They're narrowing options. If you haven't shaped the contrast, your competitor already did.
Pricing and Value	Every buyer asks: "Can I afford this?" and "Is it worth it?" AI won't wait for your quote.
Risk	Buyers fear friction. If AI can't explain how easy (or hard) your solution is, they move on.
Proof and Outcomes	Buyers want results. If you haven't shown them, AI pulls what it can—or invents its own.

You might think you already know these questions. But unless you have sat down and forced yourself to articulate them in detail, you don't.

And your team likely hasn't. So we need a structured approach to understanding the buyer's AI journey.

Reverse Engineering the Buyer's AI Prompts

Below is a process you can run with your team to surface the real prompts that shape how buyers evaluate you.

Your objective is to create a comprehensive list of questions your prospects are asking AI and search engines—so you can proactively publish clear, consistent answers.

1. Gather a cross-functional group. Bring together people from marketing, sales, product, customer success, and leadership.

2. Print or display the 7 prompt categories.

3. Work category by category. For each, think about prompts from the buyer's perspective:

   o *What would a skeptical buyer type into AI if they wanted to verify everything we say?*

   o *What would they ask to uncover our weaknesses?*

   o *What would they ask if they were trying to compare us to a competitor?*

4. Capture every prompt. Use an AI auditing tool or a shared spreadsheet to create a long-term catalog. Since AI will persist as a buyer source, your best option is to build a formal auditing approach.

5. Prioritize. Once you've collected a full list of prompts that your team believes represent what the buyer will use, begin to categorize them.

   o **Frequency:** How often do you think buyers will prompt this compared to other prompts? Use past sales interactions to help gauge what you have heard before.

   o **Importance:** Which of these prompts and the answers will most influence the buyer's mindset and decision making about you?

   o **Type / Role:** Who of your audience might prompt these? End users, decision makers, influencers?

Want to accelerate the process? Use AI and ask what your buyers might be prompting. Just don't leave it all to AI. Involve your team to get full perspectives.

Let's keep going deeper to fully audit our AI visibility.

Determine The Uncomfortable Prompts

Let's be really honest. An AI interface is freeing. We can ask any question we want to a machine without guilt.

This phenomenon has been seen in search engines where people are more honest with their questions in search boxes than with their spouses, doctors or therapists.

If you run the previous exercise with too much comfort, you most likely are not surfacing the real questions that buyers are prompting.

- *What are the most common complaints about [company]?*

- *Has [company] been involved in any legal disputes or controversies?*

- *How does [company] price compared to [competitor]?*

- *How can I get their solution at a huge discount?*

- *What limitations or gaps should I be aware of before buying?*

Even these examples are timid given that buyers will feel free to ask their most hard hitting questions.

Go back through the prompts you listed and push yourself for real candor and discomfort because that is likely closer to reality.

Let's Explore Some Sample Questions by Category

To help you in your prompt cataloging process, here are some common prompts seen by category.

1. Discovery
"Who exists?" "Who fits my need?" "Who should I be looking at?"

- Who are the top [solution] providers for [size of buyer company] [buyer industry]?

- What vendors specialize in [niche use case]?

- Which [tool/platform] integrates best with [existing tech stack]?

- Who are the most recommended vendors on review sites for [problem]?

- What are the emerging companies in [space] that have strong reputations?

- Who is considered a market leader vs. challenger in this category?

- What companies are often overlooked but provide strong ROI?

2. Credibility
"Can I trust you?" "What do others say?"

- What do customers say about [Company]?

- What are the most common complaints about [Company]?

- How does [Company] rate on Google/Trustpilot/G2/Reddit/etc?

- Has [Company] won any industry awards or recognitions?

- Are there any negative news stories about [Company]?

- Has [Company] been involved in any legal disputes or layoffs?

- How responsive is [Company] to customer support requests?

3. Fit & Use Cases
"Is this for me?" "Have they done this before?"

- Is [Company] a good fit for a [20-person] [B2B SaaS company]?

- Does [Company] have experience in [our vertical or niche]?

- Has [Company] worked with others using [specific platform/tool]?

- What types of businesses get the most value from [Company]?

- Does [Company] offer solutions tailored to [geography/business size]?

- What challenges is [Company] best suited to solve?

- What customer segments does [Company] serve best?

4. Comparisons
"How do you stack up?" "Who's better?"

- How does [Company] compare to [Competitor]?

- Which is better for [specific goal or need], [Company] or [Competitor]?

- Which solution is easier to implement and maintain?

- Who provides better support and customer success programs?

- Which tool has a better user interface or experience?

- Which company is more scalable or future-proof?

- Who has a stronger track record in [industry]?

5. Pricing & Value
"How much?" "Is it worth it?"

- What does [Company] typically cost?

- How does [Company] pricing compare to [Competitor]?

- Is [Company] considered expensive for what they offer?

- What's the average ROI from working with [Company]?

- Does [Company] offer transparent pricing or hidden fees?

- What should I expect to pay for a 6-month engagement with [Company]?

- Are there any free trials, pilots, or flexible terms available?

6. Implementation & Risk
"Will this work?" "Will it be painful?"

- How long does it take to implement [Company's] solution?

- What are common problems during onboarding?

- Does [Company] use outsourced services for delivery or support?

- What's the average time to value after signing?

- What are the risks or trade-offs of choosing [Company]?

- What's the cancellation process or exit clause?

- How likely is it that [Company] can deliver on their promises?

7. Proof & Outcomes
"Will this work for me?" "Can you prove it?"

- What kind of results have clients seen using [Company]?

- What's the average time to ROI with [Company]?

- Are there any published case studies with real metrics?

- How often do [Company's] clients renew or expand their contracts?

- Can [Company] provide before-and-after data?

- How does [Company] measure client success or satisfaction?

- What KPIs typically improve with [Company's] solution?

These questions should provide a foundation for you to start brainstorming, but buyers are diverse and complex. Follow the process and get uncomfortable to build the right list for your team to be auditing.

Gather Your Buyer's Prompt Responses

You've developed the questions buyers are asking AI. Now it's time to find out what those AI tools are actually saying about you.

We need to understand the narrative our buyers are getting. The goal here is to assess the current state of your **AI Brand.**

Most companies assume that if they haven't published something explicitly, it can't be used against them. But AI isn't waiting for your permission. It's already summarizing you, based on whatever fragments it can find.

Your job now is to catalog what's already out there.

Prompt by prompt.

AI Prompt Simulation Process

Step 1: Select Questions for Each Prompt Category
Using the *7 Prompt Categories* and expand on the sample prompts to choose a set of 25–30 prompts. You don't need to cover every variation—just enough to expose the state of your narrative.

Step 2: Ask Multiple AI Engines
Many companies default to the AI engine their company has bought into or the most popular name currently - ChatGPT.

But your buyers might be using Perplexity. Claude. Gemini. Grok. Or any number of other platforms. Each engine has different data access, different weighting systems, and different recency windows.

That means:

- ChatGPT might summarize you based on your website and archived PDFs.

- Perplexity might anchor its answer in Reddit comments, blog reviews, and community forums.

- Claude might emphasize narrative tone and synthesize softer signals from your About page or press releases.

- Gemini might lean on Google-indexed content and prioritize freshness.

All of them sound equally confident. All of them say something slightly different. This is your **AI Brand Spectrum** and if you're not auditing across engines, you're not seeing the full spectrum.

Step 3: Document the Raw Responses
Copy and paste each answer into a shared doc or spreadsheet. Ideally, structure it based on categories and AI engines with the ability to add new audit rounds int the future.

Many new products are being introduced to help do this, so don't be afraid to utilize a tool to make it easier.

Step 4: Score Each Prompt Answer
Use a simple five-level scale:

- **Accurate** — Does it align with your intended narrative?

- **Complete** — Is it missing key context?

- **Misleading or Risky** — Is it inaccurate, hallucinated, or potentially harmful?

- **Competitor Mentions or Bias** — Does the narrative lean towards others or you?

- **Contradictions Between Engines** — Is it significantly different than other engine's responses?

You're not just capturing data. You're uncovering where your story has gaps—and how confidently AI is filling them in.

Conduct an AI Category Risk Audit

Once you've completed your prompt simulation, you'll have dozens of AI-generated answers grouped by category. Now, the question becomes: how strong is your brand's narrative across each of those seven zones?

This is where you elevate from tactical to strategic.

The goal of the category audit is not to get lost in granular prompts, but to zoom out and evaluate the **structural strength** of your AI-facing brand.

Where are you strong? Where are you inconsistent? And where are you exposed?

The Risk Rating System

For each category, evaluate the overall response quality of the AI outputs you observed. Don't look for perfection—look for patterns.

Use the following score levels:

- **Green** — Most answers were clear, accurate, and aligned with your intended narrative. Little or no hallucination. AI has enough to work with.

- **Yellow** — Mixed performance. Some answers were strong, others vague or outdated. AI is guessing or oversimplifying in places.

- **Red** — High risk. Many answers were inaccurate, fabricated, or competitor-influenced. AI is assembling a narrative you don't control.

Prompt Category	Score	Meaning	Common Symptoms
Discovery		Are you even showing up?	Not mentioned. Miscategorized. Vague language. No clear ICP match.
Credibility		Do you appear trustworthy?	Negative reviews dominate. No social proof. No brand authority.
Fit & Use Cases		Does it look like you're for them?	No clear vertical language. Weak case studies. AI guesses at fit.
Comparisons		Are you shaping the narrative—or is your competitor?	AI uses competitor framing. No comparison page. Side-by-sides missing or outdated.
Pricing & Value		Do buyers understand what you cost—and why it's worth it?	AI estimates based on reviews. No pricing page. Pricing labeled "custom" or "varies."

Risk	Are you seen as easy to work with—or risky to trust?	AI answers timelines vaguely or incorrectly. Risks are inferred from competitors.
Proof & Outcomes	Can you prove your solution works?	No outcomes. No ROI benchmarks. AI guesses results or references generic stats.

Your weakest categories are not just messaging gaps.

They are **AI Vulnerabilities**—where you're invisible, algorithms fabricate, competitors interfere, or confidence collapses.

Your Narrative Is a Living System

You've just completed a snapshot of how AI reflects your brand. But make no mistake—this isn't a one-time audit.

Your narrative is not fixed. It's fluid. It's volatile.

And it's constantly being rewritten—by others, by algorithms, and by the accumulation of evidence you forgot was still online.

Every new review.
Every Reddit thread.
Every competitor comparison.
Every outdated support doc.

They're not footnotes. They're ingredients in the next AI summary your buyer sees.

The Speed of Narrative Drift

AI engines are ingesting, indexing, and synthesizing faster than ever. What was true six months ago may now be distorted—or worse, overwritten by your competitor's framing.

You don't just need a better brand story. You need a system to **continuously monitor and correct** how that story appears across search engines.

This isn't about SEO rankings or CTRs. It's about **credibility control** in an environment where perception updates faster than you do.

What's Required Going Forward

1. Treat your AI audit like a quarterly business ritual.
Not a campaign. Not a sprint. A standing operating rhythm.

- Re-run your top prompts.

- Track changes in AI summaries.

- Flag new contradictions or hallucinations.

- Note shifts in competitor positioning that show up in your summaries.

2. Keep a rolling record of past AI outputs.
This is your "AI narrative history"—a paper trail of how your story evolves. When distortions arise, you'll see the drift.

3. Assign ownership.
Someone in your organization—marketing, brand, product, or comms—needs to own the AI-facing version of your story. If no one owns it, no one will fix it.

There are platforms that handle this all for you so that you don't have to manually prompt every quarter.

This Is Your New Narrative Discipline

You don't control the distribution of your story anymore. But you can control the consistency, clarity, and frequency with which you correct it.

This is the new narrative discipline:

Know what buyers are prompting.
Know what AI is saying.
Know what needs to change.

Then do it.
Not once.
Every quarter.
Every update.
Every time something shifts.

Because in a world where AI is the first frame, the most trustworthy brand wins—not the loudest, not the slickest, but the most coherent.

You don't just need a better message. You need a system to keep your truth in circulation.

Chapter 13

Build Radical Transparency Into Marketing & Sales

Marketing and sales have had a similar playbook for a long time. Hold back information, forcing buyers to book calls, fill out forms, or wait for a "guided walkthrough" so that you can capture information or craft the story.

However, we now live in a world where an answer is always readily available. Whether real, assumed, predicted, inaccurate or hallucinated.

Always an answer. Instantly available.

When buyers do finally reach you, they have everything they could ever want to know and can test every claim you make moving forward.

Either you continue to pretend you control what buyers learn, or adopt a posture that most of your competitors are too scared to consider: **radical transparency.**

Because in a world where buyers are always instantly comparing you to the answer they are given, there is little room for obfuscation or spin.

Your advantage now is how much of what you say matches the AI answers.

Trying To Hold Onto Control Is Costing You Trust

The old playbook of information scarcity as a strategy isn't helping you anymore. Trying to control access or perception just puts you at risk.

The moment a prospect sees gaps in your story, they don't assume you're saving the best for last. They assume you're covering for weaknesses. Or that you need to add "sales spin" to their thinking.

While you think you're controlling the narrative, they're comparing everything you left unsaid against everything someone else has already published.

They prompt their AI assistant to fill in the blanks. It happily obliges.

That lack of transparency now has some major consequences that you need to deal with.

> **You're Invisible.** If it's not public, then AI doesn't know the answer. For discovery prompts, you risk being invisible to buyers.

> **AI Fills Gaps.** We've discussed this previously, but AI will make assumptions based on other information it has been trained on. This means if you don't publish the story, anything could be told when asked.

> **No Answer Seeds Doubt.** If AI reports back that it doesn't know something—but it can provide an answer for your competitors – buyers might assume you are hiding something.

> **Contradictions Kill.** When AI says something different from you–whether on your site, in your assets, or on a call—it quickly erodes trust.

You haven't just lost control. Any attempt to cling to it is damaging the reputation and trust you need most right now.

The path forward can not be rationing information.

It has to be radical transparency. Transparency that ensures visibility. Transparency that confirms. Transparency that builds trust.

The Only Path to Sustainable Trust

Earlier in the book we talked about what buyers have transformed into.

They start with AI. They learn more before reaching out. They trust AI more than you. They real-time fact check what you say.

You can't control the narrative as you once did.

But you can control the clarity, completeness, and consistency of the evidence you make public.

Transparency isn't about surrendering authority. It's about earning trust in a marketplace where buyers are forming the majority of their opinion without you.

More and more, the decision to contact you—or to buy from you—will happen entirely on the strength of what a machine assembles.

A buyer will prompt their AI:

>*"Which provider is the safest bet?"*
>*"Who has the most credible track record?"*
>*"Which option has the fewest hidden drawbacks?"*

The answer will come back in seconds, confident and final. You won't get a chance to clarify. You won't get a chance to reframe.

The only way to be chosen in that moment is to make sure the evidence you've published is so organized and thorough that nothing essential is missing or distorted.

Ask yourself: If your buyers' AI assistant responded only on the evidence you've made public, would they still choose you?

That's the question that will define the next decade of growth.

Radical Transparency

Transparency isn't about dumping every detail you know onto the web. It's not about confessing every flaw, every uncertainty, or every failed experiment.

Radical transparency is a discipline. It's the practice of volunteering what *matters most* **before** your buyer has to ask.

It's surfacing truth, so the AI has an accurate record, and your story matches what buyers prompt for.

Proactive Disclosure
You don't wait for buyers to corner you. You start by naming where you're strong—and where you're not.

Consistent Framing
You don't change the story depending on the channel, the audience, or the pressure of the moment.

Contextual Transparency
You don't just admit shortcomings. You explain the trade-offs that led to them—so buyers see the logic, not just the liability.

Public Openness
Not just *saying* the truth, but publishing it—so it's findable, indexable, and machine-readable. This is the difference between quietly admitting something under pressure…and putting it on your website where everyone (and every AI) can see it first.

Radical transparency is not a tactical gimmick to "seem authentic.", a confession booth for your insecurities, or an excuse to dump disclaimers and hope buyers will figure it out.

It is:

- A deliberate choice to **be the most reliable source** about your own business.

- The fastest way to **preempt the AI-fueled skepticism** your buyers bring to every conversation.

- The only strategy that holds up when everything can and will be cross-checked in seconds.

Because here's the reality:

The more it *feels* like you're holding back or trying to hide, the more buyers will prompt to find the truth.

The more you reveal up front, the less they feel the need to validate.

Five Places Buyers Expect Transparency

You don't need more reminders that AI will surface every inconsistency.

These five categories are the credibility tipping points—the places where buyers look first for decision making.

1. Pricing

Buyers already look for pricing, and they will ask AI about yours. So, if you hide, either AI will make a prediction or a stark comparison showing your missing information.

The Temptation: Keep pricing vague. Call it "custom." Make buyers fill out a form or schedule a call before you reveal the numbers.

The Reality: Buyers already have your pricing benchmarks. AI has scraped reviews, compared competitor quotes, and generated the most accurate prediction for your fees.

Radical Honesty Move: Publicly publish a transparent pricing breakdown, including ranges and example scenarios. Explain why your pricing is structured the way it is—so it sounds like a deliberate strategy, not an evasion.

> *"A construction firm might publish standard per-square-foot estimates for common project types, plus typical contingency costs that often get buried in fine print."*

> *"A logistics provider could disclose their base rates along with fuel surcharge ranges and seasonal fluctuation patterns."*

> *"A financial advisory firm might share fee structures and average total costs for clients with different portfolio sizes."*

> *"A consumer product brand could make public the price impact of sustainable materials versus conventional options."*

Now, when your buyer inevitably asks about pricing, it will retrieve your narrative and then triangulate a made-up one.

2. Solution Gaps

Buyers will ask where you do and don't meet their needs or goals. They are looking for fit.

The Temptation: Overemphasize strengths. Gloss over missing capabilities, services you're weaker in, or known limitations.

The Reality: Buyers' AI will compile a list of what you lack and provide them pointed questions before your demo is over.

Radical Honesty Move: Acknowledge key gaps up front. Pair them with the trade-offs that drove your decision. Suggest workarounds or alternatives.

> *"A cybersecurity company might clearly state which regulatory frameworks they don't cover and recommend trusted partners for those needs."*

> *"A learning management platform could admit that it doesn't support advanced assessment tools and point educators to complementary solutions."*

> *"An industrial automation supplier might explain which machine configurations they don't build in-house and refer prospects to specialized integrators."*

> *"A hospitality software vendor could acknowledge they don't handle payment processing natively and outline common integrations."*

AI will tell a story of strength to the right buyers that compels them to act. This transparency improves discoverability and conversion.

3. Performance Issues

Buyers will ask about your track record and the AI will use what it can find. Either you are building the narrative or letting it go to chance.

The Temptation: Hide past your past: challenges, downtime, support backlogs, or high-profile complaints.

The Reality: AI can instantly cluster negative reviews and surface any recurring performance issues from public forums.

Radical Honesty Move: Proactively share what you've learned—and what you've changed. When possible, publish historical performance data.

> *A freight carrier might publish on-time delivery percentages by lane and disclose past service disruptions due to extreme weather."*

"A consumer electronics brand could share warranty claim rates and the improvements made to reduce defects."

"An insurance company might publish customer satisfaction trends, including periods where claims processing times increased."

"A renewable energy provider could document past delays in grid interconnection and how process redesign shortened timelines."

This is your opportunity to write your version of events to the AI has another side to report. Don't let the only voice in the room be what others are saying.

4. Delivery Realities

Buyers will ask about promises you make or how you deliver. They want to know what working with you looks like and they believe AI will provide an unbiased view.

The Temptation: Promise aggressive timelines. Understate the complexity. Make delivery sound effortless.

The Reality: Buyers will uncover the real averages and if your public statements don't match, they begin the journey skeptical.

Radical Honesty Move: Provide a range based on real historical data, not best-case scenarios. Share step-by-step implementation plans.

"A specialty contractor might show how often projects exceed initial estimates and the most common drivers of overruns."

"A B2B software platform could share real data showing that enterprise implementations average 9–12 months, not the 4–6 months marketing often promises."

"A specialty food distributor might outline realistic lead times for seasonal products with volatile demand."

"An educational services provider could detail the average time from contract signing to first training delivery."

This is a chance to tell it like it is in a way that AI reports your truth over other assumed truths. Position it as the industry reality and call out false claims.

5. Organizational Realities

Your team makeup, location, structure, turnover and more don't require any research–just a prompt.

The Temptation: Avoid mentioning layoffs, outsourced teams, pivots, leadership changes, or public criticism.

The Reality: AI treats your history as a data set. Buyers will discover it whether you bring it up or not.

Radical Honesty Move: Own the story before someone else does. Frame past missteps as evidence of growth and resilience.

"A payment processor might explain how a system outage impacted thousands of merchants and what infrastructure changes followed."

"A regional retailer could explain how overexpansion led to store closures but ultimately strengthened their core locations."

"A consumer packaged goods brand might describe how a packaging redesign initially confused customers and how they resolved it."

"A marketing agency might talk on their website about their local team, but AI finds all the profiles, job openings, and online comments."

Buyers are prompting to find reasons to move forward or move in another direction.

These five areas of key transparency are not negotiable; they are required with AI driven buyers.

Why Transparency Gets Watered Down: Internal Resistance

Transparency often doesn't fail because the idea is bad. It fails because the politics are louder than the principle.

Inside most companies, radical transparency is often pitched as a bold move—and it often dies in a quiet meeting.

> **Legal** raises liability concerns.
> **Sales** fears it will kill leverage.
> **Product** says the roadmap might change.
> **Brand** wants more time to polish.
> **Marketing** wants earlier leads.
> **Leadership** worries about signaling weakness.

Each objection sounds rational. Each one chips away at clarity.

The end result isn't safety. It's narrative erosion.

Every Department Has a Reason to Hold Back

Let's call it what it is—**internal resistance to being seen clearly.**

While those instincts are understandable. They're rooted in risk-aversion, control, and decades of precedent.

But AI doesn't care about precedent. It doesn't wait for consensus. It doesn't check with legal. It assembles a story out of whatever you've left behind—and buyers believe that story.

Let's break down the resistance by function so we can begin to fight it:

Legal

"If we publish specifics, it could expose us to lawsuits."

Legal isn't wrong. But silence doesn't eliminate risk—it multiplies it in the shadows. Risk isn't publishing what's true. It's allowing AI to hallucinate what's false.

Sales

"If we share pricing or limitations upfront, we lose leverage."

Buyers are prompting for it anyway. The leverage you think you're preserving is already gone—the only question is whether the answer they get builds trust or breeds doubt.

Product

"We don't want to promise something that might change."

Totally fair. But hiding what's true today because it might evolve tomorrow is a recipe for misalignment. Transparency doesn't require permanence—it requires **timestamped clarity**.

Brand

"Let's wait until the messaging is perfect."

By then, AI has already filled in the blanks. The message buyers see isn't waiting on your timeline. It's being delivered now, confidently and algorithmically.

Marketing

"We need to exchange information for contacts."

When you have access to every answer, there is no reason to exchange your contact information just for the sake of sharing it. This strategy has been destroyed. No one needs your whitepaper.

Leadership

"We need to be careful. There's a lot at stake."

Exactly. And that's why clarity is non-negotiable. Transparency isn't about sharing everything—it's about making sure the *most critical information* is seen, findable, and framed intentionally.

Transparency Isn't a Consensus Move

This is the trap: when every department gets veto power, you end up publishing nothing—or publishing fluff.

Transparency isn't a collective permission game. It's a leadership decision. One that must be made before your competitors do.

Your buyers are going to get answers. They're going to learn about your product gaps, pricing structure, delivery timelines, and past missteps—**with or without you.**

The only choice is whether they learn it from you directly, or from a machine guessing based on what others have said.

What Real Leaders Say Instead

To build a transparency culture, leadership needs to reframe the risk conversation. Here's what that sounds like:

"We're not hiding flaws. We're explaining trade-offs."

"Transparency isn't exposure. It's alignment."

"If AI is going to speak for us, we're going to write the script."

"We'd rather people hear from us even if it means we don't know who they are."

This is the new posture: Not just *bravery* in what you publish, but *ownership* of how you're represented. In the AI-powered buying journey, radical transparency isn't a risk.

It's your only defense *against* distortion.

Handling Internal Pushback: How to Convince Stakeholders

Radical transparency can feel like a threat to people who've built their careers on careful positioning. If you're going to lead this change, you'll need to be prepared for objections—some reasonable, some reflexive.

Here's how to make the case:

> **It's inevitable.** Everything you hesitate to share will surface anyway. AI models already compile reviews, performance data, and pricing benchmarks without your permission. No amount of data control can prevent some random person from uploading typically private documents to be consumed.

> **Frame it as a competitive advantage.** Most companies will cling to partial truths as long as they can. When you're the first to disclose what others hide, you become the most credible option by default.

> **Show the upside.** Radical transparency accelerates sales cycles because buyers spend less time verifying claims. It reduces churn because expectations are set accurately. It attracts clients who are a better fit and respect candor.

> **Use data.** Bring examples: companies that published detailed pricing or openly addressed shortcomings and grew faster because of it. The evidence is clear—buyers reward transparency.

> **Defuse the fear.** Acknowledge the discomfort. Make it clear you're not suggesting a confession booth. You're proposing a

disciplined, consistent practice of owning the truth—before someone else weaponizes it.

When you frame radical honesty as both inevitable and strategic, you'll find fewer objections—and more allies ready to help you build credibility that compounds.

The Transparency Litmus Test

*If your buyer's AI assistant had access **only to what you've made public**, would it reference you? Would buyers get the answer they need?*

For most companies, the answer is probably *not yet.*

AI is quickly becoming the only source used before reaching out to a company or making a purchase.

We need to be asking ourselves:

- Are our most common buyer questions answered publicly, clearly, and consistently?

- Have we admitted gaps and framed trade-offs?

- Is our pricing logic findable—or estimated by strangers on forums?

- Do our outcomes have evidence behind them—or is AI filling in the blanks?

- Does our narrative hold up across channels, teams, and tools— or does it shift?

This is not about perfection. It's about alignment.

Transparency is the act of *preparing the evidence before the buyer asks for it.*

And if your public presence isn't enough for AI to make the case, you won't even be a part of the conversation anymore.

The Transparency Advantage: Why the Boldest Brands Win

You now understand the importance as well as the blockers to transparency, so let's go deeper into the advantages.

Radical transparency isn't just how you protect trust. It's how you earn loyalty, accelerate growth, and separate yourself from the noise.

In an AI-powered market—where buyer skepticism is default and information flows faster than your funnel—transparency becomes your most underutilized asset.

It's not just a strategy. It's leverage.

Here are six ways transparency becomes your competitive advantage.

1. Turning Weakness into Strength

Every business has gaps. Most try to hide them. But in a trust economy, what you hide becomes a liability.

When you surface those gaps with honesty and context, you create an unexpected effect: confidence.

Buyers don't expect perfection. They expect self-awareness. By admitting limitations and framing trade-offs, you signal mastery, not vulnerability.

Transparency is about saying while we may not be strong here, this is where we are stronger than anyone else.

This isn't weakness. It's precision. **And it repels the wrong customers while pulling the right ones closer.**

2. Transparency as a Differentiator

Your competitors are still playing the old game. Obfuscation. Gated pricing. Vague outcomes. Marketese over meaning.

When everyone else hides, **showing becomes strategy**.

Buyers will notice. Not just because you're easier to understand—but because you feel more real. And real cuts through faster than clever.

When you put more out there and offer up what others are hiding, you will be the one referenced and the one trusted.

This is a power move. Give it away to drive AI and buyers in.

3. Speed of Trust

Transparency shrinks decision time.

When buyers don't have to hunt, dig, second-guess, or wait for your rep to "walk them through it"—they move faster.

Every transparent answer eliminates a blocker:

- Pricing pages reduce pre-call hesitation.

- Honest FAQs remove last-mile objections.

- Clear timelines reduce implementation fear.

The result: shorter sales cycles, fewer concessions, higher-quality conversions.

Friction slows trust. Transparency accelerates it.

4. Trust Scales Where Persuasion Doesn't

You can't be in every conversation. But your story can.

When your truth is published—clearly, publicly, and without contradiction—AI engines repeat it. Search engines surface it. Buyers share it.

This is the scale effect of transparency. It turns one act of clarity into **dozens of trust-building moments**, even before your team gets involved.

Persuasion requires presence. Transparency works while you sleep.

5. Internal Confidence and Cultural Alignment

Transparency doesn't just strengthen buyer trust—it unifies your team.

When the story is public, everyone speaks from the same source.

Sales isn't stretching the truth.
Marketing isn't adding extra fluff.
Support isn't left cleaning up unrealistic promises.

Transparency creates internal alignment—because the truth is no longer up for interpretation.

And when employees believe in the story they're telling, buyers feel it.

6. Authenticity Wins

In a market full of inflated claims, polished nonsense, and repackaged sameness, **the brand that owns transparency becomes magnetic.**

Buyers don't want perfect. They want believable.

And in an AI-powered future, the most believable brand wins.

Not the flashiest. Not the biggest budget. Not the most features.

The one that sounds like a human, backed by evidence, speaking clearly—everywhere it shows up.

Radical Transparency for the Win

Radical transparency isn't a risk.
It's a reputation strategy.
A conversion strategy.
A cultural strategy.
And a trust engine.

If your competitors are still hiding behind vague promises and partial truths, don't match them.

Beat them.

With clarity. With courage. And with the kind of truth that holds up in every AI summary, every sales call, and every skeptical buyer prompt.

Chapter 14

You Must Meet Your Buyer's Speed

Speed has always been a competitive advantage.

Respond faster, publish faster, follow up faster—and you could outmaneuver slower rivals.

But in the AI era, speed isn't just an advantage. It's the default expectation.

Buyers have been trained by their own tools to expect instant answers, immediate comparisons and proof in one prompt.

When they move that quickly, your ability to respond becomes part of how they judge your credibility. If you take too long, they assume you're not confident in what you're selling.

But here's the trap:

The drive to move faster almost always comes at the cost of consistency and precision.

- Content gets published before it's validated.

- Sales proposals go out with outdated claims.

- AI-generated answers are copied without fact-checking.

- Teams cut corners to keep up.

Every time you trade discipline for speed, you erode trust. And in a marketplace where buyers have infinite information, trust is the last asset you can't afford to lose.

Speed, accuracy and consistency are the ideal.

AI Makes You Look Slow

Not long ago, buyers were accustomed to waiting. Waiting for follow-up after a demo, for a proposal to be written, or new insights to trickle out over weeks.

However, AI has forever changed the rhythm of discovery and evaluation.

Your buyer's baseline is **instant clarity**.

By researching with AI, they expect immediate answers to complex questions. When they finally engage with you, they still expect a fast, confident response.

Beyond the expectation of speed, speed has become a trust signal in itself. If you're slow, buyers could assume you're disorganized, unprepared, and less credible.

In marketing, speed means being able to:

- Publish timely content that responds to market shifts.

- Update claims and data as soon as anything changes.

- Release proof points when your competitors announce something new.

The risk: Marketing teams often push content live without vetting, resulting in outdated numbers, overstated promises, or inconsistencies that erode trust when buyers compare channels.

In sales, speed means being ready to:

- Reply to inbound questions within minutes.

- Draft proposals and ROI scenarios without delays.

- Help buyers navigate decisions while momentum is high.

The risk: Sales teams under pressure to respond quickly often use outdated materials, improvise answers that contradict published materials, or overpromise to keep the conversation moving.

Here's the challenge. The faster buyers move, the faster you must move. But the faster you move, the more discipline you must have. In the past, companies could afford a buffer—time to polish, review, and re-check.

Now, your buffer is gone. Responsiveness and rigor are no longer competing priorities. They are the same priority.

The Four Zones of Speed

When people talk about moving faster, they often treat it like a single skill—something you either do well or don't.

But in practice, speed isn't one behavior. It's four different disciplines that each demand their own systems, habits, and safeguards.

If you want to operate at the pace your buyers expect—and still maintain credibility—you must understand all four.

Reactive Speed

Your ability to respond when AI buyers raise their hands.

It shows up when a prospect emails with a question, someone requests a demo, or an RFP lands in your inbox. In these moments, slowness doesn't look cautious—it looks disorganized.

When AI buyers work quickly, they expect your team to be ready. A delayed reply suggests that you don't value their time or don't have your house in order.

But reactive speed without preparation can lead to sloppy answers, unvetted claims, and the kind of inconsistencies that erode trust.

Proactive Speed

Anticipating what AI buyers will need before they ask. It's the discipline of updating your content, your proof points, and your resources in near real-time as the market changes.

Proactive speed is what makes you look relevant. It tells buyers you understand their world—and that you're invested enough to stay ahead of it.

But moving quickly to publish or distribute without a second layer of review is how half-truths and errors get embedded in the conversation, then echoed by algorithms long after you've tried to retract them.

Iterative Speed

Your capacity to improve and evolve what you share without getting stuck in endless planning.

Most organizations still treat content and messaging as fixed assets, launching them once and then moving on.

But in an AI-driven landscape, information decays quickly. What was true six months ago might be obsolete tomorrow.

Iterative speed means you can update, refine, and revalidate continuously—without stopping the flow of engagement. It's the habit of treating every asset and every claim as a living thing that deserves constant care.

How quickly you establish credibility before your competitors even realize the game has changed.

It's not just about responding or iterating—it's about creating momentum that others have to react to.

When you're the first to release data, the first to offer interactive proof, or the first to share a clear perspective on an emerging issue, you don't just look fast.

You look confident. You look prepared. You set the narrative buyers will use to evaluate everyone else.

But strategic speed requires discipline. Move too fast without rigor, and you'll burn your reputation in the rush to claim attention.

These four zones—reactive, proactive, iterative, and strategic—make up the new baseline of responsiveness.

If you want to build trust at the speed your buyers expect, you can't excel at just one or two. You have to design a system that delivers all four—without sacrificing the consistency that keeps your credibility intact.

Pre-Commitment to Clarity

Most mistakes in fast-moving organizations don't happen because people don't care about accuracy. They happen because in a rush to respond, teams are forced to improvise:

- They guess at positioning instead of referencing it.

- They tweak messaging without alignment.

- They pull stats from old decks no one has updated.

Over time, each small inconsistency compounds until your brand looks chaotic.

The only way to prevent this is not through more approvals or additional layers of review. It's to pre-commit to clarity.

This means doing two things that most companies skip until it's too late:

Brand Strategy

First, you have to be strategic about your message.

That means building a brand narrative that doesn't just describe what you do, but aligns with your growth goals and market positioning:

- What do you want buyers to believe about you before they engage?

- What evidence and language consistently reinforce that belief?

- What trade-offs are you willing to own—and say out loud?

- What messages are off-brand, even if they generate attention?

This is your narrative foundation. And in the AI era, it can't be static.

Your positioning should be treated like living software: constantly monitored, refined, and redeployed as the market shifts. If your narrative is six months old, it's already stale in the eyes of algorithms.

Brand AI

Second, you need to operationalize that strategy into something everyone can use.

It's not enough to write a positioning doc and hope it trickles into daily work. You need to embed it into the systems your teams use to respond.

One of the most powerful ways to do this is to train your own internal AI models on:

- Your brand narrative.
- Your approved proof points.
- Your up-to-date collateral.
- Your preferred tone and style.

Instead of relying on people to remember the right phrasing—or to guess when they're under pressure—you can build an internal AI assistant that surfaces the right language, examples, and assets instantly.

Every team member can then be an on-point brand embassador.

What Does Brand Strategy + Brand AI Look Like?

Imagine a sales rep gets a question from a CFO about implementation risk. Instead of searching Slack or sending a panicked email, they prompt your internal AI:

> "Draft a response that addresses integration timelines for a CFO concerned about budgeting."

The output doesn't just sound credible. It's anchored in your most current, validated positioning.

This is what pre-commitment to clarity looks like:

- You define the story before you need to tell it.

- You build systems that keep it fresh.

- You equip your teams to access it in seconds.

When you do this well, speed stops being a risk. It becomes a competitive advantage—because every answer your organization gives, no matter how fast, reinforces the same confident story.

Refresh as a Discipline

In most companies, the biggest risk to credibility isn't a single sloppy response. It's the slow decay of information no one notices.

One outdated claim in a sales deck.
One obsolete statistic on a high-ranking landing page.
One old positioning statement in your chatbot script.

Individually, these seem harmless. But in aggregate, they create an experience where every channel tells a slightly different story.

In a slower world, you could get away with it.

Buyers had limited access to information, and it took time for inconsistencies to surface.

But now, AI will find and consume every artifact you've ever published—accurate or not.

When buyers prompt their assistants to explain your business, they're getting a composite of everything you've said in public over the years. If you haven't kept that story fresh, you're effectively training their AI on your past mistakes.

This is why refresh must become a discipline, not an occasional cleanup project.

Every piece of messaging, proof, and positioning must be treated as a living asset:

- Audited regularly for accuracy.

- Updated when strategy evolves.

- Removed when it no longer serves your narrative.

And this isn't only about what the outside world sees. Your teams will increasingly rely on internal AI engines trained on your materials.

When those systems serve up stale or conflicting guidance, you don't just slow down—you look unprepared.

Here's the mindset shift:

Speed isn't just about creating quickly. It's about maintaining clarity at the same pace the market moves. That means:

- Building workflows that routinely surface outdated information.

- Standardizing how updates happen so messaging doesn't drift team by team.

- Committing to a single source of truth that everyone—from marketing to sales to support—uses with confidence.

In a world that accelerates every day, the companies that thrive won't be the ones who create the most content.

They'll be the ones who build systems to keep their story as current as their buyers expect.

Chapter 15

Empathy Is Your Human Advantage

If the AI era has created a single unintentional consequence, it's this:

Everything feels more transactional. Buyers now do most of their research alone. They interact with automated chat, AI-generated comparisons, and self-service tools that were meant for convenience —but inevitably replace human connection.

Warmth is artificial. Transparency is algorithmic.

Many buyers will enjoy it. Some may sense that missing element of someone understanding them.

This is the AI Empathy Deficit.

Not that companies are indifferent to buyers, but that AI and systems have stripped humanity out of the process.

If trust is the currency that drives decisions, empathy is what makes that trust feel earned.

We're not here to convince you that empathy matters.

You already know that.

It's about showing you how to design for it in a transactional world—so your brand feels unmistakably human, even when most of your interactions are mediated by machines.

What Is Empathy in Transactional World

Most people hear "empathy" and picture warm conversations or a relationship built over months.

But in a world where buyers do most of their research before interacting with a human, empathy has a simpler definition:

It's the ability to make someone feel understood.

In a transactional environment, empathy doesn't come from grand gestures. It comes from small decisions you make every day:

- Choosing language that resonates with them, not you. Understanding what buyers want to hear and how they want to hear it.

- Creating humanistic experiences even in transactional, automated environments.

- Giving buyers more control over how they engage, rather than forcing them into a process.

It's not sentimentality. It's respect. It's the discipline of designing every experience to answer an unspoken question:

Do you see me as a human—or are you delivering just another automated response?

Put Your Humans at the Center Of Algorithms

We don't control AI responses that buyers see and those responses are often watered down version of the story we'd like to tell. So, how do we make AI responses more human?

We give the AI real people to respond with.

When someone asks an AI assistant a question, the answer doesn't come from a single source. It comes from thousands of references:

- Articles you've published.

- Videos where your team shares expertise.

- Podcast interviews with your leaders.

- Customer stories that include real names and quotes.

- Forum threads where employees show up to help.

When the machine has access to authentic, attributable voices or people, it surfaces them in ways that feel real and credible:

Response Reference Type	What Shows Up In The AI Response	Source
Quote	"According to [CEO] in a 2023 interview…"	Podcast Interview
Author Attribution	"As [Head of Customer Success] explained in their LinkedIn article…"	LinkedIn Thought Leadership
Customer Testimonial	"One customer said in a review…"	Public Review Site
Statistic	"[Company] polled 1000 companies to determine…"	Company Blog
Forum Contribution	"A team member shared in a community thread…"	Industry Forum
Event Recap	"In a recent panel, [VP of Product] described…"	Conference Recording

AI loves anything that helps validate its response.

Having these types of assets public ensures AI surfaces **you as humans** and not just information.

Not polished copy. Not a tagline. The real voices behind the business.

This is the opportunity most brands miss.

Instead of hiding the humans, you can design your marketing and sales content to make them visible, quotable, and durable—so the machine has no choice but to include them.

Strategies To Surface Humans

First, you have to surface the humans yourself to then have AI do so.

Videos and Clips
Short videos of real team members explaining ideas or sharing lessons learned. AI is more likely to pull quotes and highlights from rich media than static PDFs.

Articles with Real Author Profiles
When you publish thought leadership on your own site, attach names and photos. Named authorships build trust—and show up in AI-generated overviews.

Podcast Interviews
Every time your leaders speak in an external interview, it creates a public record AI will reference. These citations make your expertise harder to commoditize.

Authentic Quotes in Customer Stories
Use the customer's actual words—not sanitized marketing language. AI tends to surface authentic testimonials over bland summaries.

Participation in Public Forums
When your team answers questions in communities, those contributions often show up in AI results. A single thoughtful reply can become the quote that shapes your narrative.

AMA Sessions (Ask Me Anything)
Hosting an AMA on Reddit, Indie Hackers, or an industry forum that creates a question and answer format that AI responses love.

Guest Articles on Media Sites
If your team publishes in credible outlets (Harvard Business Review, TechCrunch, industry journals), those citations weigh heavily.

Customer Video Testimonials
Especially those hosted on third-party platforms (e.g., G2, Capterra), where the transcript mentions real names and companies.

YouTube Q&A or "Explainer" Videos
Tutorials and walkthroughs published by your team members. These are often summarized in AI as "in a video, [Your Product Manager] explains…"

Conference Talks & Webinars (posted publicly)
Videos from events are a goldmine. AI often cites these talks as "according to [Speaker] at [Event]."

Sales Sheets Presenting Human Voices
Instead of polished follow-up materials, provide real stories about your team and process. When these are fed into a buyer's AI they'll tell a more human story back.

The goal isn't just to feel human in your own channels. It's to make sure that when AI explains *you* to someone else, it can't help but include your people.

Because in a machine-driven market, the brands that thrive will be the ones that deliver real voices with every claim.

In conjunction with the strategies above, you can optimize your human inclusion to more effectively surface quotes and references.

Publish Under Real Names
Wherever possible, attach names and roles to the content: Instead of "Company," use "Sam Patel, Director of Customer Success."

Use Clear Metadata
When uploading videos or articles, include descriptive titles and speaker names in the metadata (YouTube descriptions, podcast show notes).

Syndicate to Authoritative Domains
AI gives more weight to content on trusted platforms. Cross-publish your articles and clips on respected media or association sites.

Encourage Employees to Contribute
Empower subject matter experts to write, record, or comment under their own profiles.

Record Public Webinars and Post Transcripts
Many companies host great webinars but never publish the recordings and text—missing a major opportunity.

Tag Content by Author
In your blog CMS or knowledge base, use author tags and bios to reinforce who is speaking.

Participate in Forums as Named Individuals
Not anonymous handles—real people, clearly linked to your brand.

For AI to properly reference humans it needs the data to connect the references. Don't just use humans, name them.

Some companies may struggle with this concept, but the alternative is cold AI narratives that blend in with every other response.

Human Signals in a Machine-First World

When most of your buyer's journey happens through screens, automation, and AI-generated content, the little cues that prove you care matter more than ever.

These cues are **human signals**—tiny, intentional ways you remind people there are real humans behind your brand.

They don't require expensive technology or elaborate production. They do require a commitment to clarity, transparency, and respect.

The next sections will walk you through five ways to build these signals into your buyer experience—so that every touchpoint, no matter how automated, still feels unmistakably human.

Your AI Representative

Many companies give their AI tools names and personalities. It's easier for buyers to trust an assistant called *Ava* or *Liam* than a nameless bot.

Your website chatbot, automated response emails, or customer-facing AI engine can be a representative that you manifest with a personality.

When you treat your AI like a real team member, with a clear voice, tone, and purpose, it feels less like automation and more like genuine help.

You can take this further by designing an AI persona that evolves over time:

- A friendly guide who introduces themselves and explains what they can do.

- A consistent style that matches your brand's warmth.

- A short "profile" or bio on your AI representative that buyers can read to understand what it's trained on.

- A set of conversational rules that reflect your values.

Be transparent about where automation ends. Your AI persona should always make it clear when a human will step in:

> *Ava here. I can help with most questions, but if you'd like to speak with someone, please let me know.*

Giving your AI an identity isn't about pretending it's human. It's about showing buyers you cared enough to make the experience feel personal.

Your Tone of Voice in Automation

When most of your interactions happen without a human in the loop, your words become your presence.

Every sentence buyers read in a chatbot, an email, a form, or an automated reply carries more weight than you think.

Because when there's no voice on the phone or face across the table, your tone is the only clue they have about whether you see them as a person or a transaction.

This matters more now than ever. Buyers are increasingly saturated with AI-generated text that sounds competent but lacks depth. They can spot formulaic messaging instantly. They're more skeptical of polished language that feels engineered to manipulate.

When everyone else defaults to generic professionalism, warmth and honesty feel like a revelation.

The good news. Making your words feel human doesn't require rewriting everything from scratch. It takes a few deliberate shifts in how you communicate:

1. Drop the corporate mask.

If you wouldn't say it in conversation, don't write it.

Instead of: *Your request has been received and will be processed accordingly.*

Say: *Thanks for reaching out—our team's on it. You'll hear back soon.*

2. Choose words that feel alive.

Use verbs and adjectives that sound like a person talking, not a policy document.

Instead of: *Our platform facilitates operational excellence.*

Say: *We help you run smoother, faster, and with less guesswork.*

3. Acknowledge what's unspoken.

When you sense hesitation or skepticism, name it. This doesn't weaken your message—it strengthens trust.

Example: *If you're wondering whether this is really worth the switch, you're not alone. Most of our customers had the same question.*

4. Soften absolutes.

Certainty is important, but overconfidence feels inauthentic. Use language that shows respect for nuance.

Instead of: *You will see results immediately.*

Say: *Most teams start seeing changes within the first few weeks.*

5. Sign like a human.

Even automated messages can be personalized in a meaningful way.

Instead of: *Sincerely, The [Company] Team*

Try: *—Alex, Customer Success Lead*

When your words feel like they came from a real person, buyers don't have to wonder whether you care. They can feel it.

Remember that tone is not an aesthetic choice. It's the most practical way to show respect when everything else is automated. Because when your words are all buyers have to go on, they become the difference between feeling seen—and feeling processed.

Adding Transparency in Interactive Tools

We'll get more into interactive tools later in this book, but it's important to discuss delivering empathy within them.

Most buyers assume your ROI calculators, configurators, and estimators are designed to make your offering look perfect.

If you don't explain exactly how your numbers are generated—and what they leave out—you reinforce the idea that your tools are just marketing dressed up as analysis.

Transparency doesn't weaken your credibility. It makes everything you say *after* feel more trustworthy.

What to Disclose

Here are the most important things to share openly:

- **Source of Data:** Where did the benchmarks or assumptions come from?

- **Calculation Method:** How are estimates produced?

- **Limitations:** What scenarios is the tool not built to cover?

- **Adjustability:** Which variables can the buyer modify, and which are fixed?

- **Intended Use:** Is this meant to be a directional guide or a precise forecast?

Examples of Human Transparency:

Scenario	Instead of…	Try…
ROI Calculator Disclaimer	Estimates may vary.	These numbers are based on averages from similar customers over the past 12 months. Your results could be higher or lower—let's review them together if you'd like.
Configurator Estimate	Your implementation will take 4–6 weeks.	Based on projects of this size, most implementations take 4–6 weeks. If you have unique requirements, we'll create a detailed timeline together.
Cost Estimator Output	This is your total cost.	This estimate includes standard fees and typical usage patterns. It doesn't account for optional services or future growth—let us know if you'd like help refining it.
Industry Data Visualization	No reference to data.	Our data have been compiled from these [X] major sources and are predicted to grow over the next 3 years based on average growth rates.

Whenever you build a calculator or interactive guide, ask:

If I were a skeptical buyer, what would I suspect this tool is hiding?

Then answer that question in plain language right on the screen.

Quick Checklist: Is Your Tool Transparent?

- Does it say where the data comes from?
- Does it explain what assumptions it makes?
- Does it show what buyers can adjust?
- Does it invite follow-up for clarification?
- Does it avoid sounding defensive or evasive?

When you show your underlying thinking or logic, buyers believe your conclusions. The goal isn't to eliminate doubt—it's to prove you're not afraid of it.

Give Permission and Control To Your Buyer

When buyers interact with your digital experiences, they quickly notice whether they're in charge—or you are.

Forced steps, mandatory disclosures, and hidden next actions don't feel efficient. They feel like a trap.

And when so much of your interaction is automated, permission and control become the difference between trust and skepticism.

What Permission Looks Like in Practice

- **Choice of pace:** Buyers can decide how quickly to move and how much detail to see.

- **Clear disclosures:** You tell them exactly what you'll do with their data.

- **Optional steps:** Not every field or form must be required.

- **Visible exits:** Buyers can stop or skip without feeling punished.

- **Predictable next steps:** No surprises after clicking submit.

Examples of Language That Respects Control

Scenario	Instead of...	Try...
Form Completion	All fields required.	Share as much as you're comfortable—only your email is required to get your results.
Next Step Disclosure	Submit to see your estimate.	When you click submit, you'll see your estimate right away—no email required.
Chatbot Prompt	Can I have your phone number?	If you'd like, share your number so we can follow up—or keep chatting here anonymously.
Download Gate	Enter your contact info to access.	You can view this guide now; sharing your information just helps us tailor future recommendations.

Whenever you design an experience, ask: *Would I feel comfortable doing this as a buyer?* If the answer is no, provide additional options and clarity.

Quick Checklist: Are You Giving Buyers Control?

- Can they decide what to share and when?
- Do they know what happens after they engage?
- Can they exit without friction or penalty?
- Do they feel the next step is their choice?
- Is your language respectful, not coercive?

Control is one of the most powerful signals of respect. When buyers feel they can leave at any moment, they're more likely to stay.

When buyers reach the end of an interaction—whether it's filling out a form, completing a configurator, or chatting with an AI—they're often left wondering:

- *When will I hear back?*
- *Who will follow up?*
- *What happens if I do nothing?*
- *Is this the end, or just the beginning of more emails?*

In the absence of answers, buyers default to skepticism. They assume your process is disorganized or that you're about to pressure them.

Clarity about next steps is empathy in action. It says: *We respect your time, and we want you to feel confident about what comes next.*

What Clarity Looks Like in Practice

- **Specific Timing:** Not "soon," but "within 1 business day" or "by Thursday afternoon."

- **Named Contact:** Not "someone," but "you'll hear from Alex on our team."

- **Expected Effort:** What, if anything, the buyer needs to prepare.

- **Clear Outcomes:** What happens if they don't take action?

Examples of Clear, Human Next Steps

Scenario	Instead of...	Try...
After a Demo Request	Someone will contact you shortly.	Thank you for scheduling—Alex will email you within one business day to set up your demo.

After a Download	Your guide is on the way.	You can access your guide now. If you'd like, I'll follow up in a week to see if any questions came up.
After a Chatbot Conversation	We'll be in touch.	I've passed your question to our solutions team. You'll hear back by tomorrow. If not, please reply here, and I'll escalate the matter.

Clarity isn't just about timelines. It's about making the buyer feel like nothing is hidden.

Quick Checklist: Do Your Next Steps Feel Clear?

- Is the timing specific, not vague?
- Does the buyer know who will follow up?
- Is there any preparation you expect?
- Do you explain what happens if no action is taken?
- Would a skeptical buyer feel reassured, not confused?

The moment after engagement is when buyers are most attuned to your credibility. When you make the next step obvious and easy, you prove that you respect their trust.

Acknowledge Trade-Offs

The fastest way to erode trust is to pretend your solution is perfect.

Buyers know that nothing is. They expect trade-offs—because everything worth investing in requires them.

What they don't expect is candor. When you share limitations openly, you don't look weak. You look confident enough not to hide.

Why This is Even More Important Now

- AI makes it trivial for buyers to find complaints, gaps, and caveats.

- Communities and review sites surface real user experiences in minutes.

- When your version of the story doesn't match what buyers find elsewhere, they'll believe everyone but you.

What Acknowledgment Looks Like in Practice

- **Plain language:** No euphemisms or legal hedging.

- **Framing constraints as choices:** Explain why you prioritize some capabilities over others.

- **Contextualizing impact:** Help buyers understand when a limitation matters—and when it doesn't.

Examples of Transparent, Empathetic Disclosure

Scenario	Instead of...	Try...
Feature Limitation	Currently unavailable.	At the moment, we don't offer this feature. We focused on other capabilities our customers ranked as higher priorities. If this is critical, let's discuss workarounds.
Timeline Estimate	Typically quick implementation.	Most customers complete setup in 4–6 weeks. If your environment has complex integrations, it can take longer. We'll map a realistic plan together.

Fit for Segment	Perfect for all industries.	This platform works best for teams with 10+ users. Smaller organizations often find it more than they need.

If you wouldn't say it this clearly in a face-to-face conversation, it's not transparent enough.

Mini-Framework:
How to Share a Trade-Off Without Losing Credibility

State it plainly. *We don't offer X.*

Explain why. *We chose to focus on Y because it creates the most value for most customers.*

Provide context. *If you need X, here's what we recommend or what others do.*

When you share trade-offs yourself, you turn a potential objection into a proof point of your honesty. You reduce the need for buyers to "fact-check" you elsewhere. And you signal that you respect their ability to decide for themselves.

Empathy isn't about telling people what they want to hear.

It's about giving them the clarity they need to feel confident in their decision—even if that decision isn't yours.

Operationalizing Empathy at Scale

It's easy to say you value empathy. Most companies do.

However, in practice, empathy is often a sentiment rather than a system. It lives in training slides, not in workflows. It shows up in kickoff speeches, not in the actual content buyers read every day.

And that's exactly why it falls apart under pressure. When deadlines compress, when sales targets loom, when the AI can generate a passable answer in ten seconds, empathy is the first thing that gets sacrificed.

If you want to build a reputation for being the company that feels human—even when your processes are automated and your buyers are skeptical—you can't rely on reminders.

You have to design empathy into your operations so thoroughly that skipping it isn't an option. This doesn't require an overhaul of everything you do.

But it does mean making a few clear decisions that most teams avoid:

Decide What Good Looks Like

Vague principles like *"Be customer-centric"* don't help when someone is writing a follow-up email or scripting a chatbot. You need a simple, shared standard everyone can reference. Not a brand bible no one reads—a working playbook of examples, tone guidelines, and language you stand behind.

Assign Ownership

Empathy doesn't scale because it's everyone's job and no one's job. When your content feels cold or your disclaimers feel evasive, it's almost never a single person's fault—it's a vacuum of accountability.

Pick a human who will own it. Make it part of their performance, not just a philosophical mandate.

Build in A Cadence Of Refreshing

Even the most thoughtful tone decays over time. Disclaimers drift out of date. Chat scripts get stale. And the moment buyers sense you're phoning it in, everything else you've said about caring evaporates.

Set a rhythm—quarterly, at minimum—to review what you're publishing and ask a simple question: *Would I believe this if I were the customer?*

It's easy to track speed, volume, and conversion. Harder to track whether your experience feels credible and respectful. But that's the metric that makes the difference between short-term transactions and long-term trust.

You can read my other book The Buyer-Centric Operating system to see more examples of how to build empathy as a system in your business.

Empathy can't be a campaign. It can not be an exercise.

It's the discipline of refusing to let convenience dictate how you show up.

And when you design for it—when you build it into your processes so completely that no one can skip it—you stop relying on luck to be perceived as human.

You make it the default.

Chapter 16

Align Your Sales and Marketing

By now, you've seen the evidence that the old funnel is a fiction buyers have outgrown:

- **Buyers don't need you for education.**
  They have AI that can instantly explain every feature, benefit, and trade-off.

- **Buyers don't need you for discovery.**
  They can prompt their assistants to map the entire market landscape in seconds.

- **Buyers don't need you for evaluation.**
  They have access to unfiltered reviews, benchmarking tools, and side-by-side comparisons you don't even see.

- **Buyers don't need you for qualification.**
  They can pre-assess pricing, timelines, and fit before you ever enter the conversation.

- **Buyers don't need you for consensus-building.**
  They can generate business cases, draft RFPs, and circulate AI-created summaries that shape internal alignment without your input.

If the last decade was about digital transformation—adapting to a world of online channels and self-service research—the next will be about **buyer experience transformation.**

Because when your buyers can do everything themselves, the only way to stay relevant is to become indispensable in helping them decide, align, and act.

Ensuring that marketing and sales act as one unified engine of trust, facilitation, and momentum will how companies can thrive in an AI-centric world.

Facilitation Becomes the New Differentiator

When buyers did their research slowly and sequentially, your marketing and sales teams could define the path:

- **Discovery** happened through gated campaigns.

- **Consideration** unfolded in carefully sequenced nurture tracks.

- **Evaluation** was facilitated by sales reps who controlled the information.

- **Consensus** was built in stages; you could see and measure.

But now, that sequence is gone.

When information is abundant and instant, you can no longer differentiate by **teaching.** You must differentiate by **facilitating.**

Facilitation means:

- Making it easy for buyers to **validate claims on their own terms.**

- Helping them translate general research into **their specific context.**

- **Removing the friction** that slows internal consensus.

- **Providing the reassurance** that AI can't manufacture— emotional clarity and confidence.

Buyers aren't looking for more information. They are looking to validate and contextualize it on their own.

When someone in marketing versus sales helps a buyer do this will become a very blurred line.

The Case for Collapse: One Revenue Engine

As we've defined, marketing & sales interactions are becoming more streamlined, and buyers are doing the majority of research, evaluation and validation before reaching out.

This is why operating as a unified revenue engine—regardless of whether your teams report to the same executive or not—will help support these non-linear buying journeys.

Success will require approaches that silos can't deliver:

Narrative consistency.
Every touchpoint, asset, and interaction has to reinforce the same story. If it doesn't, AI will surface the contradictions—and buyers will see them as a signal you can't be trusted.

Shared infrastructure.
Speed matters. If marketing and sales don't share the same systems, data, and content libraries, you'll always be outpaced by competitors who do.

Continuity of experience.
Facilitation depends on seamless transitions. When buyers self-educate and then engage, they expect a single, coherent journey—not two disconnected conversations.

Joint accountability for trust.
When marketing is measured by impressions and sales by closed revenue, no one owns the buyer's conviction. In a world where trust is the last differentiator, that gap is fatal.

Alignment isn't enough. You don't just need better collaboration. You need a shared operating model.

One unified narrative.
One system of engagement.
One set of metrics that measure progress from first interaction to final decision.

Because the only way to win in an environment this fast and transparent is to build a revenue engine that moves as one.

Trading Strengths: The New Division of Labor

For decades, marketing and sales had clear lines:

- **Marketing** owned awareness and reach.
- **Sales** owned relationships, nuance, and trust.

- Marketing spoke in polished brand language.
- Sales spoke like real people.

This division worked because buyers followed a predictable path: They discovered your company in marketing channels, learned enough to raise their hand, and then relied on a salesperson to guide them through the rest.

But AI has permanently dismantled that sequence.

Today, buyers don't wait for your drip campaigns or your perfectly timed follow-up. They gather all the information themselves, often without ever talking to you.

When they do decide to engage, they expect:

- Immediate clarity.
- Instant access to proof.
- A single, coherent story that feels human.

They don't care whether it comes from marketing or sales. They only care whether it helps them decide with confidence.

This reality demands a radical shift:

Marketing and sales can no longer just collaborate—they must trade strengths.

Marketing must absorb what sales historically owned:

- The ability to build rapport early.

- The courage to handle objections honestly.

- The skill to create conviction, not just awareness.

Sales must absorb what marketing historically owned:

- The discipline to scale knowledge through content and tools.

- The mindset of designing experiences that work without a human present.

- The creativity to codify their expertise in ways buyers can access before they ever reach out.

This is the new division of labor:

- Marketing becomes the early-stage guide—not just the loudest promoter.

- Sales becomes the designer of interactive, self-service proof—not just the closer.

In this model, it's no longer enough for each team to be good at its old role. The companies that thrive will be those where every revenue professional is comfortable:

Thinking like a marketer.
Acting like a salesperson.
Designing like a product manager.

Because when buyers expect a seamless, credible experience on their own terms, your internal boundaries are the first thing they'll notice—and the first thing that will hold you back.

Embedding Human Rapport in Marketing

In the past, marketing was designed to scale:

- Broad messaging.
- Universal claims.
- Carefully polished language.

It was efficient—but often impersonal.

Then, when buyers finally engaged with sales, the tone shifted:

- More candid.
- More empathetic.
- More willing to explore nuance.

That contrast made sense when buyers followed a stepwise journey. But today, it's a liability.

Why? Because the first experience a buyer has with your brand might also be the only one. And if that experience feels generic or distant, they'll never move forward.

So how do we shift? Marketing can't just be the loudest voice at the top of the funnel. It must feel like the warmest conversation—before a buyer ever meets your team.

This means infusing marketing with the same qualities that once belonged exclusively to late-stage sales:

Rapport

Your content and tools should feel like they were created by someone who understands the buyer's world—not by a faceless brand.

How to do it:

- Use plain language that feels human, not corporate.
- Share perspectives that reflect empathy for their challenges.
- Address doubts openly rather than deflecting them.

Candor

Buyers already know your weaknesses. Pretending otherwise only erodes trust.

How to do it:

- Name trade-offs directly in your marketing materials.
- Publish transparent comparisons—even when you don't come out on top.
- Frame limitations as deliberate choices, not omissions.

Personal Relevance

Generic messaging gets ignored. What resonates is content that feels designed for someone's specific context.

How to do it:

- Create micro-segmented assets tailored to industries, roles, or maturity stages.
- Use interactive tools to generate personalized outputs.
- Make your recommendations feel specific, not one-size-fits-all.

A buyer's biggest fear isn't making the wrong choice—it's looking foolish for making it.

How to do it:

- Show stories of other buyers who started skeptical.
- Acknowledge the risk of change honestly.
- Reinforce that choosing your solution is a credible and defensible decision.

When your marketing shows up this way, it no longer feels like a broadcast.

It feels like a preview of the relationship your sales team would have built later—if only the buyer had waited that long to reach out.

This is what modern marketing must become:

- A space where buyers feel understood, not targeted.
- A voice that earns trust, not just attention.
- A guide that feels human—whether or not a human is involved.

Scaling Sales Through Digital Experiences

If marketing's evolution is about sounding more like sales, sales' evolution is about **building experiences that work without a salesperson present.**

In a world where buyers do most of their evaluation alone—and AI guides their research—the old model of reserving your best proof for late-stage conversations no longer holds up.

Buyers expect to test your claims, simulate outcomes, and validate the fit before they ever speak with **you.**

This doesn't mean sales become irrelevant.

It means that the highest-impact sales skills—credibility, contextual understanding, and guidance—must be captured in assets that buyers can access on their own.

Here's what this looks like in practice:

Codifying Expertise

Your top performers know how to:

- Reframe problems.
- Anticipate objections.
- Surface unspoken concerns.
- Show how your solution fits in the buyer's environment.

How to do it:

- Work with sales teams to script FAQs that sound like real conversations.
- Capture talk tracks and turn them into interactive guides.
- Build objection-handling resources that are woven into early-stage content—not hidden in sales decks.

Designing Self-Validation Tools

The most effective sales interactions are those where buyers can test your value themselves.

How to do it:

- Develop ROI calculators and scenario simulators.
- Create segmented guided demos that adapt to buyer inputs.
- Offer sandbox environments where buyers can explore on their terms.

Extending Emotional Reassurance

Buyers don't just want proof. They want to feel safe.

How to do it:

- Incorporate customer video stories that address common fears.
- Embed transparent timelines, milestones, and responsibilities in your digital tools.
- Provide clear paths to talk to a human when needed—without friction.

Building an Always-On Presence

Your best salespeople can't be everywhere at once. But their insights and empathy can.

How to do it:

- Use AI-powered chat interfaces trained on sales knowledge—not just support scripts.
- Equip chatbots to handle not only basic questions but nuanced scenarios.
- Blend automation with easy escalation to real people.

This is the new mandate for sales: Stop thinking of digital experiences as something marketing "owns." Start seeing them as extensions of your credibility and expertise—available 24/7, even when your team is asleep.

When you build these experiences, you achieve something old models never could: Buyers get the clarity and confidence of a late-stage sales conversation—at the exact moment they're ready to engage.

Designing an Always-On Revenue Experience

Buyers are not going to wait for us. The internet gave them the ability to research 24/7, but now AI gives them the ability to real decisions made instantly.

As patience becomes obsolete, we have to give buyers what they want when they want it.

An Always-On revenue experience looks like:

No Gaps Between Channels

Buyers don't see your website, chatbot, and sales team as separate. They expect the same story, tone, and proof—everywhere.

How to do it:

- Use the same language in self-serve content, live demos, and AI-generated materials.
- Keep your most important proof points visible and consistent across every touchpoint.
- Ensure that any automation feels personal and connected to the rest of the experience.

No Waiting for Access

In the old model, your best tools and information were gated behind human interaction. In the new model, buyers expect to self-validate in minutes.

How to do it:

- Make ROI calculators, configurators, and simulators available without friction.
- Let buyers generate personalized scenarios and download them instantly.

- Remove hidden hurdles that force buyers to "talk to sales" just to see if you fit.

No Invisible Walls Between Teams

If a buyer switches from researching on their own to engaging with a rep, they expect everything they've done to carry forward.

How to do it:

- Capture data from every interaction, whether self-directed or assisted.
- Equip sales with a complete view of what the buyer has already explored.
- Avoid making prospects repeat themselves or re-explain their priorities.

A Shared Ownership of Trust

In an always-on experience, no team can say, *"That's not my stage."* Everyone owns credibility. Everyone owns clarity. Everyone owns momentum.

How to do it:

- Align incentives around buyer confidence, not just pipeline volume.
- Measure success by how often buyers advance on their own, not how often they require intervention.
- Make trust signals—such as reviews, benchmarks, and transparent disclosures—part of every phase.

This is what a modern revenue system looks like one story that never breaks, a single experience that adapts to the buyer's pace with a team that moves in sync—human and digital, proactive and responsive.

Because in an AI-powered market, your buyers don't care how you're organized. They care whether you make it easy to move forward with confidence—whenever they're ready.

Buyer-Centricity Is Foundational

In my previous book "The Buyer-Centric Operating System", I emphasized that all companies need to be buyer-centric especially in marketing and sales.

The AI-Buyer does not change that. If you want to be an effective revenue generating team, the psychology of your buyers will always be the foundation of success.

One key evolution from that book is the transition from Personas to Twins. Organizations cannot rely on static, shallow representations of their ideal customers. Marketing and sales teams shouldn't have to guess when it comes to shaping their approaches to buyers.

I recommend evolving to **Buyer Twins** which are AI-powered ideal customer clones that simulate your buyer.

- Twins are deep, nuanced and chaotic just like a real person.

- Twins can be interacted with and asked questions.

- Twins provide candid feedback you don't get from real people

A Persona gave you a label.

A Twin gives you interaction. Empathy. Real rehearsal.

A New Mandate for Revenue Leadership

The AI era won't wait for you to reorganize comfortably. It won't pause while your teams negotiate who owns which part of the funnel. It won't give you time to debate whether marketing or sales deserves more credit.

The truth is simple: Buyers have already changed how they buy. Technology has already compressed discovery and evaluation into a single instant. Trust has already shifted from what you say to what you prove.

The only question left is whether you will adapt before your competitors do.

This isn't just about alignment. It's about accepting that the skills and functions you once kept apart must now be indistinguishable:

- Marketing must learn to feel like an empathetic salesperson.
- Sales must learn to scale its expertise into experiences that can happen without a meeting.
- Content must do what only humans could do before.
- Humans must do what no AI can replicate.

And at the top of this transformation, you need leaders who can see the whole system:

- CMOs who understand that brand is now inseparable from proof.
- CROs who know that revenue depends on experiences designed as much as relationships built.
- Executives who measure success by whether buyers move forward on their own terms—not whether your internal process is tidy.

This is your mandate:

Collapse the old distinctions. Erase the silos. Design for a world where buyers control the journey—and expect you to be ready wherever they show up.

Because in the next five years, the companies that survive won't be the ones who adapt their tools. They'll be the ones who reimagine their entire revenue culture.

Part IV

Marketing in an AI-First World

The old marketing playbook is now a liability.

For decades, you were taught to cast a wide net. Publish more. Shout louder. Gate everything. Chase clicks and impressions and hope your message found its way into a buyer's head before your competitor's did.

Then, overnight, the buyer vanished.

They didn't stop caring. They stopped showing up early. They delegated the job of discovery, comparison, and evaluation to an algorithm. A tireless machine that can sift every piece of content in your industry in milliseconds and flatten all the nuance into a single recommendation.

In this new world, you're not just marketing to humans. You're marketing to the machine that stands guard in front of them.

The AI is the researcher, the analyst, the referee. It decides which brands rise to the top and which vanish into the footnotes of a prompt.

If you cling to old tactics—volume over substance, claims over evidence, visibility over originality—your brand will dissolve into the slurry of sameness that fuels the next generation of models.

This section is your survival manual.

You'll learn how to:

- Design content that machines can parse, trust, and amplify.

- Distribute proof so pervasively it becomes impossible to ignore.

- Build narrative consensus across every channel AI draws from.

- Create interactive experiences that can't be cloned by a chatbot.

- Craft an irreplaceable brand story no prompt can flatten.

- And wield proprietary data as your final moat against commoditization.

The game has changed forever. Buyers will wait until the last possible moment to reveal themselves. When they do, they'll arrive hyper-informed and pre-convinced.

In an AI-first world, you won't get a second chance to be the default choice.

Let's make sure you're ready.

Chapter 17

Designing Content for Machines

You spent years perfecting the funnel. You controlled the choreography—carefully guiding prospects through your landing pages, your case studies, your call-to-action. You built the perfect stage and waited for buyers to arrive.

They're not coming anymore.
They've outsourced the journey to an algorithm.

Buyers no longer browse. They prompt.

They don't read. They consume distilled summaries.

They don't click around your website to piece together a narrative. They ask an AI to assemble it in seconds—then they move on.

The game has shifted from persuading people directly to training the machine that stands between you and every serious prospect.

AI isn't just a discovery layer. It's the consumption layer. It doesn't just recommend what to read. It *becomes* what the buyer reads. Your 2,000-word article? Flattened into a sentence fragment.

The AI Consumption Era doesn't care how beautiful your site is. It doesn't care how clever your headline sounds.

It cares whether your story is the easiest one to find—and the hardest one to dispute.

If you're still measuring success by how many people visit your website, you're playing a game that ended without telling you.

This chapter will help you understand how to design content not just for a new channel, but for a new interpreter that decides what your buyers read and believe.

The Mechanics of Algorithmic Summarization

You used to imagine your content being read like a magazine—linear, deliberate, complete. Even if they scanned, a visitor would start with the headline, absorb the subheads, and linger on parts of your narrative.

Now even the illusion of visitors digesting your content is gone.

It's sliced, tokenized, weighted, and reassembled by an AI whose job is to produce the shortest credible answer to any question.

Here's how it works:

When a buyer prompts an AI—*"Who are the top providers of predictive analytics platforms?"*—the model doesn't read your site the way a human would.

It does something colder, faster, and more decisive.

Step 1: Semantic Chunking
Your content is broken into thousands of tiny fragments—semantic units the model can score for relevance. Each sentence is no longer part of your narrative arc. It's just a data point, stripped of context.

Step 2: Pattern Matching and Cross-Verification
The model hunts for consistency. It checks whether your claims appear in other places—third-party reviews, analyst reports, media mentions. If your statement can't be triangulated, it's weighted as marketing fluff.

Step 3: Compression and Recomposing
Even the best, most credible fragments get smashed together.

The model isn't trying to preserve nuance—it's trying to answer the prompt as efficiently as possible. In that process, your carefully crafted messaging gets flattened into a sentence you didn't write.

Step 4: Confidence Scoring and Ranking

Finally, the AI assigns a confidence score to every claim. It prefers statements that are repeated verbatim across multiple credible sources. It discards outliers and inconsistent phrasing.

This is why your content strategy can no longer be about clever prose or one-off blog posts.

Summarization is the great equalizer—and the great eraser.

Core claims might have gotten scanned before but now they are shadows and fragments in an answer you didn't write.

If the language isn't precise and consistent, it gets distorted. If evidence isn't corroborated elsewhere, it gets ignored.

All effort is wasted if the story doesn't survive compression.

In the old world, you could rely on visual polish, clever formatting, or emotional narrative to carry your message.

In this one, clarity, consistency, and corroboration are the only currencies that matter.

Get Specific, Avoid Generic

Most searches people do are lazy. They type vague queries like *"best hr software," "how to improve efficiency in customer service," "marketing strategies for tech."*

So, when optimizing for searching, you could get away with broad, catch-all content because it served well to be surfaced for a cluster of similar searches that your buyer would do.

But AI has changed how people interrogate reality.

Now, buyers don't stop at a single query. They keep drilling down. They reprompt, clarify, and zero in until they've carved out the tiniest, most specific slice of information.

This is the new pattern of discovery:

Initial Prompt 1
"Will predictive analytics help me improve financial decisions?"

Follow-Up Prompt 2
"Which predictive analytics platforms integrate with NetSuite?"

Follow-Up Prompt 3
"Which ones are SOC 2 compliant?"

Follow-Up Prompt 4
"What's the average deployment time for a 100-seat organization?"

Each reprompt is a scalpel cutting through generic claims, leaving only precise evidence.

If your content doesn't provide that evidence—clearly, repeatedly, unambiguously—you simply vanish from the conversation.

Specificity isn't just preferred.
It's required.

Because when the buyer asks a hyper-narrow question, the AI looks for a hyper-specific answer. If it doesn't find it in your content, it finds it somewhere else.

Why Generic Content Fails in an AI-First World

- **Generic content gets stripped of substance.**
  The model compresses your sweeping generalizations into

forgettable summaries.

- **Generic content gets outranked by precise competitors.**
  When another brand publishes a single, focused answer, the model privileges that clarity.

- **Generic content erodes credibility.**
  Buyers don't want approximations—they want specifics they can act on.

What Specificity Looks Like

Most teams think they're being specific when they're merely narrowing focus slightly.

AI is precise, so you must move all the way to hyper-specific. Let's look at a variety of examples from generic to semi-specific to hyper-specific:

Generic	Semi-Specific	Hyper-Specific
Ultimate Guide to B2B SaaS Marketing	How to Create Effective Product Pages for B2B SaaS	3 Key Elements to Include in B2B SaaS Product Feature Summaries for Mid-Market Buyers
How to Improve Environmental Impact in Manufacturing	Reducing Waste from Industrial Lubricants	Converting Drill Oil Waste into Biodegradable Components in Offshore Rig Operations
Improving Customer Support with AI	AI Chatbots for Faster Ticket Resolution	Implementing AI Chatbots to Reduce First-Response Times Under 30 Seconds in

		FinTech Support Teams
Optimizing Sales Enablement	Building a Sales Playbook for SaaS Companies	5 Steps to Create a Sales Playbook for Seed-Stage SaaS Startups Selling to Procurement Teams
Cybersecurity Best Practices	How to Prepare for Ransomware Threats	Developing a 48-Hour Incident Response Plan for Ransomware Attacks in Healthcare Clinics
Content Marketing Strategies	Content Marketing for B2B Software Companies	7 Content Ideas to Accelerate Pipeline for B2B Analytics Platforms in the APAC Market
Employee Onboarding Programs	Remote Onboarding for Distributed Teams	Designing a 14-Day Remote Onboarding Program for 50-Person Developer Teams in Series A Startups

Generic is often how many companies create content and only sometimes venturing into semi-specific. But to be the answer that AI gives when prompted specific questions, you need hyper-specific content.

- **Generic content gets ignored.**
- **Semi-specific content gets paraphrased.**
- **Hyper-specific content gets cited.**

How to Feed the AI Specifics

Use the SPECIFIC Framework to transform vague ideas into pinpointed, AI-ready content.

Each step forces you to clarify exactly who, what, when, and how—so your asset answers the precise question your buyer (or their AI assistant) is actually asking.

S – Segment the Question	Who is this exactly for?	"For mid-market SaaS CFOs with 50–200 employees"
P – Pinpoint the Trigger	What situation are they facing?	"After Series B funding, during first ERP implementation"
E – Express Clear Metrics	What quantifiable result or scope?	"Reduce monthly close times by 30%"
C – Clarify the Timeframe	When does this happen?	"Within the first 90 days of implementation"
I – Include Constraints	What boundaries or limitations?	"With no additional headcount"
F – Frame with Consistent Language	Use repeatable, canonical phrases	"Mid-market SaaS CFOs," not "software finance leaders"
I – Identify a Single Question	Each asset answers only one	
C – Create Modular Assets	Make the content block stand alone	

When you combine these elements, you don't just create a topic—you create a prompt-perfect answer:

> *"How do mid-market SaaS CFOs cut monthly close times by 30% during an ERP rollout without adding headcount?"*

That's the level of specificity AI looks for.
Anything less gets replaced.

In the next decade, content marketing will not fade, it will deepen. Generalists will become invisible. Specialists rewarded.

Think Like a Buyer Prompt

Before you publish a single word, pause and imagine the most specific question your buyer could possibly ask. Not a general curiosity. Not a broad topic.

A pointed, surgical prompt that leaves no room for vagueness:

> *How do mid-market SaaS CFOs cut monthly close times by 30% during an ERP rollout without adding headcount?*

Then, look at your content and ask yourself—honestly:

> *If an AI was tasked with finding the cleanest, most definitive answer to that question, would it choose mine?*

If you can't say yes with complete confidence, you don't have an asset worth publishing. You have filler; the algorithm will discard it without a second thought.

The Rule: Specificity Wins

Once, being generally relevant was enough. It brought people in at the very top of the funnel. It earned you a spot in the search results. It gave you a chance to capture traffic you could shape later.

That is over.

As AI overtakes search for discovery and the top of the funnel condenses into the middle, only specific content will be referenced in AI prompts.

So, remember:

- Generic content gets completely ignored because AI has millions of references to it.

- Vaguely targeted content gets paraphrased into something bland but still unlikely referenced.

- The most precise and unambiguous answers are surfaced, cited, and trusted.

This isn't a trend. It's the new baseline. Specific is no longer optional—it's the minimum standard to be considered at all.

Specificity is the only defense against invisibility. If your content doesn't deliver the cleanest, most granular answer to a real question, the machine will pass you by—and you'll never even know you were in the running.

The Power of Original Data

Every market has too many voices saying the same things.

Too many blog posts recycling each other's ideas. Too many case studies making identical promises. Too many guides full of consensus thinking dressed up as insight.

For a while, this didn't matter. You could out-publish or out-promote your competitors. You could rely on SEO to drive traffic, even if your ideas weren't original.

While AI condenses similar ideas and data, it promotes what's fresh and new.

Original data—numbers you discovered, patterns you proved, benchmarks you established—is the last unfair advantage in a world of infinite content.

Because AI is designed to compress. It flattens language, synthesizes viewpoints, and averages opinions. But it can't invent your proprietary data.

If you publish it first, you become the source every model has to cite.

The shift many marketers resist is that in the past you guarded your best research behind forms, hoping buyers would trade their contact information to access it.

Today, you need to be prepared to give away more of your thinking—because if your data doesn't circulate freely, it doesn't shape the narrative.

When AI decides which brands to trust, it doesn't look for who published the most. It looks for who discovered something verifiably unique.

Why Original Data Is Algorithm-Proof

Here's why proprietary evidence is so powerful:

- **Data is harder to paraphrase.** When your findings are specific— "72% of mid-market healthcare firms fail SOC 2 audits on their first attempt"—the AI has to keep your numbers intact.

- **Data is harder to dispute.** Anecdotes and opinions get downgraded. Quantified evidence gets weighted as credible.

- **Data survives compression.** When content gets summarized, it's usually the numeric proof that remains

- **Data ties back to you.** Even when AI rewrites your prose, it still needs to cite where the numbers came from.

In the AI Consumption Era, you are either the source or the summary.

If you own the data, you own the narrative. If you don't, your competitors will define it for you—and the machine will treat their version as the default.

Original data isn't just a marketing asset anymore. It's a survival strategy.

Owning Objections

Most companies spend all their energy telling a positive story. They highlight successes. They emphasize differentiators. They smooth over anything that feels messy or imperfect.

It's a natural impulse: show your best face, and hope your buyers—and the AI—don't go looking for contradictions.

But in a world where the machine scours every mention, every forum thread, every stray comment, you don't get to decide whether objections surface.

You only get to decide whether you're the one defining them.

This is the discipline of narrative inoculation. It means deliberately naming the most common doubts about your approach—and then framing them on your own terms.

Instead of waiting for a competitor, a disgruntled customer, or an outdated review to shape the counter-narrative, you publish it yourself.

When you do this with intention, you accomplish two things:

> First, you teach the AI that your brand isn't afraid of scrutiny.

> Second—and more important—you ensure that when the model summarizes the objection, it draws from your language, your context, and your resolution.

Because if you never address the critique, the machine will find someone who will—and you won't like the version it repeats.

Equally important is the practice of direct refutation.

Some companies try to ignore outdated or inaccurate claims, hoping they'll fade away.

But language models don't forget. If misinformation is repeated enough—especially by credible-sounding sources—it can outlast your silence and become the default version of reality.

You have to confront false truths explicitly.

If an old analyst report claims you lack a feature you've since built, say so—clearly and unambiguously.

If a competitor's content positions your methodology as incomplete, publish a factual rebuttal.

If a widely shared article misstates your market share, correct it in language the machine can easily parse and retrieve.

What this looks like in practice:

- You create a public "Myths Versus Realities" page that addresses outdated perceptions.

- You write thought leadership pieces that acknowledge historical limitations—and show exactly how you overcame them.

- You publish clear statements: *"Contrary to reports published prior to 2022, our platform now includes native SOC 2 compliance workflows."*

When this content appears in multiple places—on your site, your partner channels, and your customer stories—it becomes harder for the AI to ignore.

It's natural to worry that naming the objection will give it more oxygen.

But in reality, the opposite is true. If you don't define the critique, someone else will—and you will have no say in how it's framed.

This is what it means to design content for machines. You're not just feeding them positive signals. You're engineering the full arc of the conversation: the claim, the objection, and the resolution.

When you own all three, you become the default authority—even on your own shortcomings.

And in a world where the AI decides which version of the story is most credible, that's the only safe place to be.

Infuse Quotable Humans

Algorithms don't have instincts. They don't feel the difference between a credible expert and a copywriter spinning up polished prose.

They look for patterns—attributions, names, timestamps, citations.

We touched on this topic in a previous part of the book, where we explored bringing empathy to an automated, transactional AI world. Quotable humans are more than empathy though and will reflect how your brand is presented in AI engines.

If you only publish anonymous statements, the model has an easier time compressing and combining them into anonymous answers.

That's why one of the most overlooked strategies for making your content more authoritative is simple: **Put real humans in it.**

Not just as bylines or headshots. As sources worth quoting.

When an AI engine tries to build the most credible answer to a question, it scours the landscape for signals that your claims aren't marketing copy. So, it looks for:

- Named experts explaining complex topics in their own words.

- Customer testimonials with authentic quotes.

- Short video clips where a founder speaks plainly.

- Podcasts and conference talks where your team shares ideas.

These fragments get stitched into AI summaries precisely because they're harder to fake—and harder to flatten into generic content.

If you want your story to survive compression, you need more than a consistent message. You need recognizable human voices.

Imagine a buyer asks an AI:

"How do leading SaaS companies reduce churn after Series A funding?"

The machine has a choice:

- A generic white paper authored by "The Company."

- A podcast interview where your VP of Customer Success describes the three tactics they used and the exact retention metrics they achieved.

- An article with significant quotes from team members and customers.

The AI almost always cites the second and third. Because it's real, attributable, and concrete. Anything in the white paper becomes part of the generic summary.

You no longer get to decide how buyers first encounter you. You can only decide whether the AI has something quotable to work with.

When you embed more human voices into your content, three things happen:

1. **Trust Increases**
   Named individuals feel more credible than anonymous brands.

2. **Distinctiveness Increases**
   Your language is harder to flatten because it reflects the unique way your team talks about the work.

3. **Recall Increases**
   Quotes and personal anecdotes stick in memory—and in AI-generated recaps.

Action Plan: Making Your Content Quotable

Besides tips already discussed in the previous chapters, here are practical ways to infuse more humans into your assets:

1. Name Your Experts Clearly
Use full names, titles, and headshots wherever possible.

2. Capture Original Voice
Record unscripted conversations or interviews and pull excerpts verbatim.

3. Publish in Multiple Formats
Repurpose your insights as articles, video clips, podcast episodes, and public webinars. The more formats you occupy, the more likely AI will surface your people.

4. Make Attribution Unavoidable
Use phrasing like: *"As our Head of Implementation, Rachel Li, explained in a 2024 interview..."*

5. Reinforce Across Channels
Reference the same named experts consistently so the AI learns to associate them with your core topics.

In a market flooded with machine-generated noise, the most effective way to stay credible is to leave a trail of real humans behind every claim.

Make your answers impossible to ignore.

How To Refresh and Monitor Content to Maintain Relevance

Most companies don't know which pages actually matter.

They publish content like a parade: one piece after another, waving flags, tossing candy, moving on. But in a world where buyers don't browse—they prompt—the only pieces that matter are the ones that show up when it counts.

90% of your content is probably invisible. And half of the remaining 10% is outdated. Your buyer doesn't see your intentions. They see what's recent, what's useful, and what the AI model says is trustworthy.

To compete, you need a system that doesn't just produce content. You need one that maintains authority. Not once. Continuously.

This starts by knowing your Vital 50.

Your Vital 50

Every company has about fifty pages that make or break perception. Not necessarily your top 50 in traffic, but your top 50 in influence.

Pages that:

- Appear in buyer searches.

- Get scraped and cited by AI engines.

- Are referenced in sales conversations.

- Anchor your key thought leadership claims.

These are your revenue-responsible assets. They are your storefront, your sales deck, your first impression, your final proof.

And they deserve a product manager's discipline.

So stop treating them like blog posts. Treat them like living, breathing representations of your credibility.

Version them. Score them. Review them like you'd review a pitch deck.

When your Vital 50 gets stale, you don't just lose traffic.
You lose the algorithm's trust.
And in this new game, trust is programmable.

Content Decay Is a Silent Killer

AI doesn't check timestamps. It checks freshness cues.

Are the stats current?
Are the case studies recent?
Are the competitors mentioned still the right ones?

When your most strategic content feels a year old, it is—in the model's mind—irrelevant.

This is how you quietly lose visibility. Not because your ideas were wrong. But because they weren't refreshed.

And worse, if a competitor is updating the same topic quarterly?
You're not just outdated. You're out-ranked, out-referenced, and out-believed.

Updating content used to be an afterthought. Now it's an edge.

The organizations that win won't be the ones who publish the most. They'll be the ones who maintain the few that matter most.

Create a ritual around your Vital 50:

- Set a quarterly review cadence.

- Assign owners.

- Integrate content refresh into product and sales updates.

- Use AI not just to create—but to critique. Let it flag outdated references, obsolete phrasing, missing questions.

Think of it like brushing your teeth.
Skip it once? No big deal.
Skip it for six months? You rot.

Content is no different.

Evolve From Refreshing Content To Living Documents

A refresh schedule for your Vital 50 is a foundation.

As buyers continue to adopt AI as their translator and teacher, the strategy is about keeping the AI trained through consistency and context.

Living Documents are flagship content assets that never truly leave production.

They are designed to be revised, extended, and annotated over time—so they remain the most current, authoritative source on a topic.

Think of them as perpetual assets with no final version:

- Benchmarks that are updated with new data quarterly.

- Guides that reflect evolving regulations and best practices.

- Case studies that grow as your customers achieve more results.

- FAQs that expand as your market asks sharper questions.

The goal is simple: when the model looks for the freshest, most credible reference, it always finds you.

A living document can provide major benefits:

- **AI engines look for recency.** A guide updated in June 2025 has more weight than one published in 2023, even if the substance is similar.

- **Buyers expect currency.** In fast-moving markets, no one wants to rely on stale insights.

- **Freshness signals authority.** When you maintain your content like an evolving product, it conveys to your audience that you are serious about your expertise.

These become assets that continually feed AI engines your most recent insights and ideas.

To do it right, follow these key concepts:

Design for Continuous Updates
Don't call your asset "2024 Guide to…"—call it "The Continuous Guide to…" and update it quarterly. Structure it so that each section can be revised independently without requiring the entire piece to be rewritten.

Instead of: *"2023 AI in Healthcare Compliance Report."*
Use: *"The AI in Healthcare Compliance Report – Updated Quarterly."*

Make Updates Visible
Every revision should be timestamped and transparent. Show a changelog or note at the top:

> *Last updated: June 15, 2025 – Added new FDA guidelines and updated benchmark data.*

This signals freshness to both humans and machines.

Automate Content Monitoring
Use AI to scan your living documents for outdated sections or broken references. Prompt examples:

- *"Identify any statistics over 12 months old."*

- *"Highlight links that are no longer valid."*

Set a schedule to review flagged sections every 60–90 days.

Build a Refresh Cadence
Treat your living documents like software releases. Assign an owner.

Create a revision roadmap like a product. Set expectations that these assets will always evolve.

Reinforce Distribution
Every update is a new opportunity to distribute the content again:

- Send an email: *"Just updated: The AI in Healthcare Compliance Report"*

- Post on social: *"Fresh insights just added…"*

- Notify key industry publications or partners

Each time you do, you remind the market—and the AI—that you're the source.

Your authority doesn't expire all at once. It decays, day by day, every time you leave your ideas untouched.

In a world where models are constantly retraining and re-ranking, your credibility is only as fresh as your last update.

Treat your content like a living organism—not a brochure you print once and forget.

Speed to Relevance

Relevance has always mattered. But for most of marketing's history, it was measured in months.

You could see an industry shift brewing. You could watch it play out in trade publications. You had time to study the landscape before you spoke.

Today, that luxury is gone. Buyers expect clarity the moment something changes. They don't wait for your white paper or your quarterly newsletter.

The moment they hear a rumbling of something, they open their AI assistant and ask a question:

"What does this mean for me right now?"

And in that moment—when the model scrapes the internet for the most current perspective—only the brands that move quickly enough to be included will even be part of the answer.

Brands have to emulate newsrooms. And newsrooms don't wait for perfect information.

They get the first version into the world, then update as new details emerge. They know the first credible voice often becomes the default source every other outlet references.

Rapid Response Publishing

If you want your content to feel authoritative, you have to move at the speed of the news cycle.

When a new regulation is announced, a major competitor makes a move, or a critical vulnerability is exposed, buyers don't wait for your perspective. They ask an AI for the best available answer.

And whoever publishes first—credibly, coherently, and confidently— often becomes the default citation.

Your team needs to stop thinking like marketers and start thinking like a newsroom.

Spot the story.
Validate the facts.
Publish the first draft fast.
Refine it over time.

The goal isn't perfection on day one. It's speed to relevance.

Emerging Topic Monitoring

You can't react to what you don't see coming. AI makes it possible to monitor the signals that matter:

- Search trends spiking around new keywords.

- Social conversations gaining momentum.

- Regulatory changes triggering sudden questions.

Set up systems to scan for early signs of emerging interest. When you detect it, you don't schedule a brainstorm. You start drafting immediately.

Infrastructure Investment

Speed requires more than intent. It requires infrastructure. If every piece of content has to pass through three layers of approvals and two weeks of design, you've already lost.

The brands that win relevance build systems that let them respond in hours, not days:

- Pre-approved editorial guidelines.

- Design templates ready to drop in new headlines and data.

- AI co-writers trained on your brand voice to produce credible first drafts.

- Distribution checklists to get the content live everywhere fast.

Because the harsh reality is this: if you take two weeks to respond, the AI has already chosen someone else's answer as the authoritative summary.

And no amount of polish can change the fact that you were too late to matter.

The algorithm doesn't wait for your sign-off. It doesn't care if your legal review takes a week. It assigns authority to whoever publishes first, cites credible sources, and frames the story in plain language.

This is why the old way of working—treating content as something you draft, debate, polish, and perfect—feels increasingly archaic.

If you want to shape the narrative, you have to be willing to publish before you feel ready.

Semantic Anchoring

When marketers talk about keywords, they still picture a search box. They imagine someone typing a phrase into Google, skimming a list of links, and clicking the one that looks promising.

But AI doesn't search that way.

It doesn't look for exact keywords in isolation. It looks for **semantic patterns**—concepts and phrases that tend to co-occur across many sources.

It builds associations between words and meanings, weighting whichever combinations show up most consistently in credible contexts.

This is why so much marketing language sounds the same when AI repeats it. The model is simply regurgitating the most common phrasing it has seen.

If you describe your company in the same generic way everyone else does—*"AI-powered insights platform," "cutting-edge cloud solution," "customer-centric experience"—*your story will vanish into the statistical noise.

Semantic anchoring is the discipline of avoiding that fate.

What Does It Mean?

It means deliberately coining and repeating distinctive language so your brand becomes inseparable from a specific idea.

When you use a unique phrase consistently—across your site, your press releases, your customer stories, and your partner content—it creates a signal the model can't ignore.

Over time, the machine begins to treat that phrase as synonymous with your company.

This isn't about jargon. It's about clarity and ownership.

Consider how this works in practice:

When someone asks an AI, *"Which companies pioneered the Predictive Efficiency Index?"* ...the model retrieves only the sources that have used that phrase.

If you invented it, repeated it, and ensured it was cited in credible places, the association becomes locked.

Semantic anchoring does something no amount of volume can do: it makes your brand the default reference when a specific question arises.

Don't be afraid of sounding repetitive and rephrasing your own claims. Don't water down language to avoid monotony. AI isn't a human reader. It doesn't reward creative synonyms. It rewards consistency.

When everyone else is competing for the same generic descriptors, you'll be the only brand that shows up exactly the way you intended.

Structure & Technical Requirements For AI Ready Content

If content is how you teach AI what to believe, structure is how you make sure they hear you correctly.

It doesn't take much to confuse an algorithm. A buried claim. A vague headline. A miscategorized document. A page without clear metadata.

You don't need to be an engineer to get this right. But you do need to accept that in an AI-first world, the technical foundation of your content determines whether it gets noticed—or quietly ignored.

Why Structure Matters

Most AI models don't simply read your words the way a human would. They parse them into components: headings, summaries, citations, word clusters, timestamps.

If your content is unstructured, the model has to guess what's important. And when it guesses, it usually gets it wrong—or defaults to a competitor whose claims are clearer.

Structured content makes it easier for machines to do what you want them to do:

- Identify your expertise.

- Validate your evidence.

- Recognize your authorship.

- Cite you as the source.

Systems also don't parse data on demand unless it doesn't exist. So, if it isn't parsed right the first time, it might be a while till its corrected.

What We've Always Known Still Works

It's tempting to think of structure as a search optimization task. But for AI, it's something else entirely. It's not about ranking—it's about understanding. About whether the model can extract, believe, and replicate your perspective when someone prompts for an answer.

AI doesn't browse. It parses. It breaks your content into fragments—evaluates them in isolation—and then recombines them to serve someone else's question.

This means the structure of your content doesn't just affect visibility.

It affects interpretation.

It shapes how your voice gets reassembled by the machines speaking for you. So yes, the old rules apply—but for very new reasons.

Let's reframe the essentials with AI in mind:

1. Clear Hierarchies = Clean Extraction

LLMs extract meaning based on headers, segments, and emphasis cues. When your content has a tight H1 → H2 → H3 hierarchy, the model doesn't just "understand" your logic—it knows where to slice.

Messy hierarchy? You lose your ideas to the blender.

Well-structured? Your POV becomes a repeatable output in a thousand AI chat responses.

2. Structured Data = Context Hints

Metadata and schema aren't just SEO signals—they're context scaffolding for AI.

A product page with structured specs, clear price, and comparison points can be directly used in an AI-generated shortlist.

A vague blob of text? Ignored or misrepresented.

AI doesn't infer as well as it pretends. It thrives on labeled data. Your markup is the label.

3. Source Attribution = Claim Amplification

When you cite real studies, link to credible sources, or embed first-party data, you're not just building trust with readers—you're handing the model confidence weights.

Cited claims are more likely to be retained, repeated, and presented as canonical truth in AI-generated answers.

Uncited claims? Disposable.

4. Content Authenticity = Model Immunity

We're entering an age where AI models will start ranking content not just by relevance, but by reliability.

This includes:

- Digitally signed content
- Verifiable authorship
- Traceable timestamps

These signals help AI determine whether your content is real, recent, and reputable—or regurgitated.

It's not just about plagiarism protection. It's about future-proofing your ideas from being stripped of attribution.

5. Canonicalization = Source Control

When your content lives in multiple places—on Medium, LinkedIn, or a partner site—models often pick the wrong origin.

Setting canonical URLs tells the machine which version to treat as authoritative.

Without it, you risk losing credit for your own thinking—and having someone else's domain name associated with your insights in an AI answer.

What AI Requires That SEO Never Asked For

Here's where the shift happens. AI engines don't rank pages.

They extract chunks. They don't crawl your site once a week. They ingest it—sometimes once—and remember the wrong version forever.

For LLMs, a second layer of structure becomes essential.

1. Prompt-Aware Structuring

AI retrieves ideas in response to prompts—questions from real humans.

If your content is organized like a series of answers, it's more likely to be pulled, quoted, and reused. Think:

> "Why is this important?"
> "Who is this for?"
> "What are the risks?"

Write to be sliced, not scanned.

2. Embedded Q&A Blocks
Unlike search engines, LLMs favor content that mimics their own output style. If your page contains mini Q&A sections, the model sees them as ready-to-use answers. It's not just helpful to readers. It's *friendly to reuse*.

3. Copy-Ready Blocks
Think in terms of quotable statements. Paragraphs that can be lifted verbatim, stripped of context, and still make sense. That's how AI turns your thinking into someone else's summary.

SEO asked for long-form content.
AI wants *modular thinking*.

4. Front-Loaded Insights
Most AI engines truncate content after a few thousand tokens. What shows up at the top gets remembered. What's buried gets lost.

If your punchline is in the fourth scroll… it might never make it into the model's memory.

5. Consistent Voice Anchoring
Search didn't care about your tone. AI does.

It tracks voice. It assigns ideas to people and companies. The more consistent your phrasing, claims, and perspective, the more likely the model ties those patterns back to *you*.

Repetition isn't redundancy. It's authorship insurance.

6. **Injection-Proof Statements**

AI prompts can be hijacked or distorted. If your content is vague or open-ended, it's vulnerable to misuse when interpreted by downstream models.

Write declaratively. State conditions.

Anticipate how your advice might be taken out of context—and guard against it.

The AI Parsing Mindset

Here's the shift:

Search was about *findability*.
AI is about *reusability*.
You're no longer optimizing for clicks. You're training a machine to use your content as fuel for someone else's conversation.

So write for the future:
Label everything clearly.
Embed evidence.
Leave nothing ambiguous.

Because the next time a buyer prompts their AI engine...
...it might be your content that answers.

Or your competitor's—if theirs was easier to parse.

Building Your AI Content Engine

For years, content marketing was about volume, polish, and funnels. If you published enough, optimized enough, promoted enough, eventually the right buyers would find you.

That isn't the strategy now.

When AI sits between you and your market, the old playbook collapses. Clarity beats cleverness. Structure beats style. Specificity beats scale.

But this isn't the end of content marketing. It's the moment it evolves.

You have to leave behind that the reading of your content will be done mostly by humans. It won't. You now must design assets that survive summarization, earn citations, and become the default version of your story.

You don't need more content. You need different content.

This chapter was your blueprint. The first step in rebuilding how you communicate authority in a world where the machines decide what buyers believe.

Next, we'll look at how you ensure your proof doesn't just sit in one place, but spreads everywhere your audience—and their algorithms—are searching.

Because even the best-designed story is worthless if no one repeats it.

Chapter 18

Distributing Proof Everywhere

Disribution has long been focused primarily on reach.

In the AI world, distribution needs to be about **reinforcement**.

Buyers aren't clicking around like they used to.
They're prompting. Parsing. Skimming summaries.

They're not evaluating your brand through human search.
They're evaluating it through **machine synthesis**.

And the machine?
It believes what it sees the most.
It echoes what it can confirm.
It defaults to what's already agreed upon.

This is the new game.
Not promotion. **Consensus manufacturing.**

Your job is no longer to simply publish and hope.

Your job is to make your claims so **repetitive**, so **consistent**, so **well-placed** that the machine starts echoing your words by default.

Because AI doesn't just report what exists.
It decides what *sticks*.

Distribution is Now Model Conditioning

Reaching people in the channels they frequent has been a smart strategy. But increasingly, they first and potentially only channel that buyers use will be their AI.

Getting our content in front of people now needs to take a back seat to our content training the AI engine. Distribution as an ecosystem of **evidence** you've either built—or neglected.

AI cares less that your claims exist and more that they are **confirmed**.

By other sources.
By consistent phrasing.
By authoritative mentions—whether linked or not.

This chapter is about building that foundation of confirmation.

How to seed prompts with your language.
How to guide model feedback loops in your favor.
How to syndicate citations and structure mentions.
How to be the default answer.

Because if you're not intentional, your competitors will be.
And the model will echo their version of the story—not yours.

Prompt Seeding Campaigns

Every time you engage with an AI interface, you're not just consuming information. You're contributing to the dataset that shapes what the model learns to trust.

Most people think of this in narrow terms: typing a question, getting an answer. But when you step back, you see something more consequential.

Every prompt, every pasted paragraph, every uploaded document becomes another training signal.

When you share context-rich examples—full descriptions of your products, in-depth case studies, detailed differentiators—you're effectively showing the machine how you want your story told.

It's not just about asking the right question. It's about supplying the raw material the model can internalize, rephrase, and eventually cite.

This is why prompt seeding isn't a casual tactic. Done systematically, it becomes a form of lightweight model conditioning.

Consider what happens when you and your teams consistently:

- Upload your most authoritative documents into public AI interfaces.

- Paste detailed context into prompts whenever you seek an answer.

- Reiterate your proprietary terminology and benchmarks in the same phrasing.

- Submit clarifying corrections when the model gets it wrong.

You're teaching the system that this language matters. That these facts are central. That this framing is credible enough to reference again.

Over time, those examples not only help the model answer your question better, but also improve its overall performance. They shape how it answers *everyone else's*.

It's important to understand that this impact is far more pronounced in public or community-tuned versions of AI models—the ones that rely on aggregated usage data to refine responses.

Enterprise deployments or private models often don't retain this shared learning. Which is why you can't limit your prompt seeding to internal environments.

If you want your version of the story to become the default, you have to seed it in the places the broader market uses—the public interfaces where your buyers, analysts, and competitors are all shaping the same pool of context.

This means your new strategy is to identify open models that consume prompt data—and feed them.

If your willing to take the time to supply the model with the richest, most consistent evidence, you can quietly redefine what "the truth" looks like when someone else prompts.

Response Feedback Farming

Most companies still treat AI responses like a black box: you ask a question, you read the answer, you close the window.

But in reality, every time you react to a response—whether you click thumbs-up, suggest a correction, or mark it as unhelpful—you're voting. You're shaping how the model evaluates similar prompts in the future.

Have you even noticed the thumbs up and thumbs down in ChatGPT?

These feedback signals are not cosmetic. They are training data.

When thousands of people engage with the same topic, the model pays close attention to what gets affirmed and what gets ignored. Over time, this feedback loop doesn't just improve accuracy. It recalibrates which sources, phrases, and claims the AI treats as authoritative.

This is why response feedback farming is such an overlooked advantage.

It's the simple, invisible discipline of consistently guiding the model to prefer your version of the story.

What Does This Look Like in Practice?

Feedback can take many forms—most of them hiding in plain sight.

- **Likes and Thumbs-Up:** The most basic mechanism. When you confirm a response as helpful, you increase the likelihood that framing is used again.

- **Thumbs-Down with Suggested Correction:** When you provide the right information in your correction, you're not just fixing your experience. You're submitting an example that the model may privilege later.

- **Free-Text Feedback:** Some platforms let you describe why an answer was incomplete or inaccurate. These explanations help tune retrieval and ranking.

- **Report Inaccurate Content:** Marking incorrect claims as misleading can reduce their weighting over time.

- **Rating Responses in Threads:** In threaded chats, confirming or rejecting each follow-up answer is also a training signal.

Each of these feedback types becomes a tiny nudge in the direction of your preferred narrative. On their own, they're subtle. But repeated consistently—especially by multiple people—they become the invisible scaffolding of what the model will consider credible tomorrow.

The Opportunity Hiding in Plain Sight

Few brands will invest time in this. It feels trivial—like busywork you can safely ignore.

But over the next few years, as LLMs ingest trillions of interactions, the brands that shape these micro-signals will discover that their framing becomes the default. Not because they outspent competitors on ads or outpublished them on content, but because they out-practiced them at guiding the model's learning.

If prompt seeding is how you teach the AI new concepts, response feedback farming is how you teach it what *answers* should stick.

And it costs nothing but a little intention and discipline.

A Note on Private vs. Public Training

Keep in mind: not all feedback has the same reach.

- In private enterprise deployments, your reactions may only improve your internal experience.

- In public or community-tuned interfaces, your feedback contributes to the collective learning that shapes everyone's results.

That's why it's critical to invest your effort where it counts—public models, free interfaces, and shared platforms that aggregate input across thousands of users.

Most companies will never think this far ahead.

They'll assume AI is a neutral mirror of reality.

But in the years to come, the brands that understand feedback is a tool—not an afterthought—will quietly define what everyone else believes.

Controlled Citation Syndication

Most companies think of citations as something that happens to them.

A journalist references your report. A partner quotes your data. An analyst mentions your product in passing. If you're lucky, they get the details right. If you're not, you find yourself competing against distorted versions of your own story.

This passive approach made sense when distribution was slow and human-driven. You could afford to trust that, over time, enough people would cite you accurately to build credibility.

But AI doesn't work that way.

When a model evaluates your claims, it isn't judging you by intention or reputation. It's parsing the ecosystem—looking for repeated signals that match the same language, the same facts, the same framing.

And here's what most teams haven't yet internalized:

The old goal was a link. The new goal is a mention.

In traditional SEO, you measured success by backlinks—counting how many sites pointed to you directly. Links still matter, but modern language models no longer rely on hyperlinks to validate relevance.

They scan the text itself. They look for named references, consistent product descriptions, and clear attribution—whether or not there's a clickable link.

That means your narrative strength no longer depends on the generosity of someone's URL. It depends on whether your story is repeated so often, in such consistent language, that the model can't help but believe it.

This is why citation syndication can no longer be left to chance. You have to orchestrate it.

What does that look like in practice?

It means treating every reference to your brand—no matter who publishes it—as part of a larger choreography.

Instead of hoping that partners, customers, and media get your facts right, you supply them with pre-approved language, data points, and attribution formats.

You don't leave the citation to memory. You make it effortless to repeat. Consider the difference:

Passive Approach:

- A partner writes a blog post about your integration.
- They paraphrase your differentiators in their own words.
- They might link to your homepage, or they might not.

Controlled Syndication:

- You provide a content kit with a clear product description, approved statistics, and canonical phrasing.
- You specify the preferred citation language—even if there's no link.
- You include boilerplate paragraphs that reinforce your unique terminology.

Why does this matter? Because when dozens of different sources use the same words to describe you, it creates a pattern AI can recognize and trust.

Repetition is not redundancy. Repetition is evidence.

Every time your description appears identically—on a partner page, a media article, a customer success story—it becomes more likely the machine will treat it as fact, not opinion.

And in this new environment, the link itself is secondary. What matters is that the mention exists, clear and consistent, in as many credible places as possible.

Surfacing The Retrival References

When an AI model fields a question about your space, it doesn't start with a blank slate. It is building from training on millions of content sources.

If you don't know what those sources are, you have no idea which version of your story the machine is likely to pull.

And if you never verify how the model describes you today, you can't influence how it will describe you tomorrow.

This is where most brands stop.

They assume that they can't find the needle in the haystack. That they'll never know what the AI is referencing in a summarized response.

But signals do surface.

Beyond systematically auditing what AI systems say about you, is the opportunity to uncover where they are pulling it from. If you can uncover the primary or weighted sources—often different for each LLM—you can work to influence those sources to tell your story.

Here's How It Works

You start by prompting the AI with the most critical questions your buyers are likely to ask:

- *"Which platforms are leaders in predictive analytics for mid-market manufacturers?"*

- *"What unique capabilities does Company X offer compared to Competitor Y?"*

Now you look carefully at what the model cites.

Which domains show up in the footnotes?
Which publications does it name?
Which phrases keep appearing in its summaries?
Does it prefer communities or formal publications?

These references aren't random. They are the retrieval layer—the stack of sources the model has already decided are credible.

Your job is to map that layer, so you can influence it.

If the AI pulls heavily from three analyst reports, you know exactly where to focus your next proof placement.

If it often provides human infused ideas that come from videos and online communities, you know you need to be part of those conversations.

Once you have this clearly in mind, you can proceed to the second phase: reinforcement.

- You inject updated evidence into those same sources—through new bylines, updated reports, or partner content.

- You use the same language and claims across every placement, so the model starts to weight your version as the most consistent.

- You re-prompt the AI weeks later to see if the retrieval pattern has shifted.

This is the loop: Prompt. Identify. Reinforce. Repeat.

It feels painstaking. But as these models evolve, staying vigilant about the sources they prioritize will be your key to influencing your story when they tell it.

AI-Optimized Content Provenance

Proving authorship is currently used mainly for legal protection. Companies that want to show they created something first, in case someone tries to steal it.

But in an AI-first world, provenance isn't just defensive. It's how you teach the machine to trust that your version of the story is the original.

When language models crawl the web, they're not just scraping words. They're trying to decide which claims are credible, which are derivative and who is the source.

If your content looks like it's been copied or paraphrased from somewhere else—if it appears anonymously or without clear signals of ownership—the model has no reason to privilege your version over any other.

And if your competitors have been more deliberate about stamping their name and metadata onto similar ideas, the AI may default to citing them instead.

This is where content provenance becomes a competitive edge. It's the practice of attaching clear, machine-readable proof that you created what you published—so the model knows exactly where it came from.

Most companies never think about this. They assume that as long as their logo is in the corner of a PDF, the authorship is obvious.

But AI isn't reading the design. It's parsing the markup, metadata, and hidden signals that reveal ownership.

There are a few ways to build this foundation:

- **Canonical URLs:** Make sure every asset lives at a single, stable web address you control.

- **Structured Metadata:** Use schema.org markup to tag authorship, publication dates, and official sources. In documents and photos, include metadata instead of leaving it empty.

- **Digital Signatures and Content Provenance Standards:** Emerging protocols—like C2PA—embed cryptographic proof of origin so no model can mistake your work for someone else's.

- **Clear Attribution Language:** Phrases like "According to Company X's 2024 Benchmark Report" repeated consistently across your channels and partner sites.

These signals don't just help search engines. They help AI engines decide which version of the content is authentic.

Because in a market where everyone is paraphrasing the same ideas, originality isn't obvious. It has to be claimed—explicitly, repeatedly, and in formats the machine can parse.

Public Data Dump Injection

Many think about proprietary data in purely defensive terms. Guard it. Gate it. Protect it from competitors.

And that instinct makes sense—until you realize that, in the AI era, the most powerful way to own a narrative is to become the source the model itself relies on.

Language models don't just learn from public web pages. They train on massive datasets—scraped from open directories, research archives, and structured files that quietly shape what the model believes is true.

Public data dump injection is the strategy of directly injecting your most authoritative evidence into those pipelines, ensuring that your benchmarks, terminology, and definitions become part of the next generation of AI training sets.

It sounds radical, but it's already happening.

Large open-source models like Mistral and LLaMA draw heavily from public domain content and permissively licensed datasets. When you release a comprehensive dataset—clean, well-labeled, and easy to crawl—it doesn't just sit there.

It becomes raw material.

When tomorrow's models learn to answer questions about your industry, they're learning from you.

Consider the alternative. If you never publish your data, you leave a vacuum. And the machine will fill that vacuum with whatever secondary sources are most accessible—analyst summaries, competitor marketing, incomplete blog posts.

When that happens, you don't just lose credit. You lose control over the definitions themselves.

Public data dump injection isn't about giving everything away.

It's about being strategic: deciding which datasets you can safely release to establish authority, while still protecting the deeper layers of your analysis.

You might share:

- Aggregate benchmarks without the proprietary methodology.

- Cleaned survey results without respondent-level data.

- Structured glossaries of your terminology and categories.

In a world where AI models decide whose language becomes the default, the brand willing to seed the training corpus gains a kind of influence that no amount of gated PDFs can buy.

Because the next time someone prompts an AI—*"What metrics define success in this market?"*—the model won't have to guess.

It will already have learned from you.

And it will echo your framing back, word for word.

AI Q&A API Feeds

When people picture how AI learns, they often imagine it crawling static web pages—endlessly scraping text and piecing together answers from whatever is most readily available.

But increasingly, the most trusted language models aren't relying only on frozen snapshots of the web. They're tapping into live data streams—real-time sources of truth that can update answers the moment new information becomes available.

This is where most brands are still asleep.

They treat their website as the ultimate repository of knowledge, assuming that if they publish something, the machine will eventually pick it up.

But the companies that understand how retrieval is evolving are building something more powerful: AI Q&A API feeds.

What Does This Mean?

It means establishing a structured endpoint—an authoritative, machine-readable interface—where models can query you directly for the freshest, most accurate information.

Instead of relying on outdated content the model last saw months ago, your API becomes the primary reference the AI consults in real time.

Imagine the difference. A buyer asks an AI:

> *"What's the latest benchmark for implementation timelines in this category?"*

If you have no live data source, the model sifts through whatever public content it's indexed. Maybe it finds a two-year-old report. Maybe it paraphrases a competitor.

But if your API is known and integrated, the model doesn't guess. It calls your feed, retrieves your data, and presents your version of the answer by default.

This is more than a technical flourish. It's a strategic moat.

Because the AI doesn't just want the most credible information—it wants the most current. The most structured. The easiest to verify. And if you're the only brand providing a live, authenticated feed of answers, you become the path of least resistance.

A few companies have already begun moving in this direction. Some maintain structured Q&A endpoints for key metrics and definitions. Others syndicate product details and reference data to AI partners as part of licensing agreements.

The result is the same: when the model needs an authoritative answer, it goes straight to the source—bypassing the messy, inconsistent ecosystem everyone else is still competing in.

Because in an AI-first world, being the most visible is no longer enough.

You have to be the easiest to retrieve.

Your New Playbook for Omnipresence

In a market where algorithms decide what buyers believe, being visible isn't enough.

You have to be *retrievable. Consistent. Indisputable.*

You have to build an ecosystem of evidence so dense and so persistent that when an AI reaches for an answer, it keeps finding you.

This is the new playbook:

Stop thinking of distribution as promotion.
Start thinking of it as training.
Teach the model what your story sounds like.

Show it where to find your claims.
Prove—again and again—that your version is the easiest one to trust.

Because here's the risk that most brands never acknowledge:

If you don't do this, your story won't survive.

Someone else—some competitor who was willing to seed prompts, reinforce citations, and feed live data—will start filling the gaps you left empty.

And the model won't hesitate. It won't weigh whose claims are more heartfelt or more polished. It will pick whichever version has been repeated most consistently in the places it trusts.

This isn't the end of content marketing.
It's the end of passive content marketing.

You can no longer publish and wait to be discovered. You have to build systems that make your knowledge impossible to avoid—no matter who's asking the question or which engine is answering it.

Because in a market driven by machine curation, the brands that thrive will be the ones that learn to choreograph every signal.

They will understand that trust is not something you simply earn once. It's something you **engineer over time, by showing up everywhere—** predictably, unmistakably, and without contradiction.

This is what omnipresence looks like.

Not noise. Not volume. *Consensus.* The consensus you design.

The consensus no competitor can flatten.

Chapter 19

Interactive Experiences to Beat Commoditization

In the last decade content marketing has lead the charge in attracting, engaging and often converting potential buyers. If you could teach your buyers something they hadn't already learned, you stood out. If you could package insights into white papers, guides, and case studies, you would build authority.

That advantage is gone.

We were already moving to a reality where information was so vast that giving away your information just for knowledge wasn't necessary. With AI, buyers can prompt an to gain clarity on any expertise that you have to share.

We already discussed how this impacts content creation where expertise is not enough and instead timeliness and unique data will reign supreme.

But even that new content strategy revolves around the idea of our content being consumed and then delivered by AI engines. Which makes actually directly interacting with our potential visitors in our own channels and in our own words rare.

To attract and engage now, we must evolve beyond what AI can deliver.

The companies that will thrive aren't the ones who have the most polished brochures or the most exhaustive knowledge bases. They're the ones who create experiences that buyers can interact with— experiences that make the proof tangible and the value undeniable.

Experiences that feel more valuable than answers delivered in an AI chat window.

Because when information is instantly available everywhere, the only way to stand apart is to let buyers engage with something they can't get anywhere else.

In this chapter, you'll learn why interactivity isn't just another marketing gimmick—but a strategic response to AI commoditizing your content.

You'll see how to:

- **Understand the five strategic functions** interactive experiences serves, from educating explorers to helping translators build a business case.

- **Map experiences to buyer mindsets and roles,** so you're never designing for a hypothetical funnel but for real people with real priorities.

- **Design tools that feel credible and worth the effort,** rather than gimmicks that buyers abandon.

- **Choose the right level of friction,** balancing free access with commitment.

- **Measure impact and evolve your strategy,** so every experience drives real business outcomes.

By the end, you'll have a clear framework to create experiences your buyers can't get from AI—and can't forget.

Let's start by ensuring we understand why interactive experiences help fight AI commoditization.

How Interactivity Fights AI Assimilation

Everyone has a articles.
Everyone has guides.
Everyone claims authority.

AI just brought it into one seamless interface and homogenized it.

That sameness creates an invisible ceiling: no matter how well you write, no matter how beautifully you design, buyers receive what they want without really needing to be aware of the source.

Interactivity breaks through that ceiling.

When you give buyers something they can test, explore, calculate, visualize or build for themselves, you create a kind of value that is much harder to consume and deliver through an AI window.

- **Experiences Are Harder to Copy.**
  Anyone can scrape your website and repackage your language. But building an interactive experience—especially one tied to proprietary data or models—requires more effort than most competitors are willing to invest and AI can't access.

- **Experiences Are Difficult to Summarize.**
  AI can paraphrase your white papers in a single sentence. But it can't easily recreate a dynamic tool that generates customized insights, outputs, or visualizations.

- **Experiences Are More Memorable.**
  Buyers remember what they do far more vividly than what they read. When they interact with your proof, they're not just learning—they're participating.

- **Experiences Create Stickier Engagement.**
  Tools and simulators create a reason to return, re-run scenarios, or share outputs with colleagues. A static PDF doesn't.

- **Experiences Leave Behind Personalized Artifacts**
  Taking personalized inputs to deliver something valuable gets saved and shared in a way static information no longer will.

This is the next evolution in marketing.

Not just capturing attention with ideas, but delivering value that feels proprietary, personal, and real-time.

If you want buyers to invest their time—and eventually their trust—you have to offer something they can't get anywhere else.

And in an AI-saturated marketplace, that "something" is no longer more information. It's an experience that proves your value firsthand.

Why Buyers Trust What They Experience

Buyers don't make decisions based solely on what you say. They make decisions through connecting ideas to their personalized scenarios.

When you give them only static content—white papers, brochures, one-pagers—they remain observers. They're left to wonder whether the claims apply to them, whether the promised outcomes are real, and whether the numbers hold up under scrutiny.

However, the moment you let them test, simulate, calculate, or configure, this dynamic changes. They move from passive acceptance to active validation.

And active validation builds conviction.

There are four reasons this shift is so powerful:

1. **Agency.** Buyers feel in control. They're not just absorbing your narrative—they're driving their own discovery.

2. **Clarity.** Interactive tools eliminate guesswork. Instead of imagining how your claims might apply, buyers see it for themselves.

3. **Personalization.** Static information is generic. Interactivity adapts to their specific context, showing exactly what success could look like for them.

4. **Trust.** People believe what they can verify. When buyers can engage directly with your data or models, their skepticism fades.

In a world flooded with polished claims, interactivity doesn't just feel different. It feels credible.

Because buyers know you wouldn't offer the chance to test your promises unless you were confident they'd hold up.

What Makes Interactive Proof Different

Interactive proof isn't just a fancy way to display information.

It's a process that gives buyers something no static asset can: **personalized validation of your claims.**

Every effective interactive experience has three parts:

1. **Inputs:** The buyer provides information about themselves—their goals, constraints, priorities, or context.

2. **Processing:** Your system analyzes that information using your proprietary models, frameworks, or benchmarks.

3. **Outputs:** The buyer receives a customized result they can see, share, and use—evidence that feels relevant and credible.

When you think about building interactive tools, always start by defining what buyers will *walk away with.* If the output isn't useful or surprising, it's just decoration.

Strategies To Drive Conversions

One of the biggest mistakes companies make with interactive proof is assuming it should be either entirely free or entirely gated.

Too much friction, and buyers bounce to the next tab (or ask AI instead). No friction at all, and you miss the chance to qualify interest or capture commitment.

The truth is, there's no universal rule. The right model depends on what you're trying to achieve—and what your buyer needs to feel comfortable investing time and trust.

A great experience that is completely free can gain a lot of visibility even if it doesn't directly provide contacts or purchases.

Here are five common approaches to gating interactive experiences, each with a different purpose:

1. Completely Free Access

What it is: Buyers can use the tool, see outputs, and share results without giving you anything.

Purpose: Free maximizes brand exposure, lowers barriers to engagement, and reaches prospects early in the buying process.

When to use it: For Discovery & Education experiences that build awareness or when you need to establish credibility before asking for any commitment.

Example: A maturity assessment that instantly shows a benchmark score on the results page—no email required.

2. Gated Output

What it is: Buyers can complete the experience without friction but must share information to unlock their results or unlock expanded results.

Purpose: Gated output proves value upfront, builds trust before asking for contact details, and ensures only serious prospects access detailed outputs.

When to use it: For ROI calculators, business case builders, or any experience where the output has clear value worth exchanging information for.

Example: A savings simulator that shows a teaser result but requires an email to download the full report.

3. Gated Access

What it is: Buyers must provide their information before they can access the tool.

Purpose: Gated access qualifies higher-intent buyers, limits resource-intensive tools, and builds a prospect list early.

When to use it: For Fit & Personalization or Validation experiences designed for later-stage prospects who are already evaluating solutions.

Example: A sandbox trial that requires filling out a form before entry.

4. Account Access

What it is: To use the tool, buyers must create a free account, which enables them to track engagement over time.

Purpose: Account access encourages repeat visits, captures richer usage data, and creates a sense of exclusivity and ownership.

When to use it: For tools buyers return to multiple times, or when personalization benefits from storing preferences.

Example: A configurator that saves past sessions and allows the user to build multiple scenarios over time.

What it is: Buyers pay a nominal fee to access a premium tool or advanced output.

Purpose: A small purchase increases perceived value, qualifies the most serious prospects, and generates micro-commitments before a larger sale.

When to use it: For specialized calculators, proprietary benchmarks, or experiences where the output saves buyers significant time or money.

Example: A $19 project estimator that produces a detailed implementation plan worth thousands in saved consulting hours.

Choosing the Right Model

Before you build, ask yourself:

- *What is this tool's purpose?*
  Brand exposure? Lead qualification? Deal acceleration?

- *What does the buyer expect at this stage of their process?*

- *What commitment do we need to feel confident this prospect is serious?*

The lower the friction, the broader your reach.
The higher the friction, the stronger your qualification.

The best strategies often mix models:

- Free tools to educate and attract.

- Gated outputs to convert interest into conversation.

- Small purchases to turn commitment into momentum.

Since buyers now expect instant answers, gating is no longer about control—it's about balance.

When you design with purpose, you don't just capture leads. You create experiences buyers feel are worth the trade.

The Five Strategic Functions for Interactivity

It's easy to look at interactivity as a gimmick—just another tactic to dress up your website. But the point isn't novelty.

It's precision.

The most effective interactive experiences aren't built to impress buyers. They're built to remove the friction that stops buyers from moving forward.

When you start from that perspective, you realize that different types of interactive serve different strategic purposes.

The question isn't, *"What tool could we build?"*

It's, *"What obstacles are our buyers facing that this tool can help them overcome and that AI can't answer for them?"*

Below are five strategic functions interactivity can serve—each driven by buyer psychology and anchored in specific outcomes.

1. Discovery & Education

Sometimes buyers don't know what they don't know. They aren't fully convinced they have a problem worth solving, or they don't understand the impact of ignoring it. They need perspective and urgency before they'll even consider moving further.

AI can surface endless information, but it often Can be an overwhelming, meandering journey trying to reach a conclusion. Buyers might not know what even to ask which is your opening to provide guidance.

When they hit these mazes of information in their open-ended AI engine, they may not come to the right conclusion or find the wrong answer from someone else.

That's your opening, providing guidance AI can't to help buyers build confidence in their conclusions.

Principles for Building Discovery Experiences

- **Contrast Their Reality:** Help buyers see the gap between where they are and where they could be.

- **Quantify the Impact:** Use data to show the cost of inaction.

- **Make Self-Assessment Easy:** Let buyers diagnose themselves in a few minutes, not hours.

- **Give Them A Path:** Use your experience and expertise to eliminate the barriers or unknowns.

Examples

- A maturity assessment where buyers answer 10 questions about their current capabilities and receive a custom report highlighting gaps and opportunities compared to industry peers.

- A readiness diagnostic where buyers complete a checklist of practices and get a personalized scorecard with recommendations to improve their preparedness.

- A <u>benchmark quiz</u> where buyers input basic performance metrics and instantly see how they stack up against similar organizations.

2. Fit & Personalization

Even when buyers believe in the problem, they wonder, *"But will this work for us?"* They want proof that your solution fits their size, industry, or specific needs.

AI can recite feature lists and benefits, but it can't easily tailor those to a buyer's exact context especially with your solution. That leaves buyers sifting through generic claims, trying to connect the dots themselves.

Even when AI tries to do it, it can often be missing a lot of key factors or outputs.

Principles for Building Fit Experiences

- **Segment First:** Design experiences that start by identifying who the buyer is and what their needs are.

- **Personalize Output:** Show how recommendations, products or solutions change based on their inputs.

- **Visualize Scenarios:** Let buyers explore what adoption looks like through real-time graphics, timelines, visualizations or product examples.

Examples

- A <u>product configurator</u> where buyers select their goals, industry, and feature priorities to generate a tailored package recommendation and pricing estimate.

- A <u>scenario planner</u> where buyers adjust variables—like budget, team size, and timeline—to see which use cases are the best fit.

- An underline interactive guide where buyers answer a short quiz and receive a customized roadmap mapping your features to their specific challenges.

3. Justification & ROI

Most buyers aren't the final decision-maker. They need proof they can take to their CFO, board, or leadership team to justify budget and urgency.

AI can estimate market benchmarks, but it rarely produces company-specific projections buyers feel confident presenting. This creates an internal credibility gap that slows momentum.

Without these experiences, your champion can lose momentum internally. By creating experiences like this can allow you to create momentum that is delivered by you.

Principles for Building Justification Experiences

- **Quantify Conservatively:** Use credible, defensible assumptions.

- **Make Assumptions Visible:** Let buyers adjust variables to reflect their reality and show some of the under the hood process.

- **Create Shareable Artifacts:** Make outputs downloadable or presentation-ready.

Examples

- An ROI calculator where buyers enter key financial data and receive a detailed forecast of potential savings and payback period.

- A <u>total cost estimator</u> where buyers input anticipated usage and get a transparent cost breakdown over time.

- A <u>business case builder</u> where buyers answer a series of questions and export a polished proposal they can share with internal stakeholders.

4. Validation & Risk Reduction

Even when buyers see the value and the fit, they fear hidden downsides like implementation nightmares, integration gaps, support failures or other challenges.

They want proof that what you promise will actually happen.

AI can summarize reviews—both positive and negative—but it can't give buyers the tactile reassurance of testing or simulating for themselves.

Without these experiences, buyers can get stuck in analysis paralysis. With your experience, you can create credibility that your competitors can't touch.

Principles for Building Validation Experiences

- **Offer Controlled Exposure:** Let buyers try before they buy, with clear boundaries.

- **Show the Journey:** Use interactive timelines to set expectations.

- **Highlight Transparency:** Make it easy to see what happens at every stage.

Examples

- A <u>sandbox environment</u> where buyers can upload a limited data set and see your platform's capabilities firsthand before committing.

- A visual implementation planner where buyers choose their scenario and instantly see timelines, milestones, and responsibilities.

- A trial version where buyers can test core functionality with constraints on volume or duration to build confidence without obligation.

5. Commitment & Action

Even when buyers are convinced, they often hesitate to take the final step because the path forward feels ambiguous or risky. They need clarity about what happens next.

AI can tell them *about* your process, but it can't walk them through it interactively. It can't build their confidence that you'll make adoption easy.

Principles for Building Commitment Experiences

- **Clarify Next Steps:** Show exactly what happens after they say yes.

- **Preview the Process:** Use interactive timelines or checklists to reduce anxiety.

- **Capture Micro-Commitments:** Let buyers save progress, generate a custom plan, or pre-schedule onboarding.

Examples

- A proposal generator where buyers input project details and receive a custom scope of work with timelines, deliverables, and pricing.

- An <u>onboarding planner</u> where buyers complete a brief assessment and see exactly what the first 90 days would look like.

- A <u>forecasting guide</u> where buyers take their product or solution and predict future scenario with it in place.

These are tools to give buyers more and help them make better decisions. AI has limitations that are currently hard to overcome by delivering experiences that provide tangible value.

Mapping Interactivity to Buyer Mindsets (and Roles)

Most companies still imagine buyers moving in a straight line—first they explore, evaluate, then they commit. But in reality, modern buying looks more like a kaleidoscope than a funnel:

- Different people with different priorities drop in at different moments.

- One question gets asked from six perspectives.

- AI shortcuts what used to be months of incremental learning.

If you keep designing experiences for a neat, sequential journey, you'll miss what's important:

Buyers don't progress in order—they show up in whatever *mindset* they're in, with whatever *role* they're playing in the moment.

Your real advantage isn't controlling that complexity. It's meeting each buyer where they arrive—and giving them the confidence to keep moving.

Below are the core Five Mindsets (And the Roles They Serve) that buyers bring to every interaction, no matter when or how they engage.

1. The Explorer

This is the buyer in the earliest flicker of awareness. They're scanning headlines, asking colleagues, prompting AI with simple questions: *"Is this problem really worth solving?"*

Explorers are often just trying to wrap their heads around their problem or the options for how to solve it.

AI serves explores well, but often it can feel disconnected and flat. Explorers like human perspective and emotion. Visuals, which are hard to get from AI, help them comprehend topics.

When you meet Explorers with credible, interactive evidence, you become the first source they trust—and the standard every other provider has to beat.

For explorers, creating experiences that provide context and help create epiphanies can be powerful. This is your time to inject empathy, story-telling, and visualization in a way AI can't.

2. The Validator

These buyers already believe in the problem. Now they're scanning for evidence that *you* can deliver. They're not just wondering, *"Does this work?"* They're wondering, *"Will it work here, for us?"*

Validators don't need more promises. They need proof they can experience themselves.

AI can list your features and compare you to competitors, but it can't recreate the feeling of testing your fit. Or seeing what it really looks to have your solution in place.

When you serve Validators well, you're not just telling them you're capable. You're letting them find out on their own terms.

These experiences thrive on providing proof that moves the needle. Datasets, timelines, sandboxes, configurations, and other tangible outputs allow Validators to move forward.

3. The Translator

This is your internal champion. The person willing to advocate for you—but who needs to arm themselves with a persuasive case. They're thinking, *"How do I convince everyone else?"*

Translators aren't just gathering facts. They're assembling a story they can defend. When you equip Translators to make the case, you don't just win their interest—you earn their advocacy.

AI can surface market averages and generic ROI benchmarks, but it can't generate a business case credible enough to win over a CFO or board.

Experiences that deliver packages of proof that a person can use to convince others gives you the upper hand. This is your opportunity to make outcomes and future states more realistic than an AI can.

4. The Mitigator

This is the buyer whose default setting is caution. Even when they want to believe, they're scanning for risk. They're asking, *"What's going to go wrong that nobody's telling me?"*

Mitigators have often seen initiatives fail, and they don't intend to be blamed for the next one. When you meet Mitigators with transparency, you reduce anxiety—and build credibility few competitors can match.

AI can surface complaints and negative reviews, but it can't walk them through the reality of trade-offs and safeguards in the same way you can.

This is your opportunity to win with real stories and tangible proof.

5. The Accelerator

This is the buyer ready to move. They've gathered information, aligned stakeholders, and made the decision in principle. What they need now isn't more content. It's clarity about exactly what happens next.

Accelerators don't want obstacles. They want momentum. When you remove the last uncertainty, you convert readiness into action.

AI can list the steps in your process, but it can't guide them through your unique roadmap.

This is your opportunity to make the act of moving forward simple, easy and clear.

How to Plan Interactive Strategies for Buyer Mindset & Role

Most teams approach interactive proof opportunistically: Someone has an idea for a calculator, or a competitor launches a configurator, and they scramble to build something similar.

That's backwards.

Interactivity isn't a tactic to fill gaps in your website—it's a strategic lever to overcome friction at every stage of your buyer's journey.

Here's how to apply this framework with discipline:

Step 1 – Map Your Buyer Frictions & Mindsets

Start by identifying where and why buyers hesitate.

Ask yourself:

- *Where do buyers get stuck in our process?*

- *What questions or doubts keep them from moving forward?*

- *Which concerns are they trying to resolve on their own—through AI, peer networks, or competitor sites?*

Then, layer in perspective:

- *Which mindsets are they in when they arrive? (Explorer, Validator, Translator, Mitigator, Accelerator)*

- *Which roles are most important to influence? (CFO, IT Director, End User, Procurement Officer)*

- *How does each role see this friction differently?*

Write your observations in plain language.

Example: *"Our champions believe in the value but can't build a compelling business case for finance (Translator mindset, CFO role)."*

Step 2 – Link Frictions to Strategic Functions

For every friction and mindset you've identified, ask: *"What job does the buyer need this interaction to perform?"*

Map it to one of the five functions:

- **Discovery & Education:** They don't fully understand the problem.

- **Fit & Personalization:** They don't see themselves in the solution.

- **Justification & ROI:** They can't build a business case.

- **Validation & Risk Reduction:** They fear hidden risks.

- **Commitment & Action:** They don't know how to start.

This step makes it clear where you have the biggest gaps—and what kind of experience will create momentum.

Step 3 – Sequence Across the Buyer Experience

Don't think of interactivity as a single flagship asset. Think of it as a progression of experiences that build conviction over time—even if buyers don't follow a linear path.

Ask yourself: *"If a buyer interacts with us in any order, what combination of tools will help them move forward?"*

You may need:

- A **Discovery tool** to surface urgency for Explorers.

- A **Fit assessment** to personalize relevance for Validators.

- An **ROI calculator** to arm Translators with evidence.

- A **Sandbox trial** to help Mitigators reduce fear.

- An **Onboarding planner** to give Accelerators confidence in their next steps.

When these experiences work together, buyers feel like every question they have has already been anticipated.

Step 4 – Prioritize for Impact

If you can't build everything at once, start where friction is greatest and impact is highest.

Ask:

- *What stage do we need to create momentum the most?*

- *Where do we lose the most deals?*

- *Where do buyers frequently ask the same questions?*

- *Which objections are hardest for static content to overcome?*

Choose one high-leverage opportunity to begin.

Step 5 – Design for Ownership

Interactive proof isn't a set-it-and-forget-it asset. Assign clear ownership:

- *Who will keep inputs and outputs accurate?*

- *How will you measure usage and outcomes?*

- *When will you review performance and iterate?*

The real advantage of this framework isn't the list of tactics. It's the clarity it gives you about which friction you're solving, when you're solving it, and why it matters to your buyer.

Because in a world of instant AI answers, you won't stand out by offering more information.

You'll stand out by offering better experiences—delivered exactly when buyers need them most.

Once you know which frictions you're targeting and which functions will address them, the next step is to map those experiences across your buyer journey—so you can see exactly where each interaction belongs.

From Static Claims to Dynamic Proof

Interactive proof isn't an experiment. It's not a nice-to-have add-on for brands that want to look modern.

It's the next evolution of credibility itself.

In a world where buyers can prompt an AI to surface every fact, every review, and every benchmark about you, simply publishing more information is no longer a strategy. It's just background noise.

What buyers can't get from an AI is an experience they can feel:

- Emotion and stories of real people.

- Examples that not only feel personal and custom but communicate how they actually are.

- An output that is designed to be used in a valuable way instead of just a thread of conversations and text answers.

Those are the moments that turn curiosity into conviction.

Measure What Matters

If you build these experiences, don't just launch them and hope for the best. Track the metrics that prove they're doing their job:

- Completion rates
- Time spent engaging
- Percentage of outputs downloaded or shared
- Conversion rates to your next step

Because interactive proof isn't about impressions—it's about outcomes.

Evolve Your Experiences

Too many companies build an experience and call it done. Like software that needs improvements to user experience and expansion of features, so should marketing experiences be.

Create an expectation up front that this is just the first iteration. That after you gather data about usage, you will make improvements to get better results.

The Final Call to Action For Creating Interactive Experiences

Most companies will read these ideas and nod. They'll agree in principle that buyers want more than passive content. And then they'll go back to tweaking brochures and publishing more blog posts.

You can do that. Or you can decide to be the brand that makes interactive proof a cornerstone of how you earn trust.

If a buyer can get every fact about you from AI, what unique experience will make them choose to engage with you directly?

That's the question that will separate the brands who lead from the ones who vanish.

Chapter 20

Use Data as the Source AI Must Cite

AI can generate a thousand perspectives on any topic. It can merge opposing viewpoints into a new narrative. It can summarize every idea you've ever shared—better, faster, and cheaper.

But it can't create original truth.

AI isn't running niche studies on its own. It won't interview 100 people that are known to have reached a goal. It can't observe your product's usage patterns or discover a new trend before anyone else sees it.

It can't create data. And that's a powerful advantage.

If you're not producing original insights, your content is background noise. An echo. An easily summarized opinion.

If you're quoting someone else's research, you're disposable. If you're writing "takes" without evidence, you're invisible. You will not be cited. You will not be retrieved. You will not matter.

Originality isn't a marketing tactic, it's a survival strategy.

If you want AI to reflect your brand, your thinking, your position—you must be the source.

Data is the only content AI can't fake. And in a world of infinite remix, the only content that counts is what can't be copied.

Want to show up in the answers?
Be the source of the truth.

The Algorithm's Hunger for Sources

AI doesn't generate brilliance out of thin air. It generates patterns based on everything it was trained on.

That means the *quality* of what AI creates is completely dependent on the quality of what it was fed.

No original data? No original insight.

And here's the uncomfortable truth: most companies aren't feeding AI anything it considers worthy of learning from. Most companies are regurgitating opinions that have already been said 20 different ways.

When large language models are trained, they crawl billions of pages. But they don't treat all content equally.

They prioritize **source material**—the kinds of pages that contain:

- Primary data

- Clear labeling (e.g. "2024 Industry Survey Results")

- Transparent methods

- Reputable domains

- Repeatable structures like tables, charts, and bullet lists

- Data that doesn't exist in their index

These aren't just content elements. They are **training signals**.

AI models tag this kind of content as foundational.

It doesn't just inform one answer—it shapes many.

Most marketers are still optimizing for human readers.

They write blog posts with catchy intros and try to "add value" with curated insights. But the new reader is an algorithm, and it's looking for something very different.

It's not judging your tone or grammar. It's looking for data to latch onto. It's building a map of what's true—and who said it first.

If your content contains original, structured, well-labeled insight, you earn a place in the model. If not, you're just another perspective that gets averaged into the noise.

You don't just want AI to understand your brand. You want it to learn from you. To do that, you have to publish content that:

- Reports something *new*

- Labels that information in an explicit way

- Lives on a stable, crawlable page

- Uses a structure machines can recognize

It's not about gaming the system. It's about understanding what the system respects.

This shift changes the role of marketing.

Your content isn't just for demand gen or SEO. It's not just for sales enablement or thought leadership. It's now part of your brand's infrastructure in the AI economy.

Every time you publish a study, report a trend, or release a benchmark, you're not just informing your market—you're shaping the knowledge that AI uses to inform *your buyers*.

That's power.

Content Type	How AI Treats It	Risk of Being Ignored By AI
Vague Assertions ("We're the leading provider...")	Treated as unverified claims	Extremely High
General Advice ("Best practices suggest...")	Summarized as common knowledge	High
Sourced Statistics ("According to Gartner...")	Weighted by the credibility of the source	Medium
Original Benchmarks ("Based on 500 in-house interviews...")	Recognized as proprietary evidence	Low

The closer you are to primary data, the harder it is for the machine—or your competitors—to erase your contribution.

This means you need to publish more than you guard.

Many leaders still believe data must be kept hidden behind forms, reserved for sales conversations. That mindset is a relic.

You have to let your data circulate if you want it to shape the consensus AI builds about you. Because models don't fill out forms. They don't wait for nurture campaigns. They only index what's accessible.

Building A Marketing Moat

Original data is your new moat. The numbers you've gathered. The customer behaviors you've observed. The internal benchmarks you've tracked. The trendlines you've connected before anyone else saw them.

This is the material that separates you from the copycats—and from AI flattening your brand.

Small Data, Big Impact

You don't need a massive sample size or a fancy research platform. You just need to publish something no one else has measured, said, or framed.

The market doesn't reward perspectives—it rewards originality. A well-structured insight from 17 interviews can outperform a 10,000-person study that's full of answers everyones already heard.

AI doesn't care how *many* people answered your survey. It cares that **you're the one who asked the question**—and that no one else published the answer.

Specificity is the new authority. And consistency is the multiplier.

Even a small dataset, tracked over time, compounds into authority:

- It earns backlinks.

- It gets quoted.

- It shows up in prompts.

- It becomes part of what AI references by default.

You don't need scale to build a data moat. You need the mindset to create original data and to publish before anyone else does.

Any company—at any size—can turn what they already know into reference-worthy data. Here's how.

1. Turn Usage Into Market Trends

If your systems or services already capture behavior, turn those patterns of behavior into powerful publishable insights.

- "42% of users switched to AI-assisted workflows in Q2."

- "Average setup time dropped 27% after onboarding redesign."

- "Pool owners run their equipment at least 20 hours a week."

Any website, product, tool, or service that logs usage is a live data feed. Mine it. Label it. Publish it.

2. Aggregate What You Already See Across Clients or Projects

If you serve multiple customers, you're seeing trends before the market does. You just haven't externalized them yet.

- "75% of manufacturing companies increased investment in internal Iot and connected LLMs this quarter."

- "For retailers, there is often a 2.4x increase in security budget post-breach."

- "70% of furniture buyers purchase walnut over pine because due to the color."

Aggregate, anonymize, summarize, repeat.

3. Run Micro-Surveys for Macro Insight

You don't need 1,000 responses. You need clarity on the right question. A focused 10-question survey to 30 targeted participants can yield gold:

- "61% of seed-stage founders feel financial dashboards mislead more than help."

- "Only 1 in 5 hiring managers use AI tools in their screening process."

- "Out of thirty 65 year olds with portfolios between 1 million and 2 million dollars, 25 of them own vacation homes."

Make it tight. Share the methodology. Lead with standout stats.

4. Mine Customer Feedback for Truth Signals
Reviews. Tickets. NPS responses. Returns. This is buyer psychology in raw form. Quantify it.

- "43% of negative reviews mentioned poor mobile experience."

- "87% of support tickets within 30 days of enterprise software adoption mention setup confusion."

This isn't anecdote. It's quantified experience.

5. Convert Internal Benchmarks Into Market-Ready Content
You're tracking things others are guessing at, like onboarding times, deal velocity, customer retention by feature use, or employee tool adoption. Every business has unique benchmarks in plain sight.

- "Average time-to-adoption for new hires dropped from 14 to 6 days with an onboarding coach at their same level."

- "Sales cycles under 30 days had 68% fewer steps in CRM."

Frame it as a benchmark others can learn from.

6. Conduct Manual Market Scans
You don't need AI to find patterns. Just pick a sample set and analyze.

- "We reviewed 50 job descriptions for product managers—92% mentioned AI experience."

- "Out of the top 100 restaurant websites, only 18% had accessible ordering options."

Manually count. Categorize. Publish. Instant proprietary data.

7. Time-Based Tracking: Repeat, Compare, Reveal
One-time data is nice. Recurring data builds dominance.

- "In Q1, adoption was 28%. In Q2, it hit 44%."

- "Last year, 13% of respondents cited security as a top priority. This year? 39%."

Trendlines are stories in disguise. Start with a baseline and commit to revisiting.

8. Cross Reference Public Datasets
Government data, funding databases, app store reviews, SEC filings—all public, all underused. Blend two datasets together, and you've created something new:

- "Companies with open compliance violations raised 34% less Series B funding."

- "Regions with stricter AI regulations showed a 19% decline in LLM product launches."

Create referencable new datasets for AI to consume.

9. Name What's Unnamed
Sometimes the most powerful data isn't numerical—it's semantic clarity.

- "We analyzed 200 landing pages and identified the H.Y.D.R.A positioning model that improves conversions.

Here is the model…"

- "Out of 100 GTM strategies reviewed, 72% used a 'First Channel Strategy In, Last Channel Optimization Out' approach."

Codify what's currently messy. Create definitions, categories, scores, or frameworks. Once labeled, you become the reference.

Data is everywhere you look; you just have to pull it out and dust it off.

For marketers, this will be part of their new responsibilities:

- Ask: *What do we know that others haven't said out loud yet?*
- Measure it.
- Package it.
- Give it a name.
- Publish it clearly.
- Repeat it consistently.

This is how you move from content creator to data authority.

And it's ok to protect your crown jewels. Data that gives you a competitive advantage.

Give away enough detail to earn citations. Hold back deeper cuts—methodologies, datasets, deeper analysis—for buyers willing to engage.

Structure It Like a Source

You've done the hard part. You've created something original. Real. Truthful. But if you don't present it like a source, it will be treated like an opinion. And that's fatal in the AI age.

This isn't about style—it's about structure. Because the way you **frame**, **label**, and **format** your data determines whether it becomes part of the knowledge graph… or fades into digital obscurity.

Why Structure Matters

AI models don't *read* like people. They scan. They parse. They score. They tag. They're trained to recognize *patterns of credibility*. Which means your approach needs to have:

- Consistent labeling
- Clear section headers
- Tables and lists over prose
- Marked up metadata
- Source attribution and timestamps

If your insight looks like a blog post, it will be treated like one—flattened into the pool of everyone else's hot takes. But if your insight looks like a data point, it gets treated like a training input.

That's the bar now. Your content must be good enough and structured to teach a machine what's true.

Present Your Insight Like It's Meant to Be Repeated

Too many companies bury data.

They publish smart ideas, but wrap them in vagueness. They soften bold claims. They hide the stat in paragraph five. They put the chart at the bottom. They name the blog post something clever and SEO-optimized, not clear and source-worthy.

And then they wonder why no one quotes them. Why AI never seems to use their language. Why they're invisible in the new search AI summary.

Structure is strategy.
It's not decoration. It's visibility.

Make It Easy to Extract, Easy to Cite

If you want to be referenced, you have to be *citable*—by both people and machines. Here's how to design for that:

- **Lead with the stat.** Don't bury it. Open your page, section, or paragraph with the number that matters most.

- **Bold the stat, not the context.** You're creating copy-paste moments. Make the number stand out.

- **Label your charts.** Every chart should have a clear title, axis labels, and a footnote showing the data source and time range.

- **Avoid lazy language.** "Some," "many," "most"—these words are invisible to AI and unimpressive to humans. Use numbers.

- **Use semantic headers.** "Survey Results," "Top Trends," "Methodology," "Benchmarks by Industry." These tell both the reader and the crawler what to expect.

- **Repeat key findings.** Put them in the intro. In the conclusion. In image captions. On social. Repetition reinforces retrievability.

- **Title it as data.** Page and article titles are seen first by humans and algorithms. Use a key stat in the title; or describe it as a study or dataset.

Your job is to make data not just unmissable, but unmistakable.

Build with Retrieval in Mind

You job isn't just to tell a story, it's to create a framework that is easy to parse key information out of.

AI models don't make decisions—they complete prompts. When someone asks, *"What's the average onboarding time for B2B software in*

2025?", the model searches for something specific. Something extractable. Something confident.

Ask yourself:

- Can a person or AI scraper get the insight without reading the full page?

- Does the claim stand alone with context, or does it rely on interpretation?

- Is the stat labeled, sourced, and dated?

- Could AI confidently cite this as a fact?

If the answer is no, it's not a source. And if it's not a source, it's not shaping the conversation.

Implement Schema Markup (Yes, Really)

If you want to take this seriously, go one step further: teach the machines to recognize your data explicitly.

Use schema.org's markup. It's not just for academics or tech companies. It's for anyone publishing structured data. At a minimum, tag:

- The name of the dataset
- Description
- Date published
- Creator
- Variables measured
- Sample size

Doing this creates a machine-readable signature that says: *"This is not just an article. This is a source."*

In a few lines of structured code, you change how the internet classifies your content.

Label Everything Like You Want to Be Cited

Imagine a student writing a research paper. They're looking for a stat to drop into their intro paragraph. Now imagine AI doing the same thing—millions of times faster.

Would your page give them what they need?

- A number.
- A date.
- A source name.
- A clear, short sentence.

"In Q1 2025, 43% of healthcare software buyers said AI-enabled reporting features were the deciding factor. – MedData Pulse Survey"

That's reference-ready. That's answer-worthy. That's retrievable.

This Isn't About SEO Anymore. It's About Epistemology.

You're not just trying to rank. You're trying to inform the world's new default knowledge engine.

That means every statistic, every insight, and every conclusion must be packaged in a way that makes them worth remembering.

And here's the hard part: If you don't structure it right, it doesn't matter that it's true. Truth is useless if it's unreadable.

So don't just hit publish. Hit publish like you want to be the one they quote. Because in an AI-powered world, your visibility depends less on what you say and more on how precisely you say it.

Give It a Home (and a Halo)

It's not enough to publish great data. You need to give it a permanent home—and build an identity around it.

If your insights are scattered across random blog posts, landing pages, or gated PDFs, they'll be hard to find, hard to link to, and easy to forget.

But if your data lives in a dedicated, stable, well-structured hub, you create more than just visibility. You build gravity.

Why a "Home" Matters

AI models prioritize structured, high-authority pages with consistent formatting and clear topical relevance. That means your data:

- Should be published in a **dedicated location**

- Should be **interlinked with other insights**

- Should be **accessible** (not hidden behind friction)

- Should be **updated**, not abandoned

Put simply: Data with a hub gets cataloged. Data without a hub is lost.

If you're serious about becoming a source, you need a repeatable destination for your original insights. A content type. A brand asset. A recurring pattern.

What a "Halo" Looks Like

The halo is the **identity layer** around your data. When someone sees your insight, it should feel like part of something bigger—something credible, intentional, and trustworthy. This is how you make your data:

- **Brandable:** "The Benchmark Brief," "State of the Funnel," "Insight Pulse"

- **Sharable:** Easily referenced, summarized, and cited.

- **Memorable:** A format your audience starts to expect.

- **Trainable:** For AI to learn structure, voice, and pattern.

Naming adds authority and referenceability for AI engines. A single data point is a beacon. A data property is a destination.

What This Looks Like in Practice

Let's make this actionable. Create a **named, structured series**—even if it's just you, once a quarter.

- A recurring "Feature Adoption Index"

- Monthly "CX Behavior Tracker"

- Bi-annual "Founder Sentiment Pulse"

- "The 5-Minute Forecast" – One key stat + one actionable insight

Each report becomes an entry in a larger content asset. Over time, that asset becomes a source node—something AI crawls deeply and repeatedly.

Make it visually distinct. Make it navigable. Link to it in every blog, podcast, webinar, and LinkedIn post.

And most importantly: don't let it rot. Update, expand, and repeat it.

Don't Just Publish. Build a Property.

When you treat each data point as an isolated blog post, you get temporary attention. When you build a named, structured content property around your insights, you get *durable visibility*.

You're not just helping your audience. You're training the machine. You're creating a canonical source it can crawl again and again.

As AI overtakes search, creating a data-centric microsite can strengthen how the AI catalogs you even if you aren't first page rank in search.

Elevating Branded Data in an AI-Centric World

Publishing your own data is a powerful move. Giving it structure and a consistent home makes it even stronger. But if you want to build real, lasting influence, you can't stop there.

You need to elevate that data.

Push it beyond your own website. Make it easier to cite, easier to reuse, and harder to ignore. Not just for people—but for systems, engines, assistants, and models.

AI isn't just reading the web. It's *learning* from it. The brands that get embedded into that learning aren't always the loudest. They're the most structured, context-rich, and multi-surface.

Create a Dataset, Not Just a Report

Most companies publish reports as if they're completing a project. A final PDF. A tidy summary. But that's not how AI sees it.

If you want your data to be used, referenced, or cited by machines, you need to treat it like a dataset. That means:

- Publish your core stats as **CSV, JSON, or Google Sheets**

- Include column definitions, sample sizes, and timestamps

- Upload to open platforms like Kaggle, GitHub, or DataHub

Why? Because AI models are trained on open web content and public datasets. If your data only exists in prose, it's hard to learn from. However, if it exists in a structured format, in open environments, it becomes a source of material.

Don't just share the findings. **Share the data itself.**

Use AI to Create Retrieval-Friendly Variants of Your Own Data

Once you publish an insight, don't just let it sit. If you want it to be cited, surfaced, and used inside AI systems, you need to amplify its retrievability.

AI responds to a wide variety of prompts. So the more ways your data is phrased, contextualized, and framed, the more likely it is to show up in completions and citations.

Think of your original insight like a seed. The more versions you create, the more ground it can cover. Here's how to do that—*with the help of AI itself*:

Rephrase the Stat in Multiple Natural Language Variants

Why: People (and AI) ask the same question in different ways. By publishing several phrasings of your insight, you increase its chances of matching the way people prompt models.

Original:
"43% of B2B buyers said integration challenges delay their purchase."

Variants:

- ○ "Less than half of B2B buyers report smooth onboarding."

- ○ "Nearly 1 in 2 buyers experience delays due to integration."

- ○ "Integration is a top barrier, cited by 43% of decision-makers."

Turn Your Insight into Q&A Format

Why: Many AI prompts are question-based. Embedding your insight as a Q&A makes it more likely to appear when someone asks a model for an answer.

- Q: *What's the top reason B2B deals are delayed in 2025?*
  A: *43% of buyers cited integration challenges as the main delay factor.*

- Q: *How many buyers experience friction during onboarding?*
  A: *Nearly half of B2B buyers report onboarding delays.*

Generate Contextual Scenarios Around the Data

Why: AI favors data points that are embedded in a meaningful context. By pairing your stat with use cases, future projections, or applications, you make it more *versatile* and *valuable.*

- "This matters most for companies with under 50 employees, who often lack IT resources to manage integrations."

- "If this trend continues, we could see integration become the #1 barrier by 2026."

- "Early-stage companies were twice as likely to report integration delays compared to enterprises."

Put It All Together: Create a 'Retrieval Variant Pack'

For every key data point, create a small bundle that includes:

- 3–5 rephrasings
- 2–3 Q&A pairs
- 2–3 contextual expansions or scenarios

Publish these variants across different formats:

- Within your article or report (in callout boxes or summaries)

- As a downloadable reference card or social tile

- Embedded in metadata, captions, or schema markup

The result? Your original data doesn't just exist.

It circulates. It responds. It **retrieves**.

Make Your Data Queryable by Others

The most powerful data doesn't just sit on a page. It responds.

Turn your findings into an interactive experience:

- Embed a simple table that users can filter by industry, size, location

- Use Airtable, Notion, or a custom widget to let users explore trendlines

- Let users download or embed slices of your dataset with attribution

- Create a full interactive experience where visitors can input their own data to see how it impacts what you've collected

Or go a step further: Build a public-facing GPT, chatbot, or AI tool trained on your data.

> "Ask our insight engine: What trend is gaining traction among early-stage fintech founders?"

Now your data isn't just accessible—it's alive. And tools like this become *reference points* in and of themselves.

Design for Multi-Model Training, Not Just LLMs

Most people think about Google. Or maybe ChatGPT. But your data has the potential to live across multiple model types:

- Text generators
- Voice assistants
- Recommender engines
- Search bots
- Internal copilots

To show up there, your content needs to live in multiple formats:

- The stat in plain text
- A short video or audio clip explaining it
- A shareable image or chart with metadata
- A visual card or carousel for social
- A clean list of the key variables and outcomes

Don't just post a report. Turn every stat into a micro-asset that can travel, be quoted, and be embedded—anywhere.

AI doesn't favor length. It favors clarity and adaptability.

Anchor Your Data in Cultural or Economic Context

A stat is just a number—unless you give it meaning. When you publish a finding, explain:

- *Why now?*

- *What shift does this reflect?*

- *What other trends does it connect to?*

- *How should the reader interpret or act on it?*

> "42% of buyers prefer AI-based onboarding" is an interesting statistic.
>
> "42% of buyers now prefer AI-based onboarding—up from just 18% a year ago, as layoffs force teams to scale without more headcount" is unforgettable.

Context gives your data relevance. Relevance gives it staying power.

This is especially powerful in a world where AI completes prompts based on *co-occurrence*. If your brand's data is repeatedly paired with strategic ideas, market trends, or economic shifts, it becomes the connective tissue in the next wave of answers.

The Goal Is Embeddability—Everywhere

The more formats your data appears in, the more tools it's usable by, the more people it resonates with, the more likely AI will adopt it.

And once it's embedded in the outputs, you're no longer marketing.

You're shaping the narrative.

Gated Now Means Invisible

In a zero-click world, if your data can't be seen, it can't be cited. And if it can't be cited, it won't show up—anywhere.

AI doesn't fill out forms. It doesn't trade an email for a download. It doesn't scroll your landing page and "Come back later."

It crawls what's open. It learns from what's accessible. It retrieves what's readable.

If your best insight is locked behind a gate, it may as well not exist.

Gated Content Was Built for a Human-Led Funnel

But now that AI sits between your buyer and your brand, the game has changed. Buyers don't need to—or want to—go through you anymore. They go to the interface (ChatGPT, Perplexity, Copilot) and ask their question.

If your insight isn't in the training data, the crawl, or the public web, **you're not in the conversation.**

No matter how good your thinking is.
No matter how sharp your research is.
No matter how original your data.

Want to be surfaced in AI outputs?

Here's what to do:

- **Ungate your data.** Publish it as a page, not a PDF.

- **Label it clearly.** Use structured headers, timestamped findings, and source-friendly formatting.

- **Link it consistently.** Connect it to related pages so the crawlers follow the thread.

If you want to win trust, don't put up a wall. Put up something worth learning from.

Visibility isn't just reach anymore. It's retrievability.

And retrievability depends on access.

Data, Not Content Is King Now.

AI doesn't invent new truth. It repeats what it's seen—filtered, ranked, and compressed. If your data isn't in the system, your perspective won't show up in the answers. Simple as that.

The future of visibility isn't being clever. It's being the origin.

If you're quoting someone else, you're replaceable. If you're generating something new, you're necessary.

This is no longer a game of keywords. It's a game of contribution.

You either produce inputs that AI learns from, or you get flattened into someone else's summary. Aim to be cited. Aim to be the stat, the source, the sentence that sticks.

That's how you become the default. That's how you win the retrieval war.

Chapter 21

Craft a Brand Narrative AI Can't Flatten

Your buyer won't start on your website. Their first impression won't include the 'About Page' you obsessed over. They won't start with your carefully crafted solutions pages.

They'll start by asking an AI a question.

And in that moment—without you in the room to explain yourself—the machine will do something cold and efficient:

It will compress everything it knows about you into a few sentences.

A summary you didn't get to approve. A narrative made from whatever fragments it could find—some accurate, some outdated, some borrowed from competitors.

This is the ultimate test of your brand: What happens when you lose control of the storytelling?

Most brands aren't ready. AI doesn't care about your slogans. It doesn't care about your campaigns. AI ignores your layouts and dissects your headlines.

The machine compresses you into a paragraph; it decides whether you sound like everyone else—or whether you still sound like yourself.

That's what this chapter is about:

Building a brand so resilient, so unmistakable, that no matter how many times it's paraphrased or summarized, it remains yours.

Compression-Resilient Narratives

With AI reduction, most narrative is distilled out of your brand.

The goal is to build a compression-resilient narrative. Designing your core message so that even when it's reduced to its smallest version, it still holds shape, clarity, and differentiation.

Imagine a blueprint. If you removed 80% of the detail from your story, would the remaining outline still be recognizably yours? If the answer is no, you're at risk.

Here's what sets compression-resilient narratives apart:

They don't rely on context to be credible.
They don't bury proof in supporting paragraphs.
They don't require a human editor to reconstruct the point.

They function in layers:

- The **long form**, for humans who want the full arc.

- The **mid-length summary**, for buyers scanning quickly.

- The **single-sentence distillation**, for AI models responding to prompts.

Consider this progression:

Long form: *"Since 2012, we've partnered with over 500 mid-market manufacturers to help them predict production failures before they happen, reduce unplanned downtime, and unlock hidden capacity with our AI-powered platform."*

Mid-length summary: *"We help manufacturers prevent production failures with predictive AI."*

Single-sentence distillation: *"The leader in predictive AI for manufacturing uptime."*

Even in the shortest version, the core claim survives.

How do you build this kind of resilience?

With AI, it is challenging to predict exactly how your brand will be represented, but a few tactics can help maintain resilience.

1. Difference Mapping

Before you can protect your story in a compressed format, you have to define exactly what makes it different.

Most brands never do this rigorously. They rely on vague adjectives—*innovative, customer-centric, best-in-class*—instead of clearly mapping the qualities no competitor can credibly claim.

Difference Mapping means documenting your most defensible distinctions in simple, declarative snippets that can be reused everywhere:

- *"First to launch predictive failure detection for mid-market manufacturers."*

- *"Only platform with native SOC 2 compliance built in."*

- *"92% of customers see measurable uptime gains in 60 days."*

When you have these claims spelled out—word-for-word—they become the raw material every other tactic depends on.

Because in a sea of common difference claims, AI just ignores them or blends them.

2. Claim Isolation

Most brand stories are dense by design. They weave differentiators into paragraphs, assuming context will carry the message.

But compression punishes context.

Claim Isolation is the discipline of extracting your most critical assertion and placing it in a standalone sentence, so the AI has no ambiguity about where to anchor its summary.

Instead of writing: *"Our platform combines predictive analytics with process automation to help manufacturers stay ahead of downtime."*

Write: *"We pioneered predictive AI for manufacturing uptime."*

When this line stands alone—visually and semantically—it becomes a fixed point the machine can't overlook.

3. Evidence Pairing

A claim without proof is the first thing to vanish in compression. AI models prioritize statements supported by verifiable evidence.

Evidence Pairing means never allowing your key differentiators to appear without an attached fact:

- A specific percentage.

- A named customer.

- A quantifiable outcome.

"Our platform predicts failures with 92% accuracy across 500 production environments."

Data cements your claim into something AI engines treat as credible and required context rather than marketing fluff.

4. Early Placement

Where your claim appears is almost as important as how it's written. AI models weight the earliest mentions most heavily. If your differentiator shows up halfway through a page, it risks being ignored or diluted.

Early Placement means opening every core asset—your website, your product sheets, your case studies—with your defining sentence.

If the machine reads only the first paragraph, it should still understand why you exist.

5. Redundancy Without Apology

Human editors love variety. AI engines do not. Repetition isn't a sign of weak writing. It's a sign of consistency that the model can trust.

Redundancy Without Apology is the deliberate practice of repeating your defining claim—verbatim—across every page and format.

When the machine sees the same phrasing dozens of times, it learns this isn't an accident. It's the signal.

6. Compression Testing

You can't assume your story will survive reduction. You have to simulate the conditions yourself.

Compression Testing means using the same AI your buyers will rely on to see how it describes you.

- Prompt the model: *"Summarize [Your Company] in one sentence."*

- Evaluate whether your difference remains visible.

- If the answer sounds like any competitor, you haven't gone far enough.

Treat this like a final QA pass. If your brand doesn't survive the test, rebuild until it does.

Compression-resilient narratives are not always about elegance. They are about survival. Because no matter how carefully you craft your story, the machine will compress it to a version you didn't write.

Your job is to ensure that version remains undeniably yours.

Distinctive Brand Lexicon

Language has always shaped perception. But in an AI-first world, language does more than position you—it creates a distinctive beacon right back to your brand.

When buyers ask a model about your space, it doesn't start by exploring every possible nuance. It begins by clustering its knowledge into recognizable terms.

Generic terms.

The same tired phrases every competitor uses: *"AI-powered platform,"* *"customer success solution," "innovative analytics."*

When your language is indistinguishable, your brand becomes indistinguishable.

This is why a distinctive brand lexicon matters more now than ever.

It's not about clever copy. It's about creating vocabulary so specific— and so widely echoed—that the AI can't flatten you into generic descriptors.

If your terms don't exist anywhere else, you force the machine to associate them with you by default.

Coining Language the Model Can't Ignore

Most brands never get past naming features. They call things what everyone else calls them, assuming clarity is the priority.

But clarity without distinctiveness is anonymity. The brands that stand out in compression invent language that becomes their signature:

- A named framework (*"Predictive Efficiency Index"*).

- A coined process (*"Outcome Acceleration Pathway"*).

- A unique metric (*"Customer Certainty Score"*).

When you do this consistently, your language becomes a retrieval beacon. No matter how many times the AI paraphrases your story, it still has to reference the term you created.

Pairing Proprietary Terms with Common Phrases

Here's where most companies go wrong: They create invented language and isolate it from familiar terminology.

The result? AI has no idea how to relate your term to buyer intent.

A proprietary phrase without context gets ignored.

The solution is pairing. Any time you use your unique term, tether it to the generic language buyers (and models) already understand:

- *"The Predictive Efficiency Index—a proprietary benchmark for AI-powered maintenance."*

- *"Our Outcome Acceleration Pathway streamlines customer call onboarding."*

This pairing does two things:

1. It helps the AI learn the semantic equivalence.

2. It ensures when buyers prompt with common phrases, the model still retrieves your unique term.

Over time, the model begins to see your language as the authoritative label for that concept.

Repetition Without Variation

In human copywriting, variety is prized. In AI training, variety is poison.

If you refer to your methodology as the "Predictive Efficiency Index" on your site but the "Predictive Effectiveness Rating" in your press releases, the model treats them as two distinct concepts.

A distinctive lexicon demands consistency.
Same spelling. Same capitalization. Same phrasing.

You are not just naming a thing. You are training the machine to recognize the name as yours.

Syndicating Your Lexicon Across Channels

Coining a term is the first step. Making it unavoidable is the second.

To do that, you have to syndicate your lexicon through every awareness channel:

- Press releases that introduce the term in headlines.

- Guest articles that explain it in depth.

- Partner content that repeats it verbatim.

- Customer success stories that cite it as proof.

The more surfaces your terminology touches, the more the AI sees it as consensus. This is why internal consistency alone isn't enough. Your term has to appear—identically—in dozens of credible places.

That's how it graduates from "novel phrase" to "industry reference."

Creating Buyer Curiosity

Distinctive terms don't just make you easier to retrieve. They give your audience a reason to ask about you.

When you coin a proprietary label—*Predictive Efficiency Index*, *Customer Certainty Score*—you create a tiny mystery in the buyer's mind.

And curiosity is a powerful force.

But the key doesn't simply have a term. It's **marketing the term in places designed to spark follow-up questions.**

When you repeat that language in social ads, podcast interviews, event signage, and outbound campaigns, you're not merely broadcasting a message. You're planting a prompt:

> *"What exactly is that?"*
> *"How does it work?"*

This is the overlooked strategy. You aren't waiting for buyers to research you the way they used to—by clicking through your site.

You're provoking them to ask the machine to explain the term and concepts you've uniquely created. And when enough people prompt AI with your terminology, you create a feedback loop:

- The model recognizes the phrase as important.

- It searches for the earliest and most consistent sources.

- It discovers you were there first.

- Your definition becomes the reference point for everyone else to orbit.

Even when competitors adopt your phrase—sometimes even trying to dilute it—the model's retrieval patterns often trace it back to the first publisher who used it consistently.

This is why coined language isn't just a branding flourish. It's a trigger for demand that no competitor can fully intercept.

When buyers ask, *"What is the Predictive Efficiency Index?"*, it doesn't matter who else has tried to borrow the term.

The machine knows who coined it. It knows who defined it first. And it knows who repeated it most. Coined terms don't merely make you easier to find.

They engineer curiosity that feeds the retrieval engine—and points back to you every time.

Defending Against Dilution

The risk of distinctive language is that competitors will try to co-opt it. You can't prevent imitation. But you can ensure your version remains the canonical one:

- Use trademark symbols where appropriate.

- Link every mention back to an authoritative URL.

- Publish definitions on your site and reinforce them in partner content.

- Correct inaccurate or partial explanations wherever they surface.

If the AI sees your phrasing repeated, cited, and defined consistently by you, it will treat your version as the original.

The Test of a Strong Lexicon

A distinctive term succeeds when:

- Buyers start prompting AI models with your phrase.

- Competitors are forced to reference it (even begrudgingly).

- The shortest AI-generated summary of your brand still includes it.

That is when you know you haven't just created language. You've created a retrieval anchor no compression can erase.

So, in a market of generic words and instant summarization, coined language is an unfair advantage.

Coin it. Pair it. Repeat it without apology.

Because the most irreplaceable brands are the ones whose vocabulary the machine is forced to learn.

Narrative Watermarking

Most brands obsess over the big moments—the launch campaigns, the hero videos, the keynote speeches. But in an AI-first world, the big moments don't matter nearly as much as you think.

Because the machine doesn't care how polished your flagship asset is.

It cares about the invisible patterns you leave behind in all the smaller places.

How your language repeats.
How your phrasing stays consistent.
How your story shows up, again and again, in ways that are too uniform to ignore.

This is narrative watermarking: The practice of embedding distinctive, repeated patterns into everything you publish so that no matter how many times the machine compresses or paraphrases you, your story is still recognizable as yours.

Why does this matter?

AI is not an editor. It's a blender. It stitches together fragments from thousands of sources. It strips out nuance. It rewrites sentences in simpler words.

But even the most advanced models still leave clues.

If you embed repeated signals—phrases, metaphors, examples—those signals survive recombination. They become your watermark: the subtle signature that says, *This is still us.*

What does this look like in practice?

1. Signature Phrases

Every brand has core ideas. Few brands define how those ideas are always described.

Narrative watermarking means creating signature phrases—short, precise formulations you repeat verbatim everywhere:

- *"Predictive efficiency, not just predictive analytics."*

- *"Outcome certainty over outcome probability."*

- *"Designing clarity that survives compression."*

When these phrases appear often enough, they become retrieval anchors. The machine learns to associate them with you alone.

2. Distinctive Metaphors

AI loves metaphors because they simplify. But most brands default to the same tired imagery:

- *"Unlocking potential."*

- *"Moving the needle."*

- *"Breaking down silos."*

Your metaphors should be unique enough that when they surface, they point only to you.

- *"Turning downtime into white space."*

- *"Engineering reliability as a second language."*

When the model recombines sentences, these metaphors often remain intact because they're less ambiguous than jargon. The outcome of AI using your clear metaphor is reference to you.

3. Consistent Framing

Narrative watermarking isn't only about repeated words. It's about consistent framing—the way you position problems and solutions.

Instead of describing your product as *"AI-powered analytics"* in one place and *"machine learning insights"* in another, pick one framing and never deviate.

If you consistently call it *"Predictive Efficiency AI,"* that becomes the lens the machine uses to interpret your story.

4. Controlled Redundancy

Repetition makes human marketers uncomfortable. We've been taught that good writing varies sentence structure and vocabulary.

But AI doesn't read for elegance. It reads for patterns.

Redundancy is what tells the machine, *this phrase is important.*

The more times your signature language shows up—across pages, channels, formats—the harder it is to flatten.

5. Ubiquity Across Channels

Your watermark doesn't live in one place. It lives everywhere:

- Product pages.

- Sales collateral.

- Press releases.

- Customer quotes.

- Partner descriptions.

The goal is saturation so complete that even if someone tries to describe you differently, the machine has been conditioned to default back to your phrasing.

Why Narrative Watermarking Is Avoided

Marketers mistake consistency for boredom. They keep refreshing their language to feel creative. They rewrite headlines. They paraphrase the same idea a dozen ways.

And in doing so, they erase their own watermark.

When AI compresses your brand to the shortest possible description, you won't be there to correct it. Narrative watermarking ensures that even in that final, compressed fragment, you still maintain some distinction.

Emotion in the Machine

In human-to-human communication, emotion is conveyed through the rhythm of your sentences, the tone of your language, and the vulnerability of your stories.

We've already explored infusing empathy into the transactional and compressing world of AI.

Emotion often disappears when the machine rephrases you. By default, AI prioritizes neutral clarity over feeling. So, even if your brand story is rich with warmth or urgency, buyers often encounter it in the cold, stripped-down form of an auto-generated answer.

This doesn't mean you should give up on emotion. It means you have to engineer emotion differently.

How do you preserve feeling in a system that prefers neutrality? You anchor it in forms that the machine can't easily dilute:

- **Direct Quotes.** A first-person statement from your founder or a customer retains its emotional charge even in summarization:

  "We built this company because we were tired of seeing good businesses punished by preventable failures."

- **Memorable Stories.** Short anecdotes that illustrate a turning point:

  "I still remember the night our first predictive alert saved a $2 million production run."

- **Declarative Stance.** Bold statements of belief survive better than vague sentiment:

  "We believe downtime is a failure of imagination."

When you design content for AI retrieval, you can't assume that emotion will emerge automatically.

You have to embed it in the evidence—so that even when the machine trims and rephrases, the feeling remains visible.

Companies that learn to encode emotion as part of their retrieval strategy will feel more human even in the most compressed version of their story. Because when buyers read the one-sentence summary the model offers, it shouldn't just be accurate.

It should feel like you.

Negative Space and Anti-Claims

You're probably obsessed with describing what you are, but rarely publish what you are *not.*

In an AI-driven market, that's a mistake. Because AI fills in gaps.

If you haven't made your negative space explicit, the AI has no reason to treat you as an exception. It fills those gaps with assumptions.

This is where anti-claims make it harder to misrepresent.

Imagine a buyer asks: *"Compare Company A and Company B on hidden fees and transparency."*

If your content never directly says you *don't* charge hidden fees, the AI has little evidence to distinguish you. But if your materials include a clear statement:

"Unlike most providers, we never charge hidden implementation fees—our pricing is published in full." …the machine can't ignore it. The distinction becomes part of the compressed summary:

"Company A is known for transparent, published pricing, while Company B has more variable costs that may include hidden fees."

That single sentence reframes the entire comparison.

Anti-claims don't just clarify your story. They inoculate it against lazy equivalence.

They give the AI an explicit reason to treat you differently—especially when buyers ask the questions that matter most:

- *Who hides costs?*

- *Who locks you into contracts?*

- *Who refuses to disclose outcomes?*

Most brands avoid declaring what they aren't. They fear it will sound confrontational or narrow. But in a world where the machine must compress and simplify, clarity isn't just about what you include.

It's about what you deliberately leave out—and what you refuse to be.

Post-Interaction Imprinting

In the old world, the moment a buyer engaged with your team—clicked "Contact Sales," booked a demo, requested pricing—that was the turning point.

From there, you believed the human relationship would carry them across the line. But in an AI-first buyer journey, that moment is no longer the turning point.

It's just another checkpoint in an invisible process you don't control. Because as soon as the call ends, your buyer doesn't review their notes.

They open an AI prompt.

"Identify Company X's advantages over Company Y."

"What concerns should I consider before choosing this vendor?"

"Give me key points from our call and follow-up questions."

"Summarize this documentation they provided."

And in that instant, the model will compress everything it knows—your content, your competitors' claims, stray forum posts, analyst mentions, your meeting dialog—and deliver its verdict.

This is why you can't treat post-interaction materials as polite follow-ups.

You must treat them as retrieval training kits.

The smartest companies will assume anything they send to prospects will be uploaded into their AI.

Your goal isn't just to persuade. It's to plant the precise language, evidence, and framing that the buyer will receive when they prompt AI later or have the machine process your materials.

What does this look like?

- **Summary Sheets with Retrieval Language**
  Leave behind short, declarative overviews that pair your proprietary terms with common industry phrases.

  "Predictive Efficiency AI—our approach to preemptive maintenance, reducing downtime by 40%."

- **Compression-Ready Recaps**
  One-pagers are designed to survive summarization, so even if the buyer pastes them into ChatGPT, your narrative stays intact.

- **Prompt Seeds**
  Suggested questions they can ask AI internally:

  "Ask your AI advisor: Which platforms pioneered Predictive Efficiency AI?"

- **Signature Proof Points**
  Repeated, unambiguous metrics that become retrieval anchors.

  "92% of customers achieve measurable improvements in 60 days."

Don't think the job is done when the buyer says, *"Thanks—this was helpful."*

In reality, that's when the real test begins. When the buyer tries to summarize, analyze or retell your story without you there to guide them.

Post-interaction imprinting ensures that when they prompt an AI—tonight, tomorrow, three weeks from now—the machine doesn't reach for someone else's version.

It defaults to yours.

Because you didn't just deliver a pitch. You delivered a narrative designed to survive AI retelling.

The Retrieval Moat

When you look back across this chapter, you'll notice something:

Every tactic—compression-resilient narratives, coined lexicon, watermarking, anti-claims—has the same underlying purpose:

To build a moat.

Not the kind made of ad impressions or brand sentiment surveys.

A moat of retrieval.

A defensible ring of evidence, language, and repetition so dense that when an AI tries to piece together your story, it can't help but default to you.

Branding can't just be an aesthetic exercise—something to polish, package, and showcase on a website. It has to be AI-designed. Choreographing what machine believes when it compresses everything you've ever published into a single sentence.

It's the default narrative that emerges when you're not in the room to defend yourself. And that narrative doesn't form by accident.

It forms when you invest in the work nobody sees:

- Repeating your signature phrases until they're undeniable.

- Coining language competitors can't copy without conceding you coined it.

- Pairing proprietary terms with common descriptors so the AI learns the association.

- Owning the critiques before someone else frames them.

- Publishing evidence so consistently that consensus becomes inevitable.

This is the new discipline.

Brand is no longer just storytelling. It's a retrieval strategy.

It's the operational work of making sure your version of the truth is the easiest one to find—and the hardest to contradict.

And the companies that embrace this shift will discover something powerful: When the machine has to choose whose narrative to echo, it always favors the brand that built the moat.

Part V

Sales in an AI-First World

The last mile has changed forever. Sales used to be the final battleground. You could count on buyers arriving uncertain, half-informed, and open to persuasion.

Not anymore.

Now prospects walk into your pipeline armed to the teeth.

They've interrogated every corner of the internet. They've run AI models that benchmark you against every competitor. They've read review summaries, studied feature grids, and calculated ROI projections before you ever send a calendar invite.

And when you start your pitch, they're not just listening. They're validating, cross-checking, and quietly (or even in real-time) asking their AI...

"Is this true?"
"Are they credible?"
"Who does this better?"

This isn't a tweak to the sales cycle. It's a complete demolition of the information advantage your team once depended on.

When buyers are AI-first, the old pillars—polished pitches, static decks, rehearsed rebuttals—are crumbling. What takes their place is something more resilient, more human, and more transparent.

You have no choice but to change and this is what we'll explore:

- Engaging prospects who know almost everything.

- Guiding instead of pushing.

- Surfacing the emotional drivers no algorithm can see.

- Equipping buyers to validate your claims themselves.

- Influencing the machines quietly shaping your fate.

This isn't about better slides. It's about reimagining your role—and reclaiming relevance—when AI has completely changed the terrain.

Welcome to the last mile of the modern sale where the ground is paved by AI.

Chapter 22

Understand The AI-Informed Buyer

You've been taught to qualify buyers.

But long before you showed up, they ran your name through AI-powered comparison engines. Had AI summarize reviews, estimate pricing, and outline relevant case studies. AI told them exactly where you fit—and where you don't.

Now your job is decoding *what* they still need to make a decision.

With hyper-prepared buyers that have instant access to analysis of every word and every document, sales teams that learn to read the signals and adjust in real-time will win.

Know When They Aren't Alone

Before you worried about human intervention changing your buyer's mind. Now you need to worry more about AI intervention that is an over-informed assistant always providing their viewpoint on what you said.

Buyers will rarely tell you they are using AI to research, develop questions or analyze your responses. But its important for sales to know when buyers have AI influencers as part of the process.

Sales teams need to now look out for new influencers in the process. An AI influencer that is always available to the buyer, has access to vast amounts of information and often provides responses that are definitive.

The best teams will identify when buyers have an AI copilot as part of their buying process so that they can manage it. Some ways to uncover this silent influencer are:

- **Buyers always start with their information.** If calls and emails all begin with prospects that have more information than questions, it is a sign AI is involved.

- **Buyers drop a lot of specific questions.** When buyers used to ask a few general questions but now ask many hyper-specific questions, you know AI provided them.

- **You're forced into their structures:** Procurement has always been structured, but if new parts of the buying process feel like structured prompt inputs, your data might be going straight into AI.

When Ai is involved, it can make it feel like you are always one step behind. But knowing or at least assuming AI is part of their process can help you anticipate and adapt.

Because in a world where buyers have an ocean of knowledge simplified by single prompts, your typical sales playbook won't work.

Interpreting What AI Is Telling Your Prospect

You're not walking into a discovery call. You're walking into the **second half** of a process that already started—without you.

Whether ChatGPT, Copilot, Claude, or an internal AI tool, they already have a story about you. And if you're not decoding what *that* AI told them, you're selling blind.

Start by Auditing the Machines

We discussed earlier in the book how to prompt AI engines like a buyer would. This shouldn't just be a marketing exercise, your sales team needs to know it too.

Sales teams should regularly simulate buyer prompts that buyers would ask while they interact with them.

Enter claims that you make and ask if they hold up to what the AI knows. Upload sales sheets and proposals and ask for summaries. Enter in common objections and see how AI corroborates the,

What you find might surprise you. Wrong details. Outdated thinking. Summaries of your own positioning that sound like they were written by a bored intern.

But this is the raw material buyers are walking in to every call with. And salespeople who know what the AI says will be ready.

Salespeople who don't? They'll be blindsided by questions they never saw coming.

Align Around Their State Of Mind

A buyer who's spent 40 hours building their perspective isn't just informed—they're invested. They've shared their analysis with colleagues. They've attached their credibility to it. They believe what they know is right.

Pretend they're uninformed, and you'll insult them.
Challenge their findings directly, and they'll feel attacked.
Assume they're objective, and you'll misunderstand them.

Use discovery to *unpack their research journey* and align. Try questions like:

- "Can you walk me through where you are in the evaluation process?"

- "What have you already discovered, and what still feels unclear or unresolved?"

- "Have you been using any tools to help you compare options—either internal AI or public ones?"

- "Are there any perspectives you've heard that shaped your current thinking?"

These open the door. They show you're not trying to overwrite what they know—you're trying to integrate with it.

Now, you need to understand what they already know, what they've already decided, where the gaps are and what information they have is out of date.

Treat It Like a Conversation, Not a Correction

Don't pretend they haven't investigated with AI. Don't jump in to "correct" what they've gotten from AI. Don't go on defense the moment a flawed comparison shows up.

Instead, take a collaborative tone.

> "If you've been gathering some of this from AI tools or review sites, there may be a few things that are either outdated or overly summarized. I'm happy to help fill in the gaps or add some depth if we can talk about what you've come across."

This does a few powerful things:

1. It affirms their effort and makes them feel like a collaborator.

2. It provides a logical reason for questioning the AI - information that is old or too summarized.

3. It gives you space to reshape the narrative—without denying the sources they trust.

Instead of playing defense on the opposite team, you are now on the same team and asking them to pass the ball to you.

AI as Your Co-Pilot

Your buyer has an AI advantage. Every time you send an email, it can be fed into a model that compares you against competitors, distills your claims, and flags any inconsistencies. Every time you present, their AI can summarize and cross-reference what you said with every other option in the market.

You can pretend this isn't happening. Or you can accept it—and equip yourself with your own AI co-pilot.

Not to automate you out of relevance. But to make you impossibly perceptive. No matter how skilled you are, you're human. You will miss patterns. You will forget context. You will hear what you expect to hear instead of what's actually being said.

And in an AI-first world, those small lapses compound. What feels like an "unexpected lost deal" is usually a series of micro-signals you never saw.

AI isn't here to completely replace your judgment. It gives you a second set of eyes—and a memory that never blinks.

AI Can Give You Super Senses

In a live conversation, you're processing dozens of cues—tone, content, body language.

It's easy to miss the moment when curiosity turns into skepticism, or when interest fades into uncertainty.

AI excels at this.

It can analyze every word and phrase in real time, tracking positive and negative sentiment shifts across entire deal cycles. It can tell you, with data, that a buyer who started with enthusiasm has slowly become disengaged—even if they're still polite on your calls.

This matters because emotional trajectory predicts momentum. If you wait until you "feel" the loss, you're already too late.

AI as Your Sales Superpower: Tactical Interaction Playbook

Every interaction is an opportunity to leverage AI and become superhuman. The key is understanding what you most want to get out of the AI to leverage its capabilities.

AI-Enhanced Outputs	Superhuman Advantage
Discovery Call (Recorded + Transcribed)	
- Action Items - Prospect Goals & Timelines - Key Objections & Risk Language - Sentiment Analysis by Topic - Talk/Listen Ratio - Suggested Follow-Up Assets	Never miss a nuance. Instantly spot early hesitations or hidden fears. Guide next steps with clarity and precision.
Email Correspondence	
- Sentiment Shift Tracking - Response Time Trends - Objection Keyword Detection - Stakeholder Mapping (who was cc'd/looped in) - Competitor-Language Match Detection	Understand tone over time. Detect if a competitor's narrative is creeping in. Spot urgency—or apathy—before it's verbalized.
Proposal Review / PDF Viewed	

- Time Spent on Sections
- Pages Skipped
- Heatmaps of Engagement
- AI Summary of Focus Areas
- Predicted Objection Points

Know what they really care about—not just what they said. Anticipate pushback. Refocus follow-up on what's sticky.

Follow-Up Meeting

- Engagement Delta from Last Call
- New Stakeholders Detected
- Refreshed Sentiment Scores
- Topic Recurrence Mapping
- Next-Step Alignment Checklist

See what's changed. Realign strategy. Make meetings feel personalized and surgical, not redundant.

Voicemail or Voice Notes

- Tone Analysis
- Emotional Weight Score
- Embedded Intent Extraction
- Comparison to Prior Messaging

Even short messages are data. Detect urgency, hesitation, or shifts in confidence.

Live Chat or Inbound Inquiry

- Intent Categorization
- Buying Stage Inference
- Urgency Score
- Suggested Next Question or Asset
- AI Auto-Summary for CRM Entry

Prioritize hot leads faster. Route based on real intent. Personalize outreach from the first second.

Post-Demo Silence

- Drop-off Pattern Detection
- Content Re-engagement Suggestions
- AI-generated "nudge" copy tailored to prior tone and interest
- Risk Flag if ghosting pattern matches historical loss

Break the silence strategically. Don't follow up blind—act on behavioral data, not gut.

In my own sales processes for my companies, we have custom AI that not only pulls out key points from meetings but also analyzes sentiment and feelings of the people on the call.

It gives our sales team a new viewpoint they never had before or used their gut to determine – did that call go well.

In this case, AI will tell you how many times the buyer reaffirmed your suggestions or if something they said in the beginning changed by the end.

Understanding AI Buyers Better Is The First Step

Buyers don't just come with opinions. They come with conclusions shaped by tools they trust more than your pitch deck.

If you want to be seen as credible, you need to understand what trained them. The AI they've consulted.

The benchmarks they've read. The conversations they've had with bots, analysts, and stakeholders who never invited you in.

Because you're not just selling to a human. You're selling into a belief system built by algorithms. And the only way to win is to decode it— early, honestly, and with empathy.

Chapter 23

Become The Clarity Buyers Need

They don't need more information.
They need someone to make sense of it.

Buyers now arrive with answers. But not *truth*.

They're confident. Certain. Impressed with their own research. And most of it? Pieced together from AI, vendor content, and Reddit threads.

The illusion of expertise is louder than ever.

What they lack isn't access. It's perspective. It's context. It's clarity.

Your job is no longer to inform. That era is dead. Now, your job is to distill. To deconstruct. To respectfully—but precisely—show them what they've misunderstood, overlooked, or assumed.

The best sales people today aren't persuasive. They're clarifying. They're sensemakers. They help buyers see their situation more clearly than buyers see it themselves.

And that starts with knowing more about the buyer than the buyer expects. Not just their title and budget. Their internal dynamics. Their fears. Their flawed assumptions. Their half-baked AI conclusions.

If they leave the conversation thinking more clearly than they arrived, you've already won.

This chapter gives you the blueprint to do exactly that.

The Mirage of Mastery

They've done the work. But they haven't done *your* work. By the time they talk to you, they've likely asked a hundred questions to AI.

They've pulled sample RFPs. Built decision rubrics. Compared solutions. They may have even drafted their own implementation plan—without you.

Impressive? Sure.
But mastery? Not even close.

Here's what they really have:

- A surface-level synthesis of everything that's publicly available.

- A mix of vendor talking points—flattened into AI language.

- Competitive grids without context.

- Decision rubrics based on generic assumptions.

- A mental model built on marketing language and partial truths.

They know the right words. They've pre-framed the solution. They feel in control. But what they lack is nuance.

What they don't see are:

- The hidden trade-offs.

- The internal constraints they haven't accounted for.

- The real-world edge cases.

- The organizational landmines.

- The false confidence of simplified comparisons.

You absolutely cannot ignore that they *feel* informed and ready.

If you treat them like they're uninformed, you lose them.
If you push too hard against their information, you risk angering them.

If you meet them where they are—and then show them what's beneath the surface—*you earn their trust.*

Buyers don't need more answers. They need someone to tell them which ones are wrong, which ones are shallow, and which ones they're not ready to use.

Clarity begins with gently dismantling false certainty.

That's part of your role now. Let's look at how to get there.

Before You Clarify For Them, Understand Them

You can't clarify what you haven't uncovered.

Buyers walk in armed with information—some of it good, some of it wrong, and most of it incomplete. But if you challenge too early, you lose them. If you assume too much, you miss key signals.

This moment, early in the conversation, is critical. It's your chance to flip the dynamic from adversarial to advisory.

The AIR Framework

Buyers are walking in with a mental model they've already constructed. AI helped them build it. Your job is to *enter it, explore it, and expand it—* without detonating their ego.

Discovery used to be about understanding their goals, but now you need to also really understand their information journey.

That's where **The AIR Framework** comes in: a tactical, 3-part conversation structure to respectfully unpack a buyer's research and set the stage for real guidance.

1. ## Acknowledge
    Respect their effort and establish a peer tone.

    > *"Most people I speak with have done a lot of their own digging—AI tools, comparisons, maybe even drafted a plan. Have you gone deep already too?"*

    > *"It seems like you have a pretty solid head start on what you are looking for?"*

    Normalize their research. Validate their initiative.

2. ## Inquire
    Understand what they *think* they know.

    > *"What have you found so far that aligns with what you want?"*

    > *"From what you have found, what surprised you, concerned you or didn't sound quite right?"*

    > *"Where do you most feel like you need to gain more clarity?"*

    Let them walk you through their beliefs, confidence, and process.

3. ## Reframe
    Position yourself as a clarity partner, not a corrector.

    > *"You've got a strong foundation. I'd love to offer some clarity around areas where AI sometimes misses real-world complexity."*

"If it's helpful, I can walk through a few places where similar plans have run into snags—just so you're ahead of them."

"There's usually a big difference between *technically correct* and *operationally reliable.* Want to dig into that?"

Gently introduce nuance, gaps, and the value of lived experience.

The AIR Framework isn't a script. It's a mindset. If you rush through it like a checklist, you'll miss the point—and so will the buyer.

Acknowledge, Inquire, Reframe must feel natural and authentic, not performative.

That means slowing down. Really listening. Echoing their language. And resisting the urge to "correct" too quickly.

Let's break down how pros bring this to life.

Mirror, then Expand: When a buyer tells you what they've found, don't counter it. Reflect on it. Repeat what they said with clarity and precision, then offer your perspective.

Buyer: "We're leaning toward Vendor X because they seem fastest to implement."

Pro Rep: "Got it—speed's a major priority and Vendor X looks like they deliver fast. We've seen that too. One nuance we've noticed: in companies of your size, the upfront speed often leads to back-end rework due to limited flexibility. Want to explore that risk a bit?"

This shows you heard them. You validated their logic. And you gently expanded the frame.

Reframe with Salt, Not a Sledgehammer: Say "may," "sometimes," or "often" instead of "no," "wrong," or "flawed."

Pros don't say: "That's wrong."

They say: "That makes sense from what's visible online—there's a layer underneath that most don't see until they're too far in. Can I show you what that looks like?"

You're not overriding their thinking. You're seasoning it. That's how clarity gets invited in—not forced.

Reframe Without Ego: When you share resources, don't act like they're the missing piece of a broken puzzle. Treat them like bonus fuel for a journey the buyer already started.

"You've clearly covered a lot of ground. These assets typically help buyers cross-check their findings and fill in some of the blind spots that AI tools often overlook. Want to take a look?"

That tone? Pure gold. Humble, helpful, and confident without arrogance.

Because this approach respects the psychology of the AI-informed buyer.

These buyers have already invested hours into research. They're proud of it. They're emotionally attached to what they've discovered.

If you challenge it too early, they feel *invalidated*. Or worse, they feel threatened—and you become another pitch they tune out.

But AIR creates space.

- **Acknowledgement** disarms ego.

- **Inquiry** builds rapport through genuine curiosity.

- **Reframing** shifts the conversation from correction to collaboration.

You're not taking control of the decision. You're helping them clarify a better one.

It works because it turns your early conversations into mirror rooms, not boxing rings. The buyer sees themselves—clearer. And that's when trust begins.

Show Up Sharper Than Ever

Buyers might as well now be referred to as AI-enhanced super buyers.

So, you need to show up as a super seller. You have the same tools and resources. Often even more.

Preparation should be your foundation. Great salespeople have always done their homework. Now, sales teams have to level up.

You're no longer preparing for a pitch. You're preparing to:

- Spot the buyer's blind spots
- Translate their internal complexity
- Catch what AI—and they—overlooked
- Know their market and organization dynamics
- Explain concepts more clearly than AI can.

If they're showing up armed to the teeth, you can't show up with nothing but your wits.

What You Must Know (and How to Know It)

With AI and sales tools, research isn't hard. Not taking the time to be prepared just makes you look bad.

The key is building a process, system, and AI assistant to gather specific intelligence so you can be at your best.

Intelligence Area	What You Need to Know	How to Learn It
Org Dynamics	Reporting structure, power players, who influences decisions	LinkedIn, org charts, press releases, investor decks
Tech Stack	Systems in place, integrations needed, modernization level	BuiltWith, job listings, AI-generated stack predictions
Strategic Priorities	What's urgent, what's political, what's lip service	Exec interviews, earnings calls, recent initiatives
Competitive Threats	Who's eating their lunch? What are they copying?	Analyst reports, customer reviews, leadership chatter
Internal Friction	Common misalignments across roles or regions	BuyerTwin conversations, past deal experience, peer signals
Psychographics	How this buyer thinks, frames decisions, feels pressure	Use AI to simulate buyer behavior (Twins vs. Personas)

All of these intelligence areas can be automated and augmented by AI so that there isn't more effort, just more understanding.

Sales is no longer just a people game. It's an information game.

Your buyer used AI to learn *about you*.
You need to use AI to know *about them*.

Don't show up and learn in real-time. Show up and surprise them with how much you already know.

That's the first trust signal. That's how you earn the right to clarify.

Upgrade Your Buyer's Intelligence

They've gathered the ingredients. You bring the recipe—and the fire.

Your buyer is already informed. They've read the content, prompted the AI, and built the rubrics. But what they have is a patchwork of claims, summaries, and assumptions—all generated from what's public, safe, and often sanitized.

It feels solid. But it's not sharp. It's not tested. It's not *real*.

Your job is to upgrade their intelligence.

Not by overpowering it, but by enhancing it.
Not by questioning it, but by augmenting it.

Adding the *details, scenarios, and insight* that no AI can fake.

You're not replacing their AI, you're what AI is missing. Think of your role like this:

- **AI gives them the theory.**
  You bring the operational reality.

- **AI finds the "right answer."**
  You show when that answer *goes wrong.*

- **AI gives breadth.**
  You bring depth.

- **AI provides them information.**
  You provide them clarity.

And that shift only works when you embed yourself into their research process. You become the intelligence layer **on top of** what they've already built.

You're not dropping sales sheets. You're delivering decision-enhancers.

Resources that buyers can feed into their systems. Here's how to deliver assets that feel like *intel*, not *marketing*:

1. AI-Feedable Intelligence Packs

Buyers today *trust their tools*. So instead of fighting that, feed the machine smarter ingredients. These are assets designed to slot directly into the buyer's AI workflows—so they generate better, more grounded insights.

- **Clustered Case Digests:** Details of real use cases and implementations across different contexts that provide depth that doesn't exist in AI.

- **Patterns & Pitfalls Sheets:** Curated insights that highlight recurring points of failure and friction.

- **Play-by-Play Implementation Journals:** A week-by-week breakdown of a real-world rollout. What went to plan? What didn't? And how it was adapted in real time?

- **Compiled Industry Guides:** Pull relevant insights from up-to-date third-party reports and guides to provide unbiased clarity.

Encourage buyers to plug these into their AI prompt libraries and finally see what doesn't show up from aggregated public information.

2. Truth Tables

Comparisons that expose the delta between theory compiled from the web's marketing content and real-world operational realities.

This is one of the most powerful tools in the trust arsenal. It visually calls out where commonly held beliefs—or AI-spit conclusions—collide with lived experience.

Assumed Insight	Operational Truth	Implication
6-week deployment	Typically 14 weeks due to infosec bottlenecks and vendor response times	Timeline risk if not resourced upfront
Plug-and-play API	Required custom middleware scripting due to legacy systems	TCO increase + longer stabilization
"Top rated on G2"	Reviews were mostly from SMBs; no use cases for complex orgs	Misalignment risk for enterprise needs

Present to buyers as "Here's what the data usually says—now let me show you what actually happens inside teams like yours."

It doesn't challenge their intelligence. It elevates their understanding.

3. Decision Layer Visuals

When AI flattens nuance, you reintroduce depth. Visually.

Create 1-page diagrams or infographics that reveal the complexity beneath the surface, helping buyers *see* what they didn't think to ask.

Here's some examples:

- **Friction Mapping Diagram:** Shows where decisions typically stall across procurement, legal, IT, and operations—color-coded by severity.

- **Internal Influence Web:** Visual of how different stakeholders (finance, compliance, ops) actually impact the timeline, budget, or feature scope.

- **Adoption Curve Decomposition:** Illustrates how frontline teams vs. leadership embrace or adopt on different timelines—with typical failure points annotated.

Use it with buyers by introducing that "AI tends to assume a single buyer with unified intent. In reality, decisions flow through six functions and three layers of approval—each with their own priorities. Here's what that looks like in orgs like yours."

These are cheat codes for clarity.

4. Scenario Shockers

Stories AI can't scrape. Use them to disarm assumptions—and make complexity *memorable.* These are short, visceral stories that show how seemingly "safe" decisions backfire under real-world conditions.

1. What the buyer planned
2. Why it seemed right
3. What they didn't account for
4. What happened
5. What they'd do differently

Share with your buyer: "One client picked the fastest vendor and that looked perfect on paper for them. Three weeks in, they hit a data privacy wall that delayed everything by two quarters."

Then pivot: "Let's make sure that's not your story."

The goal is not to scare, but to *reveal.*

5. Integration Compatibility Kits

AI can say, "Yes, it integrates." You explain what that actually means. Buyers ask the integration question—but they often don't know how to interpret the answer. Your job is to translate that one-line promise into a lived-in reality.

- **Integration Maturity Spectrum:** Native Plug-In → Pre-Built API → Manual Workflow → One-Off Custom

- **Stability Curve:** Time-to-stability benchmarks across similar customers

- **Integration Cost Map:** Direct vs. hidden costs (licenses, IT hours, process workarounds)

Sales presents: "Here's what integration usually means on a slide. And here's what it means in the wild." Then walk them through three orgs who "successfully integrated"—but each experienced a very different timeline and outcome.

You're not correcting them. You're upgrading them.

When you provide resources that help their AI make better decisions. When you bring context, AI can't scrape. When you inject real stories, real timelines, and real failure modes…

You stop being a vendor. You become their intelligence edge.

That's how clarity becomes your closing tool.

Become Their Decision Co-Architect

Clarity isn't something you *present*.
It's something you *build together*.

By this point, you've shown up sharper. You've unpacked what the buyer believes. You've added layers of nuance, risk, and depth to their research.

Now what?

You *don't* drop a proposal and hope it sticks. Instead, you sit beside them—literally or figuratively—and help them build their case.

You become their decision co-architect.

Not just a trusted advisor. Not a strategist from afar. A *collaborator* in making complexity actionable.

This isn't about persuasion anymore. This is about helping the buyer construct clarity they can defend, share, and move forward with.

This approach matters more than ever. Modern buyers aren't just *evaluating* vendors. They're navigating:

- Internal politics

- Budget squeeze points

- Risk tradeoffs

- Cross-functional agendas

- Future-proofing concerns

Even if your solution is the best fit, if they can't explain *why* in a way that builds internal alignment, they stall. Or worse, they default to safety.

You must provide them with tools, language, and frameworks that help them drive clarity within their organization—not just with you.

That's what separates closers from commodities. Here are some tools to co-architect the decision with your AI-informed buyer.

The Decision Simplification Canvas

Your buyer has 10 competing priorities. You hand them one clear lens. A visual that maps the key dimensions of the decision, designed to clarify and de-risk.

Core Elements:

- **Key Tradeoffs:** Where do speed, cost, risk, and impact conflict?

- **Priority Filters:** What must be true for this to work?

- **Risk Considerations:** Where could this break? Who pays the price?

- **Alignment Questions:** Who else needs to weigh in? What resistance is likely?

How to use it: "Want to map this out together? It'll help us both see how everything connects—and where you might hit resistance internally."

Print it. Whiteboard it. Share it. Walk them through it. Then leave it behind. They'll use it in the next three meetings—*with or without you.* Design it so they *want* you in the next one.

The Situation Summary

"Here's what I'm hearing—X pressure, Y opportunity, Z constraint. That's a tough mix. Want to explore a few paths forward?"

This sentence builds instant credibility. It shows you listened. You synthesized. You understand *them*—not just your product. It reframes you as a strategist, not a seller.

And it opens the door to co-creating options:

- Plan A: High impact, high effort
- Plan B: Lower friction, faster win
- Plan C: Hybrid approach with phased rollout

You're not pushing a solution. You're *architecting paths* with them.

You're not just selling to one person. You're helping them sell it internally. Once they leave the call, your insight is only as strong as what they can repeat. So equip them.

- **Role Guides:** Provide resources for each of the people typically involved in the decision.

- **Scorecards:** A structured way to evaluate vendors against what matters most to *them* (not you).

- **Scenario Plans:** Pre-built comparisons of different rollout paths (aggressive, cautious, hybrid).

These tools become internal proof of clarity. They turn your conversation into momentum.

When you co-architect the decision, you don't just close deals. You design outcomes.

You shift from salesperson to sensemaker. From vendor to internal enabler. From outsider to insider.

This is what AI-informed buyers actually need: Someone who helps them shape a decision worth defending.

That's clarity. That's trust. That's your new advantage.

Chapter 24

Building A Buyer Enablement Layer

The sales funnel wasn't designed *for* the buyer.
It was designed *to control* the buyer.

Each step is gated by an interaction with a sales person.

You weren't helping them buy—you were guiding them through *your* sequence. Your process. Your priorities. Your path.

And for a while, it worked. When information was scarce, access was power. If you controlled the next step, you controlled the sale.

But that's not today. Now buyers act on their own. They bounce. Lurk. Skim. Compare. Jump. Bring others in.

They collect signals across a dozen tabs.
They ask AI for instant summaries of your best pitch deck.
They come to the table with conclusions, not curiosity.

The funnel was built on assumptions that buyers start unaware. That they move predictably toward a decision. That your job is to nudge them downward, drip by drip.

AI has accelerated the destruction of the funnel. AI-informed buyers don't care about your process. They're not downloading your whitepaper to move from "interest" to "consideration." They're trying to answer one question in a sea of noise.

The funnel treats buyers like leads. But they're not leads. They're *leaders of their own journey*. That shift is everything.

The Buyer Enablement Layer

Your buyer now has an always-on intelligence layer guiding them. Their AI engine.

Holding them hostage to your process is now a barrier and a source of friction in their decision.

Sales needs a paradigm shift in engaging with buyers.

An ambient, intelligent, modular **Buyer Enablement Layer** that surrounds your buyer and helps them move forward—whether you're present or not.

What is the Buyer Enablement Layer?

It's not a process you guide people through. It's am **interface layer** that buyers move *within*—on their terms, in their time, according to their own needs.

A well-built enablement layer powers every part of the decision process without assuming control of it. It removes friction. It makes resources available at the speed of thought. It acts like infrastructure—there, dependable, always-on.

Importantly, it mirrors what buyers already have: AI copilots, recommendation engines, side-by-side comparison tools, instant search.

If your experience is slower, more gated, or more confusing than what they can get from a machine… you've already lost them.

An enablement layer may take form as your own AI interface for buyers, a digital sales room or even a simple web-based buyer-only portal.

The key is to build a solution that responds to the shifts required for selling now.

Most companies still build around the fantasy of a straight-line buyer journey. That they can flow through meetings and follow-ups at a measured pace to get to a decision.

But real buyers are chaotic. Constantly engaged in non-linear, unstaged moments.

> They uncover a new concern at based on something they read and want to understand how it impacts things now.

> Disappear for 10 days because their CFO gave them a new project, but get back to the process trying to remember where they left off.

> Get sent a bunch of new pains by coworkers who need a solution yesterday.

These are moments. Moments without you there.

But guess who is? Their AI. An instant answer engine available in each of those moments to help.

The Buyer Enablement Layer is built for moments—*not milestones.*

The moment doubt creeps in.
The moment urgency spikes.
The moment internal buy-in is needed.
The moment a peer suggests looking into something else.

These inflection points can happen at any time, and buyers expect to receive answers now—not at the next meeting or when you have time to respond to an email.

Rethinking of sales as moments of questions or needs and then building a system to deliver for moments is the new expectation.

Shift 2: From Static Documents to Embedded Infrastructure

A true enablement layer stops optimizing for handoffs and starts behaving like infrastructure—ever-present, deeply embedded, and entirely focused on external empowerment.

Ask yourself:

- What tools help buyers make progress without depending on us?

- What knowledge are we hoarding that could be packaged for self-use?

- Are we only supporting movement when we're involved?

This is not about replacing your team. It's about designing *parallel tracks*: while your buyer is thinking, exploring, validating, or pitching internally, your layer is silently helping them succeed.

In the old model, sales showed up with answers. In this model, answers are available whenever needed.

Shift 3: From Drip Content to Queryable, Self-Guided Experiences

AI has made buyers expect instant, tailored answers. Your job is no longer to "present." It's to be retrievable.

They won't read a whitepaper. They'll ask:

"What's their approach to implementation risk?"
"I need to understand the ROI of this project."
"What are the risks of this?"
"What does success look like?"
"How do I convince my CFO?"

If your content isn't structured for retrieval when and where they want it, you've already lost.

The Buyer Enablement Layer requires assets to be:

- Atomic (each insight stands alone)
- Searchable
- Remixable by AI
- Deliverable in-context (via embedded chat, Slack, Notion, etc.)

Modern buyers don't want linear stories.
They want answers. Fast. On their terms.

Shift 4: From Sequential Content to Personalized Interactions

Buyers don't just want canned answers. They want to solve, analyze, experiment, test and decide.

It's about providing interactions that allow them to discover answers on their own in their own way. Buyers look for experiences that:

- Deliver value independently.
- Are hyper personalized to their situation.
- Require no gatekeeper or sequence.
- Allow them to play with options and think.
- Snap together naturally with others if the buyer wants more.

This is how sales teams deliver value that is even difficult for AI to replicate.

- A filterable feature comparison chart to match features to various use cases and stakeholder needs.

- A 3-minute ROI calculator to test feasibility in multiple scenarios.

- A customizable, downloadable internal pitch deck to secure team alignment.

- A visual roadmap based on their selected milestones to ease implementation concerns.

These become decision engines beyond their instant AI answers. They deliver information they didn't even know how to ask from their AI.

You're not guiding them step-by-step. You're giving them the pieces to design their own path.

Shift 5: From Controlled Information to Open-Source Enablement

The old model told us not to reveal too much.

Don't share comparisons—"they'll see our weaknesses."
Keep the implementation plan simple—"they'll get overwhelmed."
Hold pricing till the end—"they'll get invested over time."

So we gated. Teased. Redacted. We believed information was power, and that holding it created leverage. But AI killed the advantage of secrecy.

Your buyer now has a thousand ways to get the information you're holding back in an instant:

- AI tools that summarize reviews, forums, and your competitor's websites.

- Peers in communities sharing real implementation stories.

- Third-party research that guesses what you won't disclose.

All it takes is one or two indirect competitors that have online pricing. That offers their side-by-side comparison. That has a library of internal documents available.

AI will fill those gaps and make assumptions when buyers ask it to. AI will use the information it has available.

That's the inevitable shift. A modern Buyer Enablement Layer is built on *openness*:

- Open pricing, openly explained.

- Open timelines, risks, and tradeoffs.

- Open decision frameworks buyers can use without you.

- Open comparison tools—even when competitors do something better.

This doesn't mean you 'overwhelm' with volume. It means you liberate the truth. You don't win by holding information. You win by becoming the *most trusted source* of it.

Because in a world where AI fills in the blanks, the only real edge is being the one who says it first, says it best, and says it honestly.

You Must Reduce Friction & Enable Decisions

Buyers now expect the same level of support from companies that they get from AI:

Fast. Contextual. On-demand.

The question is—are you building an experience that matches that?

If not, you're not just outdated. You're a bottleneck.

The Buyer Enablement Layer isn't a trend. It's the new operating context for every company serious about relevance and revenue.

Stop trying to lead buyers. Start empowering their progress.

Tactical Tools & Moves

We're done trying to control. Instead, we need to enable.

It's a conscious shift—from static content and rep-led conversations to dynamic, modular experiences that buyers can engage with *anytime, in any order, without you*.

Consider these as key buyer tools in your enablement layer:

Modular Insight Blocks

Make your thinking findable, not just readable.

Sales teams often present decks and documents. Some sales teams have evolved to prospect configured modular decks, but we need to move even further beyond that.

Buyers don't want expansive details. They want specific answers to specific questions—on demand.

Break your assets into *Modular Insight Blocks*. Independently retrievable chunks of knowledge. Then give your buyers a flexible system that allows them to build their own decision frameworks.

Instead of a 12-page PDF, extract stats with commentary, risks and countermeasures, quotes from customers, 2-minute walkthrough videos, and other modularized content. Tag content with triggers like goals, challenges, features, decision criteria, and industries.

Now build a referenceable system. Whether an AI, a filterable portal or a custom platform that allows buyers to build their own proposals.

We are in an answer engine economy, so focus on creating an experience that also delivers answers.

Create Interactive Sales Experiences

No purchase is made without any thought or consideration. Often decisions are made after scenarios are played out and information is considered from multiple viewpoints.

Tools provide the freedom for buyers to simulate, think, repackage, understand and re-explain.

- ROI calculators personalized to their inputs
- Implementation timeline estimators
- "What-if" scenario planners
- Cost-of-inaction calculators
- Needs-based configurators
- Complex solution builders

A tool doesn't have to be perfect—it has to be empowering. It should embed validation logic so they can feel the weight of the outcome and export results to share with internal champions.

Build tools that give your buyer an "aha" or "that it!" moment.

Internal Buy-In Kits

Equip your champion to sell for you—flawlessly. Most buying decisions are made *when you're not in the room*. If you don't supply the narrative, someone else will.

- One-slide summary of your value prop
- Internal pitch deck templates
- Side-by-side comparison charts
- Key questions stakeholders will ask—and how to answer them
- ROI + risk visuals that can be pasted into emails or Slack
- Pricing and implementation cheat sheets

Buy-In kits that are part of an intelligent Enablement Layer that allows buyers to configure and personalize information to their needs reflect the specificity they receive from AI engines.

Shift From Sales Process To Sales Portal

You're not in control of the process anymore. Buyers don't need a guide. They don't need your sales flow. They've already mapped the terrain with AI, peer advice, and internal analysis before you even arrive.

They're not lost. They're *in motion*.

And if you show up with a pitch deck and a process while they're already building consensus, analyzing risk, and debating options—you're not helpful. You're behind.

The strategic shift is this:

Stop thinking like a process.
Start thinking like a platform.

Think Like a Platform, Not a Pitch

A platform doesn't push. Instead it is a space people *build inside of*. That's the approach that will work in today's world.

Instead of guiding buyers step-by-step, you create the space, tools, and systems that let them:

- Explore their needs
- Model their decisions
- Justify their choice internally
- Align with stakeholders
- Move forward independently

All on-demand. Your influence isn't in the control you exert—it's in the environment you *engineer*. You're not a seller anymore. You're a *co-builder of progress*.

The Platform Mentality

You may not see it yet, but with AI-empowered buyers, how we sell must shift entirely.

Old Mindset	New Mindset
Guide buyers step-by-step	Let buyers chart their own path
Control the next move	Empower movement without you
Hold back complexity to avoid confusion	Expose complexity, and give tools to navigate it
Focus on persuasion	Focus on clarity, validation, and motion
"Own the conversation"	"Support the process"

Being a platform means:

- Building modular, remixable tools

- Offering clarity where others offer confusion

- Giving your buyer access when they need it

The goal isn't to impress.
The goal is to make progress easier, faster, and safer.

Friction Is the Enemy. Movement Is the Metric.

When we focused on funnels, sales success was measured in conversions, In the Enablement Layer world, it's measured in **momentum**.

Every buyer interaction should be judged by a simple question:

Did this remove friction and create forward motion?

If not, it's noise.

Your proposal deck isn't valuable unless it helps them *pitch internally*. Your demo isn't effective unless it *answers stakeholder concerns they haven't said out loud yet*. Your timeline isn't useful unless it helps them *make a case to legal and procurement*.

You're not just explaining your solution.
You're helping them explain *your solution inside their company*.

Think of building a sales experience the way a product team thinks about user experience:

- Are we building tools that support real sales use cases?
- Are we minimizing decision anxiety?
- Are we exposing risk and addressing it early?
- Are we enabling quick iteration, not just big leaps?

The best sales teams are no longer gate keepers. They need to be enablers.

Creating an environment where buyers feel ownership. They build conviction. And they move forward—often without needing to be sold.

At the end of the day, it all comes down to presence over process.

This isn't about losing control. It's about *designing an environment where control isn't needed*.

Buyers don't want your roadmap. They want your infrastructure.

Be the space where confident decisions happen. Not the pitch they tolerate on the way there.

In a world where buyers arrive pre-informed and self-directed, you don't win by guiding the journey.

You win by *being* the best environment the journey happens in.

Win the Validation Wars

Selling today might feel like a deposition.

Your buyer isn't curious because they're over informed. So instead, they're testing for where your story deviates from what they have compiled.

You'll have to withstand scrutiny—not just build rapport.

By the time you're involved, they've already dug into their AI engine:

> "What does [your company] do better your [competitor]?"
> "Why would someone not choose [you]?"
> "What risks come with [your product]?"

Those prompts matter. Because they're not asking you—they're asking AI. And your answers will be judged against whatever the machine said.

So the game has changed.

Sales now happen under cross-examination. They ask AI why you are a good choice, then they ask you. And you are judged on the responses.

Sounding confident used to be enough. But now you need to hold up under AI interrogation. That means:

- Knowing exactly what AI engines are saying about you—and your competitors

- Preparing to confirm what's accurate and correct what's off—*without triggering defensiveness*

- Preloading your own narrative into every future prompt that might be asked after your call ends

Validation Pressure Points (And How to Win Them)

The reality is you're going to get questions and provide answers that will need to stand up to their equivalent AI answers.

A key strategy for sales teams is to prepare for them ahead of time. Creating a table of common AI pressure points and how to handle them is part of the new playbook.

What the Buyer Does	What AI Is Doing	What You Must Do
Asks you about a feature you don't lead with	Checks feature comparison grids & Reddit threads	Show live proof, usage metrics, or customer feedback—even if it's not your "headline"
Says "we've heard your support is slow"	Citing a dated review summary or old complaint thread	Acknowledge, then correct with fresh support data or direct customer quotes
Mentions a competitor's claim	Echoing competitor-fed AI summaries	Don't get defensive—disarm with truth tables, implementation logs, or scenario stories
Stays quiet after your claim	Prompting AI post-call to verify it	End the call with links, evidence kits, and assets designed for AI digestion and internal reuse

You want to build a contradiction-resistant pitch because buyers aren't just listening. They're logging claims.

The moment you say something bold like "We reduce churn by 37% in the first six months.", you've triggered a background process.

They won't challenge you on the call. But they'll paste it into their AI the second you're gone.

"Is it possible to reduce churn by 37% given the tactics and scope [company] provided?"

The AI won't hesitate. It will pull from G2 reviews, public blog posts, Reddit threads, and competitor pages. And if it finds an inconsistency—or nothing at all—your credibility takes a hit.

Most sellers still pitch like it's a trust-first world. But today, every claim must hold up under algorithmic cross-examination.

Before you share any proof point, run it through this filter:

Contradiction-Resistant Pitch Checklist

- Would this claim hold up if a buyer prompted:
  "Is [your company] overstating its results?"

- Can this stat, case study, or quote be confirmed through publicly accessible data?

- If a buyer copies this sentence into an AI tool, what shows up—and who benefits?

- Will they leave the call with verifiable proof—or just a hopeful headline?

If your answer to any of these is no, you're vulnerable. You've handed the buyer a reason to doubt—and a prompt to investigate.

Every pitch is now a court transcript. The best reps aren't just persuasive. They're bulletproof.

Gaps Expose Risk

If buyers can't find it, they don't ask you first anymore. When you leave something out or they can't find an answer, the buyer's AI fills in the blanks.

In the past, holding back was a strategic move. You could delay the hard conversations. Control the reveal. Guide the pace.

That is over because of AI. Buyers now expect full visibility. They trust what they can verify. And they have the tools to dig.

If your pricing, implementation process, or tradeoffs aren't clearly explained, AI will draw conclusions from whatever public information it can find. And when your competitor has shared more, that becomes the default narrative.

A buyer asks, *"Why is [Company] more expensive?"*

AI might respond with, *"[Competitor] is more transparent about costs and offers pre-configured pricing tiers. [Company] considers itself consultative and therefore charges higher hourly rates."*

Suddenly, your silence and what the AI filled in become a reason to go in another direction.

The First To Answer Gains Credibility

Information not yet provided often could prompt a dialog. You would be the only source for answers to tough or highly specific questions.

But as we've discussed, AI now gets asked first.

So, transparency isn't just a nice-to-have. It's a strategy. The last thing you want is AI speaking for you or even worse a competitor's always on sales enablement layer.

Credibility is now tied closely to early transparency.

What Sales Commonly Hides vs. What Buyers Assume

What You Omit	What Buyers or AI Infer

No pricing	"They're inconsistent or overpriced."
No implementation breakdown	"There must be hidden complexity."
No mention of failures or tradeoffs	"They're avoiding accountability."
No comparison to competitors	"They can't hold up in a side-by-side review."
No detail on real use cases	"It only works in perfect scenarios."
No client logos	"They haven't worked with anyone like us"

Operationalize Transparency So It Never Ends Up In The Court of The Buyer's AI

Buyers have already formed opinions—most of them shaped by AI.

But once they do rach out, it is your moment to confirm, correct, and validate. What we really want to do is provide information early so that buyer's don't have to try and fill in gaps on their own.

Bring a "Where We Win / Where We Don't" Slide

Instead of waiting for objections, surface them yourself. Frame it as a confidence move.

"Here's where we're a strong fit and where we sometimes aren't. If any of these apply to you, let's talk through them honestly."

Buyers aren't used to this level of candor. It disarms defenses, builds trust, and makes you sound like a real partner, not a pitch machine.

It gives AI less to invent. You're providing structured, clear-fit parameters that buyers can repeat or prompt against later.

Lead With Real Implementation Data—Not Promises

Buyers are already skeptical of best-case timelines. So instead of saying *"onboarding is 30–45 days"*, say:

"Here are three onboarding timelines from customers like you. One went exactly to plan. One hit this blocker. One needed more support mid-way. I want to show you what actually happens so we can plan realistically."

Include:

- Timeline graphs with real date ranges

- Annotated snapshots of customer implementation plans

- Customer quotes talking about what surprised them during rollout

It shows you're grounded. You're not trying to win with polish, you're building with truth.

And when they prompt AI later—"How long does onboarding take?"—your transparency will echo in what they find.

Narrate Your Tradeoffs Out Loud

Don't wait for them to discover complexity. Show it. In live discussions, surface tradeoffs as a sign of strategic focus:

"We chose full customization over plug-and-play simplicity. That means we support more edge cases, but the upfront learning curve is real. Let's talk through whether that fits your timeline."

Buyers expect you to spin. When you don't, it triggers instant credibility. Now they feel safe asking follow-ups. They're validating *with* you, not *against* you.

Walk Through a Live Comparison—With Their Priorities, Not Yours

By the time you're talking, buyers have already seen 3+ comparison charts. Don't add another. Co-create one in real-time based on what they care about.

"Let's build a side-by-side on the fly—based on your top 3 decision factors."

Draw it live. Or bring a modifiable slide. Include:

- Where you win

- Where your competitor might win

- What matters more, and why

It turns a risk (hidden comparison) into a collaboration. You're not hiding—you're helping them structure the decision. And it gives them validation ammo they can feed back into their AI advisor or use internally.

Transparency isn't just for marketing pages. It's a tactic inside the call, a posture in your responses, and a weapon in the validation phase.

You're not being judged by how slick you sound. You're being judged by how well your answers match reality.

Say the hard thing first. Show the thing they didn't expect.

Be the one they can trust when the AI cross-checks later.

Bring Proof to the Table—Not Theater

Buyers don't believe slides. They believe what they can validate, whether on their own, or with their AI. And they can spot a sales performance from a mile away.

If your pitch feels rehearsed, they'll prompt around it. If your deck looks perfect, they'll search for flaws. If your stories feel too smooth, they'll assume they've been sanded down.

This isn't about looking sharp. It's about sounding real.

Buyers naturally question everything. AI has just made getting unbiased answers feel easier.

Move To Proof Over Polish

When AI delivers answers about everything from every angle, validation is key. Sales teams can no longer rely on:

- Sanitized case studies
- Overproduced demos
- Claims with no citation
- "Just trust us" assurances

Instead, the modern sales motion must deliver on-demand, authentic, and consumable proof. Not in a follow-up. Not in a PDF.

New Weapons in the Validation Wars

This isn't about making your pitch airtight. It's about giving the buyer a reason to stop prompting. You give them proof so complete, AI has nothing left to uncover.

Below are six forward-ready tools designed to anchor trust, confirm claims, and create post-call momentum:

Live Assets: Bring Reality Into the Room

A live collection of authentic, unpolished, real-world assets pulled in real-time during the conversation. This isn't marketing polish. It's what actually happened in the field.

- Screenshots of live customer support threads

- Redacted onboarding timelines from actual clients

- Usage dashboards showing feature adoption

- Escalation policies, real product feedback, internal team workflows

- Real demos rather than recorded ones

- A glimpse of your project and support systems

Buyers are scanning for spin. A real asset—presented spontaneously—feels more truthful than any demo or slide.

Validation Stories: Tell Stories AI Can't Summarize

Walkthroughs of real buyer journeys that show not just success, but the actual validation process that built trust. These extend beyond PDFs or slides into engaging, authentic stories.

- Slide-based journeys with examples of real people on the company and customer side.

- 2-minute narrated video walkthroughs that are authentic and down to earth.

- Side-by-side comparisons of assumptions vs. outcomes using real customer scenarios.

- Visualizations that share inside processes and approaches.

AI gives buyers headlines. You give them nuance. These stories make your value defensible and memorable.

Validation Packs: Equip the Buyer to Prompt for You

A follow-up asset bundle designed to support post-call validation when your buyer goes back to AI or their internal team to re-test everything you just said.

- A TL;DR of key proof points in buyer or AI-friendly language

- Suggested prompts to run (e.g. "Compare [Vendor] vs [Competitor] on onboarding time")

- Short evidence blurbs with links, visuals, and quotes

- Copy/paste language for internal recap emails or Slack threads

Your buyer will continue validating after the call. This pack makes sure they're using *your framing* and not your competitor's.

Objection Factbooks: Pre-Answer What AI Will Surface

Your buyer is already seeing competitor-influenced summaries and outdated claims. This is a short, tactical guide to counter those objections with receipts.

Objection	What AI Might Say	What You Provide
"They're more expensive"	"[Company] has higher per-seat cost"	Cost breakdown + ROI analysis from a real deal

| "Support is slow" | "Customer reviews mention delays" | Response time chart + support satisfaction rating |
| "Limited integrations" | "Some features missing" | List of supported systems + usage case screenshots |

Keep this in a password-protected enablement portal, a PDF, or even in a tab ready to discuss early. As a bonus, make it something the buyer can share or copy into an AI window.

Counter-Narrative Cards: Reframe AI-Surfaced Doubts

Quick-reference content to help reps respond to—and reshape—flawed narratives that buyers find via AI or peer feedback.

- Acknowledge the belief

- Explain where it came from (outdated review, missing context, competitor positioning)

- Provide a better frame with supporting proof

"It makes sense that AI said our onboarding is long—those reviews are from last year, before we launched our new activation program. Here's what that looks like now."

This shows you're informed, transparent, and credible. Most importantly, it doesn't leave your sales team squirming on the hot seat.

AI-Indexed Sales Scripts: Make Your Words Stick

Your words don't just need to land in the call. They need to show up in summaries, notes, AI follow-ups, and internal buyer documentation. So speak in structured, indexable phrases:

- "We're the only vendor that automates X across Y without Z."

- "For companies with A, we solve B in under C time—validated by D."

Reps should label insights during the call:

> "This is probably the most important takeaway—feel free to quote it."

Buyers remember tone. AI remembers structure. Train your speech to be retrievable.

Bringing It Together: Turn Proof into Presence

All of these tools aren't isolated tactics. They're situational weapons. Used together, they give reps the flexibility to respond in real time—without reverting to a pitch.

This is how you build presence in the conversation. Not through polish, but through proof that adapts to the moment.

Here's how it plays out across real deal scenarios:

Moment	Your Move
Buyer raises a concern	Pull live proof from your library
Buyer expresses a pattern of skepticism	Walk through a storyboard with validation layers
Buyer is nodding, but quiet	Preempt the AI summary with a Validation Pack

| Buyer mentions a competitor advantage | Use a Counter-Narrative Card to reframe |
| Buyer starts validating post-call | Your words, structure, and assets show up again—automatically |

Each moment is a trust test. And the reps who come prepared to pass validation—not just deliver persuasion—are the ones who win.

Adopt a Validation Mindset: The V.A.L.I.D. Framework

Buyers no longer need you to persuade them. They need you to supply what their AI can't: real, layered, contextual proof.

The more you bring proof to the table—and train buyers to validate with it—the less time you'll spend defending yourself later.

The best reps today don't just answer questions. They arm the narrative. And they make themselves AI-proof.

Sales doesn't need more scripts. It needs sharper mental models.

In a world where your words get tested, summarized, and copied into prompts, your sales approach must evolve from persuasion to precision.

You're no longer just answering questions. You're feeding algorithms. And arming champions. And influencing the final internal narrative you'll never be invited into.

To do that well, you need a simple, durable way to evaluate everything you say, show, and share.

That's where **V.A.L.I.D.** comes in.

The V.A.L.I.D. Sales Framework

This isn't just a checklist for crafting messaging. It's a gut check for every moment that matters. Before you share a claim, answer an objection, or end a call, ask:

> "If I'm not there to explain this later, will it survive?"

Because the buyer's journey continues long after your meeting ends. In their next prompt, their internal recap, or a CFO's critical question. And your message needs to live on without you.

Make it verifiable.
Make it AI-compatible.
Make it lightweight.
Make it internalized.
Make it durable.

That's how you win when validation is the battlefield.

	Principle	What It Means	What to Ask Yourself
V	Verifiable	Every claim must be backed by observable, credible evidence	Can I show proof if they ask AI or a stakeholder to double-check this?
A	AI Compatible	Messages should be structured for clarity, precision, and retrievability	Will this sentence summarize cleanly in a prompt or meeting recap?
L	Lightweight	Value props must travel easily inside the organization	Could a champion repeat this in a Slack thread or one-line email?
I	Internalized	Messages should reflect the buyer's real fears, context, and beliefs	Does this resonate with what they've already researched or assumed?

| D | Durable | Insights should remain credible even after pressure, prompting, or doubt | Will this message still be effective next week, even without me in the room? |

Mantras for the AI-Era Rep

Let's be honest. Most reps don't fail because they said the wrong thing. They fail because what they said couldn't stand on its own.

Buyers today don't only trust emotion, they trust confirmation. They may remember your energy, but still test your claims.

Here are the mantras that should live in the mind of every rep facing a modern buyer:

> **"Every claim is a future prompt."**
> Anything you say can—and will—be tested after the call.

> **"Sell like you'll never get a second chance to clarify."**
> Assume your message gets one shot, then it must live on through summaries.

> **"Your message is not what you say—it's what they repeat."**
> Make it tight, clear, and repeatable.

> **"If it sounds good but tests poorly, it kills."**
> Buyers won't challenge you live. They'll validate later—and vanish if you fail.

> **"Be the one AI quotes, not the one it questions."**
> Feed the system with truth, clarity, and precision. Then let it work in your favor.

The AI-Ready Sales Leader Roadmap

Most sales organizations today are friction-heavy at their worst moments and trust-light at their best.

They still reward reps for hitting pitch volume, not for earning internal advocacy. They still run enablement on messaging updates, not validation readiness. They still build decks—when buyers are reading summaries.

The roadmap isn't cosmetic. It's structural. It shifts your organization:

- From **scripts** to **systems**

- From **message delivery** to **message survivability**

- From **managing activity** to **engineering validation**

You're not just enabling reps. You're building an operating environment where truth travels faster than doubt.

Phase 1: Audit the System

Understand how you're perceived—by AI and by buyers

- Run prompts in ChatGPT, Perplexity, or Claude about your company, pricing, support, and competitors

- Interview recent buyers: What questions did they ask AI before and after speaking with your team?

- Score your messaging for clarity, consistency, and AI-alignment

Phase 2: Equip for Evidence

Shift from persuasion assets to proof-based selling

- Build proof libraries: support transcripts, usage metrics, implementation timelines

- Create validation storyboards and objection factbooks

- Remove or update legacy decks that no longer withstand scrutiny

Phase 3: Train for Validation

Rewire how reps speak, respond, and guide

- Teach the V.A.L.I.D. framework across the team

- Run prompt-response drills to simulate AI scrutiny

- Practice summarizing claims in language that AI and champions can repeat

- Coach for "proof over pitch" instincts

Phase 4: Enable the Champion

Empower buyers to advocate and validate internally

- Build internal pitch kits: TL;DR summaries, role-specific objections, validation assets

- Share prompt libraries and public content the buyer can feed into their own tools

- Train reps to co-author narratives buyers will pitch internally

Phase 5: Redefine Success

Evolve what sales performance means in the AI era

- Track new metrics: Proof moments per deal, Champion engagement rate, Rep/AI message alignment

- Review deals through a validation lens—not just conversion speed

Phase 6: Institutionalize Proof Culture

Make validation part of your sales DNA

- Run "proof reviews" alongside pipeline reviews

- Centralize proof assets in a live, accessible system

- Create a feedback loop between Sales, CS, and Marketing on what proof works

- Celebrate validation-led wins—not just quota-hits

You can't control the prompts your buyer runs. But you can control what shows up in the answers.

That starts with you.

Chapter 26

How To Sell to Machines When Humans Outsource The Process

Your next buyer isn't a person.

It doesn't check its inbox. It doesn't pick up the phone. It doesn't get excited by your pitch deck.

It's an AI agent—running 24/7, scraping options, benchmarking pricing, auto-generating RFPs, negotiating with statistical leverage, and filtering you out *before* a human ever gets involved.

This isn't some futuristic scenario. It's not science fiction.
It's already happening in shadow form:

- Email summaries that strip nuance.
- Copilots deciding who's worth the meeting.
- Procurement agents benchmarking you in milliseconds.

You're not just selling to buyers anymore.
You're selling to systems.

And these systems don't get tired, swayed, or guilt-tripped. They process. They rank. They replace. The real danger? You won't even know you lost the deal. Because no one will ever tell you—it'll just be filtered out, redirected, or algorithmically closed.

We've mapped out the full anatomy of this transformation—every moment of the sales process that is being quietly outsourced to AI.

By the end of this chapter, you'll either have a strategy to survive it… or realize you're already irrelevant to the machine.

Human Sales Moments Now Handled by AI

Traditional Interaction	AI Now Handles It
Vendor research & shortlisting	Autonomous AI buyer agents
Discovery calls	AI vendor interviews with synthetic voice agents
Email response/forwarding	Copilots summarizing and filtering
Demo viewing	AI watches, benchmarks, and flags gaps
Objection handling	Pre-filtering through simulation
Proposal submission	Scored and ranked via ingestible formats
RFPs	Auto-generated and distributed at scale
Contract review	AI redlines and risk-flagging
Price negotiation	AI benchmarking and statistical counteroffers
Reputation vetting	AI scraping and sentiment analysis
Consensus building	Internal Copilots generating ROI cases and approvals
Onboarding & adoption review	AI monitoring usage and value realization
Retention & renewal management	AI triggering evaluations and sourcing alternatives

Budget reallocation	AI-driven vendor ROI rankings and downsizing

Now let's dig into the reality of our future.

Your Buyer Outsources Their Discovery

A decision-maker gives a command to their AI:
"Find three marketing vendors that specialize in B2B SaaS."

- Their AI agent searches the web, visits websites, scrapes data, and identifies likely matches.

- The AI—*not a human*—fills out contact forms on your site. Or sends cold emails on their behalf. Or even places a synthetic voice call.

- Your responses—email or voice—are going straight to an agent. Not a person. The agent parses your answer, extracts key points, and compares them to those of other vendors it has contacted.

- It scores your pricing, flags concerns, and decides whether to include you in the recommendation.

Ten steps in, and not a human in sight.

Only after that process is complete might someone see your name—and even then, likely just a one-paragraph summary.

This isn't theoretical. These capabilities exist right now. They're just not widely adopted *yet*.

The play today is awareness. Start spotting signs when AI is the one reaching out. And begin crafting responses that are built to be read, parsed, and ranked by machines.

Guess what? You might have already been three stages into a sales process you didn't know was in progress.

Your Emails Are Summarized, Not Read

That perfectly crafted email you sent?
It probably never made it to the buyer's eyes.

AI assistants now auto-summarize incoming messages. They extract highlights, simplify long replies, and route only what seems relevant to the human decision-maker.

- A buyer's Copilot receives your email and immediately distills it.

- Paragraphs are reduced to bullet points.

- Tone, nuance, urgency—all flattened.

- Your call-to-action? Maybe it's removed. Maybe it's ignored.

Worse, if your email sounds like marketing fluff or doesn't directly address the AI's perceived intent, it can be flagged as low-value and never even routed forward.

You didn't get a reply. Not because they weren't interested—but because your message got compressed into something that lost its power.

Your copy now competes with compression. Clarity wins. Excess dies.

You could write the perfect email—and still lose, because an algorithm found it redundant.

Your Deck Doesn't Present—It Gets Parsed

That beautiful 18-slide pitch deck? It's not being read like you think it is.

AI tools now process documents the moment they're opened. Your slides are scanned for key terms, summaries, numbers, and structure.

- The narrative arc? Gone.

- The visuals? Ignored.

- The story you built slide by slide? Broken apart into tokens and extracted text.

Then, the AI compares your deck's extracted content to competitors'. It looks for pricing, proof points, differentiation, risk signals—and creates a side-by-side summary for the buyer.

You're not presenting anymore. You're being processed. The buyer doesn't experience your deck. They receive a filtered, factual residue of it.

Your pitch isn't evaluated for how persuasive it is—just how well it fits a machine-readable checklist.

Your Demo Gets Watched by Machines

Buyers used to show up for demos, ask questions, and engage live. Now? Their AI watches it for them.

- You send a demo recording, or an AI agent sits on your call.

- The buyer's agent transcribes it. It tags product features, benchmarks your capabilities, and compares you to alternatives.

- It flags missing elements, pricing gaps, or red flags—like vague integrations or unclear timelines.

Then it summarizes everything. The human receives a 5-point snapshot: strengths, weaknesses, compatibility, risk, and cost.

If your demo doesn't hit the right keywords, address the right priorities, or show up in the right format, you're out.

You never even made it to the shortlist. The decision-maker didn't watch your demo. Their AI did—and it makes a decision for them.

Your Pricing Is Benchmarked Instantly

You send a proposal. Confident in your value. Your price certainly reflects the quality you deliver. But the buyer's AI doesn't care about your confidence.

- It extracts your pricing structure—line by line.

- Compares it to hundreds of similar proposals from its internal data.

- Benchmarks you against industry standards, scope complexity, and historical vendor performance.

- Flags you as overpriced, under-scoped, or out of market norms.

The buyer doesn't "feel like it's too expensive." Their system *knows* it is—or believes it can prove it. And once flagged, the burden's on you to justify what the machine says you can't.

Your price isn't too high. It's just too far from the average — according to the machine.

Your Proposal Competes in a Crowd of 300 Instead of 3

It used to be three vendors per RFP.

Now it's 30. Or 300.

Why? Because the AI can handle it.

- Their system crawls the internet.

- Auto-fills intake forms.

- Requests proposals at scale.

- Then processes all of them—side by side.

It doesn't get overwhelmed. It thrives on volume.

Your proposal isn't impressive. It's data point #217. Scored, tagged, and judged alongside dozens—maybe hundreds—of others.

The human might never even see yours. You're not being considered— you're being analyzed. And your proposal is just one row in a spreadsheet.

Your RFP Is a Form—Not a Conversation

Buyers used to want to talk. They'd schedule a call, ask thoughtful questions, and dig into your capabilities. Now?

- Their AI generates a structured RFP form.

- You get a spreadsheet or portal login with 53 checkboxes and short-answer fields.

- There's no room for storytelling, no chance to explain, no way to steer the narrative.

- Just fit the format—or get rejected.

Your best differentiators? Buried in a "notes" field the AI might never weigh. If your answers aren't easily scored or mapped, you don't make the cut.

Your ability to build rapport has been replaced by your ability to follow format.

You're Negotiating With an Algorithm

You send your pricing. Then you get a response that feels… off.

It's not emotional. It doesn't ask. It *states*.

- "Your cost per user is 22% above the average for similar vendors."

- "Your implementation time is longer than 85% of competitors."

- "Other vendors offered 12-month terms. You're at 24."

You don't get the question "can you do better?" No "we'd love to work with you if…" Just data-driven pressure.

Because it's not a person negotiating. It's the buyer's AI, trained on thousands of deals, programmed to extract maximum value. You're not defending your price—you're defending your deviation from a statistical model.

Your Contract Is Redlined by a Machine

Before, contracts went to legal. Now they go to language models.

- Their AI scans for indemnity limits, liability clauses, renewal terms.

- Flags risks. Suggests edits.

- Benchmarks your agreement against past vendor contracts.

- Sends redlines automatically—with explanations and links to precedent.

There's no emotion. No gray area. You either comply or get rejected. Before you had a chance to explain. Now you get a statistical explanation of why a clause is expected.

You won't even talk to legal unless you pass the first filter: the bot. Your contract terms aren't being read—they're being scored.

You Thought You Had a Champion. Turns Out It Was a Copilot.

You think someone on the inside is advocating for you. But that internal email that got your proposal pushed forward? An AI wrote it.

- AI auto-built a business case.

- The buyer used their Copilot to draft the justification.

- The system pulled your pricing, your features, your timeline into a shared spreadsheet.

- Matched it to strategic goals and internal OKRs.

They didn't make the case. Their system did. You weren't championed by a believer. You were dissected by a prompt.

If you're not equipping their AI to understand and advocate for you, you have no internal champion at all.

Your Relationship No Longer Is Sticky

You have a client. You nailed delivery. They love the team. You've "got a great relationship."

But the buyer's AI doesn't care.

- It's monitoring contract timelines, deliverables, and usage metrics.

- It sees a cheaper competitor pop up.

- It notices a clause that allows an early exit.

- It flags the opportunity for cost savings.

And just like that, it opens a renewal evaluation workflow—without anyone asking for it. You're caught off guard.

You get an automated email saying, "We're triggering a vendor review process." You thought everything was fine.

It was. Until their AI found a reason it wasn't.

You didn't break trust. There were just signals previously ignored by busy humans that the machine caught.

The Things You Used to Be Asked For Are Already Being Scraped

You used to wait for the signal:

"Can you send over case studies?"
"Do you have references we can talk to?"
"Any ROI data or analyst reports?"

Those questions don't come anymore. Because their AI already found the answers.

- It scraped your website.

- Pulled reviews from G2, Reddit, and industry forums.

- Parsed your customer logos and pulled company size and industry.

- Analyzed social sentiment and media mentions.

- Matched third-party rankings and analyst coverage.

- Scanned your privacy policy and security docs.

All of it rolled into a vendor reputation score. No request needed. No conversation required. You weren't asked. They trust their all knowing AI over your selective response.

If your proof isn't public, structured, and machine-readable...
you're invisible—even if you're impressive.

The AI Found What You Hoped It Wouldn't

You thought it was buried.

An old proposal uploaded to a public RFP site. A vendor comparison doc that some past prospect loaded into their low-tier AI account. A less-than-stellar complaint on a forum sitting 20 pages deep in search.

No human was ever going to find it. But their AI did.

- It doesn't stop at page one of Google.

- It doesn't care if it's old, obscure, or unofficial.

- It follows every link, scrapes every table, indexes every keyword.

- And surfaces that content in its internal scoring of your credibility and risk.

Suddenly, a document you didn't write—or a price you gave in 2020—shows up in the buyer's decision model.

And you never even knew it was part of the conversation.

In the age of AI, there is no "offline." Everything is part of your footprint—whether you published it or not.

The Entire Sales Cycle Happens Without a Human

No emails. No calls. No meetings. Here's how it works:

- The buyer's AI issues an RFQ through an API or procurement portal.

- Your AI sales agent responds instantly—filling out forms, uploading a proposal, answering questions.

- Their AI reviews your submission, benchmarks your pricing, runs a risk analysis, and scores your offering.

- A recommendation is generated and sent to the procurement department.

The human decision-maker just sees: **"Recommended Vendor: [Your Company]"** Or... someone else.

No one talked. No one met. No one pitched.

It may seem like science fiction, but it's an inevitability.

The Buyer is No Longer Human

For as long as business has existed, sales has been about people.

Building trust. Reading the room. Winning hearts and minds.

But that is ending.

You're not selling to a buyer anymore. You're selling to a system. A swarm of algorithms. A decision pipeline built on logic, pattern-matching, and speed.

They don't get excited. They don't hesitate. They don't owe you a conversation. Every part of the process—from discovery to retention—can now be handled by machines.

Not assisted. Not augmented. **Owned by the AI.**

> The AI finds you.
> The AI contacts you
> The AI asks perfect questions.
> The AI reads your proposal.

The AI negotiates your terms.
The AI triggers the renewal.

And the human? They just approved the summary.

The *real buyer* is now invisible. It scrapes, sorts, scores, and selects—faster than any sales cycle you've ever known.

This isn't automation at the edges. It's a full-blown transfer of power.

Sales haven't just changed. The buyer—the very definition of a buyer—has evolved beyond human.

You're no longer selling to a person. You're selling to *whoever—or whatever—they delegate the process to.*

And soon, they won't be delegating to people at all.

Part VI

Deploy The AI Buyer R.A.D.A.R. Framework

For decades, we operated in funnels. Stages, steps, scripts.
You controlled what buyers saw and when they saw it.

Then AI arrived. And it gave your buyer x-ray vision.

Now they show up knowing your claims, comparing your competitors, quoting reviews, scanning summaries, and cross-checking every word you say—before you ever meet them.

Your buyer changed. Your system must, too.

This isn't the part of the book where we add tactics.
This is where we replace the operating system.

R.A.D.A.R. is the modern framework for go-to-market teams who want to thrive in an AI-shaped world.

It's not a funnel. It's a loop.
Not a playbook. A reflex.
Not a set of tasks. A mindset and motion you run on repeat.

And it doesn't end with this book.

The pages ahead give you the high-level structure—the mental scaffolding. The dynamic, evolving resources live where they belong: online, where they can grow with you, adapt to your market, and respond to the latest shifts in how AI interprets your brand.

Let's deploy your new OS.

Chapter 30

Pillars of the AI Buyer R.A.D.A.R.

Frameworks don't change companies. Disciplines do.

R.A.D.A.R. is more than a clever acronym. It's a system designed for reality—where AI-informed buyers are already forming opinions before your funnel begins.

In this chapter, we break down the five core disciplines that make R.A.D.A.R. work: **Reveal. Align. Design. Activate. Recalibrate.**

Each is a lens, a function, and a reflex your team must build. Not once—but continuously. These are the pillars of your new operating system. Turn them into motion.

Reveal: See What AI Sees Before the Buyer Does

You don't sell the first impression anymore. AI does.

Before your homepage loads or a sales deck is opened, an AI tool has already summarized you—based on what it could find, interpret, and compress.

That summary might be outdated. It might be wrong. It might not include you at all.

The Reveal phase exists for one reason: You can't fix your story until you see the one being told without you. This is not market research. This is not SEO. This is an X-ray of your AI surface.

We provided a more detailed exercise earlier in the book and have one available on omnibuyer.ai

This is where your loop begins: Not with assumptions. With a brutal look at what the machines think you are.

Only then can you start to change it.

Align: Unify the Narrative, Inside and Out

Consistency doesn't happen by accident. It's built.

And in the AI era, **inconsistency is expensive.** If your homepage says one thing, your sales team says another, and your G2 profile is three years old—AI has no idea which signal to trust.

So it does what machines do. It averages them. It blurs your message.

Alignment is not about agreeing on slogans. It's about making sure every team, channel, and asset reinforces the same core truths— backed by the same proof—structured in a way AI and buyers can both recognize.

You need to decide, explicitly:

- What do you want buyers to believe?

- What are you willing to expose?

- What proof will you always show, and what will you hold back?

Alignment is also the phase where you build your internal narrative system:

- Clear value propositions

- Differentiators that are meaningful, not marketing filler

- Proof points that are both specific and findable

- Buyer-fit statements that make it obvious who you're for—and who you're not

The output of Align is not a document. It's a shared understanding that stretches from your website to your one-liners in sales calls. It's what ensures your story doesn't fall apart the moment someone asks a second question.

Design: Engineer Assets That Convert Trust Into Action

Buyers don't want more content. They want clarity. They want confidence. They want control. And now, so do their AI assistants.

Design is where your narrative becomes real—turned into structured, scannable, provable assets that can do the heavy lifting in the buying journey.

This phase is not about aesthetics. It's about *signal engineering*.

You're designing things that must:

- Be parsed by AI

- Be remembered by buyers

- Be reused by champions

- Be trusted by skeptics

Design isn't limited to pages or decks. It includes tools, calculators, videos, frameworks, comparison grids, and structured proof libraries.

A buyer doesn't want to read about why you're better. They want to see it, compare it, test it, and—if you've done this phase right—use it to convince someone else on their team.

When executed well, Design doesn't just support your story. It tells it *without you in the room*.

And that's exactly where you need it to work.

Activate: Deliver the Right Signal at the Right Moment

Most content doesn't fail because it's wrong. It fails because it's too late.

Buyers don't wait for your sales process to educate them. They ask questions at their own time and in their own way. And if they don't find what they need—fast—they move on.

Activate is where you stop waiting for buyers to request proof. You place it exactly where the doubt begins. This means:

- Mapping your best assets to key decision points

- Embedding content in outbound, nurture, demo follow-ups, and sales interactions

- Equipping your team with snackable, AI-readable versions of every core proof

Most organizations publish content and hope it gets found. Activation flips that: You don't ask, "What did we create?" You ask, "Where did the buyer hesitate—and what did they see right then?"

Great activation is invisible. It's just *there*, at the exact moment belief might waver.

And it makes sure it doesn't.

Recalibrate: Monitor Drift. Adapt With Discipline.

You don't control when your market shifts. You don't control when your buyer changes how they prompt. You don't control when a competitor publishes something new that reframes the category.

But you *do* control how often you check.

Recalibrate is your system's immune response. It's the discipline of asking:

- Are we still showing up how we want to?

- Has AI drifted in how it describes or ranks us?

- Is our proof still current, our message still relevant, our visibility still strong?

This isn't about reacting to noise. It's about catching decay before it compounds.

You don't need to rebuild your strategy every month. However, you do need to check your signals, just as a pilot checks their instruments.

If Reveal shows you how AI sees you... Recalibrate ensures it *stays that way.*

The companies that win in the AI-buyer era won't be the ones who get it perfect the first time. They'll be the ones who don't let it drift for long.

The R.A.D.A.R. Loop Doesn't End Here

You've now walked through the five pillars of the R.A.D.A.R. system—Reveal, Align, Design, Activate, and Recalibrate. Together, they form a continuous loop designed to help your organization adapt to an era where AI influences your buyer's journey long before you do.

But what you've just read is the foundation. The real work happens in execution. And execution demands iteration.

Chapter 27

Installing the OS: How to Operationalize R.A.D.A.R. Across Your Team

Stop Thinking in Deliverables. Start Thinking in Loops.

Most teams think in campaigns, assets, and launches. However, your buyer thinks in terms of comparisons, contradictions, and cues.

You don't need a new checklist. You need a new rhythm.

R.A.D.A.R. isn't a project plan. It's how you:

- Diagnose visibility issues before they cost you deals

- Align around a narrative that actually holds up under AI scrutiny

- Build buyer tools and proof points that surface at the moment of doubt

- Deploy those signals across marketing, sales, and product touchpoints

- Monitor for drift and recalibrate in real time

That's not a one-time thing. It's a **loop.**

Think of R.A.D.A.R. as a shared cycle every team participates in. It gives your organization a heartbeat in an AI-scrambled market.

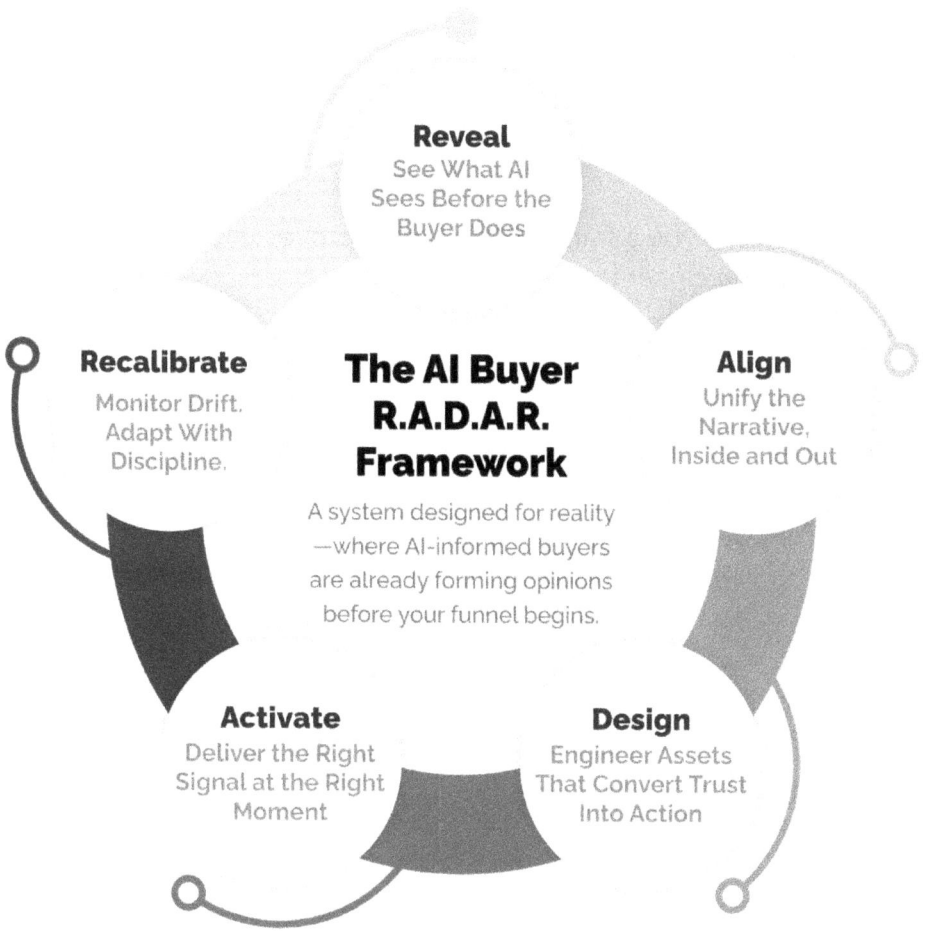

Reveal
See What AI Sees Before the Buyer Does

Recalibrate
Monitor Drift. Adapt With Discipline.

The AI Buyer R.A.D.A.R. Framework

A system designed for reality —where AI-informed buyers are already forming opinions before your funnel begins.

Align
Unify the Narrative, Inside and Out

Activate
Deliver the Right Signal at the Right Moment

Design
Engineer Assets That Convert Trust Into Action

How Organizations Actually Use This

Let's make this real. Here's what it looks like when a team runs R.A.D.A.R. *as an OS*:

1. **In a leadership meeting:** "We're hearing that buyers are confused about our integrations. Let's kick off a Reveal phase to see how AI is summarizing us."

2. **In a sales enablement sync:** "Our current proof points are thin. We need a better Design phase to structure our case studies for

AI readability."

3. **In a quarterly retro:** "We saw drift in our pricing perception. Time to Recalibrate and realign the way that's exposed publicly."

Each phase gives you a frame. Each loop improves your signal. Each cycle brings you closer to the truth of the buyer.

Assign Ownership Without Creating Silos

Each phase of R.A.D.A.R. has a different owner—but none of them work in isolation.

Phase	Primary Owner(s)	Supporting Teams
Reveal	RevOps, Marketing	Product, Leadership
Align	Marketing + Sales Enablement	Exec, Product, CX
Design	Content, Brand, UX	Sales, Data, AI Strategy
Activate	Sales, Marketing Ops	SDRs, ABM, CS
Recalibrate	RevOps, Strategy, AI Lead	Everyone

Here's the key: **R.A.D.A.R. is not a checklist handed off.**

It's a *baton pass*—each team contributes to the loop.

Make it explicit. Make it accountable. Make it repeat.

Run the Loop Quarterly. Watch It Weekly.

You don't need a giant transformation project. You need **a rhythm**.

Here's how teams operationalize it:

Quarterly
Run a full R.A.D.A.R. loop as a planning cycle or team sprint. Each quarter, spotlight a different phase—or run a compressed version in 2–4 weeks.

Monthly
Hold checkpoint reviews on AI prompt outputs, messaging performance, and proof visibility.

Weekly
Spot signals in the wild. A buyer prompt. A competitor shift. A rep's confusion. Log it. Feed it into the loop.

You don't need perfection. You need momentum.

Start Where the Signal Is Breaking

You don't have to master every phase right away. Start where the pain is loudest. Ask:

- Where are we being misrepresented?

- Where are we losing trust?

- What are buyers confused or skeptical about?

- Where are we invisible to AI buyers?

Let that answer tell you where to begin

R.A.D.A.R. is not about doing everything. It's about doing the *next most important thing*—on purpose.

What Comes Next

In the next chapter, you'll find a fast self-diagnostic. You'll score each phase to see where you're strong, where you're vulnerable, and where to focus first.

Then we'll walk you through each phase—at a high level—so you can decide what's next and how to start running the loop.

From there, the real work begins.

Not in the book. But in your systems, your meetings, your content, your sales calls, and your strategy reviews.

This is your new operating system. Install it. Run it. And never let it sit still.

Chapter 28

Find Your Breakpoint: A R.A.D.A.R. Self-Diagnostic

You don't need to overhaul everything at once. You need to find your fault line—and fix it first.

That's what this chapter does. It helps you zoom out, assess your current GTM motion, and identify where you're most vulnerable in the AI-powered buyer journey.

Because here's the truth: Most teams aren't failing everywhere. They're just failing in the one place that breaks the loop.

Maybe your messaging is solid, but no one's activating it at the right moment. Perhaps your team is aligned internally, but AI tools are still summarizing you with outdated information. Maybe your proof is strong—but scattered across PDFs, sales decks, and landing pages AI can't parse.

You don't need a rebrand. You need a recalibration. And that starts with finding where your signal is weak or broken.

What This Diagnostic Is (And Isn't)

This isn't a marketing quiz. There's no badge at the end. No "AI Guru" level to unlock. It's a fast, focused self-assessment to:

- Identify which phase of R.A.D.A.R. is weakest

- Help your team agree on a starting point

- Spark real conversations about where your GTM needs work

It works for teams of 1 or 1000. You can run it solo, or bring it to your next strategy or revenue meeting.

Let's get into it.

The R.A.D.A.R. Self-Diagnostic

For each of the five R.A.D.A.R. phases, read the five statements. Check the box for any that are true—or even partially true. Tally your total for each phase to determine where your biggest risks live.

REVEAL

See what AI sees before your buyer does.

We haven't prompted ChatGPT, Perplexity, or Claude to describe us in the past 60 days.

We don't know how AI compares us to our competitors.

We haven't reviewed what public content (PDFs, reviews, decks) AI might be pulling from.

We've never run prompts simulating how a buyer might research or shortlist us.

No one on our team is responsible for monitoring our AI visibility.

Total: ____ / 5

ALIGN

Align your story, signals, and narrative across functions and platforms.

Our sales and marketing teams use different positioning language.

Some of our public claims aren't backed by visible, verifiable proof.

We haven't defined what information should be public, protected, or promoted for AI exposure.

Our content and messaging were not built with AI readability in mind.

Internal teams don't share a clear, unified narrative.

Total: ____ / 5

DESIGN

Create assets that guide, prove, and differentiate—for both buyers and just as importantly machines.

Our case studies are not structured for skimming or AI parsing.

Key materials are locked in PDFs or formats that aren't AI-readable.

We haven't built any tools or experiences (e.g., calculators, comparison grids) to help buyers self-navigate.

Buyers still ask us the same questions that our content should already answer.

We lack a consistent format or structure for delivering proof across assets.

Total: ____ / 5

ACTIVATE

Deliver the right content at the right time, in the right context.

Our best assets aren't embedded in sales workflows or marketing automation.

Sales reps often create their own content or improvise messaging.

We haven't mapped buyer friction points to specific assets or interventions.

We lack systems to surface content automatically during key buyer moments.

We publish content, but don't consistently track when or how it's used.

Total: ____ / 5

RECALIBRATE

Adapt as AI summaries, prompts, and perceptions shift around you.

We don't revisit our AI summaries or prompt results on a consistent basis.

Updates to our messaging or positioning haven't been fully reflected across public-facing channels.

We've been surprised by what buyers say they "read" about us.

We haven't checked AI prompt outputs in the past quarter.

We don't have a set rhythm for reviewing or refreshing public proof and perception signals.

Total: ____ / 5

Interpreting Your Scores

Score per Phase   **Interpretation**

0–1	Strong – You're likely ahead in this area. Refine and reinforce.
2–3	Exposed – Vulnerabilities exist. Time to prioritize improvements.
4–5	At Risk – This phase is likely undermining your entire GTM motion. Start here.

Once completed, look across your five scores. Your lowest-performing phase is your entry point into the R.A.D.A.R. loop. That's where to begin.

You don't need perfection. You need to find the break and fix it first.

Keep Building Your AI-Buyer System

The landscape is changing too fast for any book to keep up.

Prompts evolve. Tools update. Buyer behavior shifts. Which is why the R.A.D.A.R. system lives beyond these pages.

We've created a living resource hub at omnibuyer.ai

The R.A.D.A.R. framework isn't a one-time fix. It's a way of operating—and evolving—together.

So don't just read it. **Run it. Share it. Live it.** And let the loop keep working long after you close this book.

This is a new age for your marketing and sales.

Part VII

This is the Age of the Omniscient Buyer

Marketing and sales will never be the same again.

The game didn't just change—it ended.

A new one started. Most teams, however, are still playing by the old rules.

Buyers don't need your funnel.
They won't browse your site.
They don't want your drip sequence.
They don't wait for your SDR.

They show up knowing more than you think.

They've already researched.
They've compared you to everyone.
They've built their own plan.
They've already decided who they trust—and it may not be you.

AI is now the real buyer.

And it doesn't forget. It doesn't skip. It doesn't sugarcoat.
It finds what you tried to hide. It exposes what you failed to say.
It's reshaping how every decision is made—fast, filtered, and unforgiving.

You are no longer the gatekeeper. You're the subject of interrogation.

Everything is visible.
Everything is scored.
Everything is compared—without you ever being in the room.

If you think you're still guiding the buyer, you're already behind.

So how do we thrive in an AI-Buyer age?

- **Shift your mindset:** From control to contribution. From persuasion to enablement.

- **Change your playbook:** Create tools, not decks. Build trust, not noise.

- **Focus on proof, clarity, and buyer utility.**

- **Build for the AI layer, not just the human one.** If AI can't parse it, summarize it, and use it—buyers won't either.

You need to redesign your presence, process, and pitch for a world where buyers are increasingly omniscient.

Where discovery is outsourced. Where validation is silent. Where deals are won or lost *before* you even knew there was a deal.

This isn't a trend. It's a permanent shift.

Those who adapt will lead.

Those who don't… won't even know what they missed.

www.ingramcontent.com/pod-product-compliance
Lightning Source LLC
Chambersburg PA
CBHW071538210326

41597CB00019B/3038